McCall's
DECORATING BOOK

McCall's

DECORATING BOOK

By the Decorating Editors of McCall's

Random House • McCall's

TABLE OF CONTENTS

3   Foregrounds

PROLOGUE

It's no secret that an eye-appealing and convenient arrangement of furniture and furnishings makes a room—and a home. But considering the frequent and usually costly mistakes made by brides as well as seasoned veterans, you would think the how-to of pulling together that "eye-appealing arrangement" was Classified Data locked away in a deep dark vault. Women stumble over the doorsill of interior decorating simply because they haven't opened the door. Learning *how* to open that door is complex, but not complicated, and definitely required reading. You begin simply by slowly, cautiously walking up these—

Seven Steps to Successful Decorating

THE SEVEN STEPS, once learned, can function for all creative projects from decorating a cake to designing a wardrobe. They offer a technique, a method for reaching down into your mind and bringing to the surface all sorts of facts and ideas that possibly you didn't know were there.

The dictionary's definition of "create" is "to bring into being; to originate." Everyone has more creativity than he is aware of. He is born with it just as he is born with curiosity—the two, in a way, go together. Have you ever listened to a four-year-old ask questions or watched him create wonders with a paintbrush? Unfortunately, somewhere between four years and adulthood, the child becomes conscious of the smiles, the laughs, the annoyance of the adult world over his questions, his dreams and drawings. Gradually his creative flights are throttled. He makes an effort to conform, to see things as the group does, and the amusing questions, plump green cows, purple trees and enchanting blue-faced teachers disappear.

In decorating, one of the first requirements is to dig down into the unconscious and rediscover that buried childish curiosity and creativity, that fresh way of seeing things. Once found, it should be polished up and put into use again—because all design starts inside you, not outside.

Step 1. Dream a Little

THIS HAS BECOME such a fixed habit with most designers that they may not realize they do a more than average amount of mooning. But I have never known a designer who didn't take time out for just such mulling over a project before plunging into it. Wool-gathering is part of the creative process, and ideas will dry up, will cease to come if they aren't searched for, pounced on when they appear, and cultivated. Otto Harbach said the same thing in a different way. He was struggling with Oscar Hammerstein II over a lyric. Suddenly he relaxed and said, "Oscar, we are not going to create this song. It exists right now. It is somewhere in the world. Our job is to find it."

The unconscious mind is a storehouse of ideas. A lot of your work will be done for you if you will open the door and let them drift into your conscious mind. I like to tuck a problem into a corner of my head over a weekend and just let it simmer. Often, completely without effort, a plan, a color scheme, an idea springs fullblown into my consciousness while I am weeding the petunias or pulling wild asters out of the pachysandra.

Free yourself of limitations, open your mind to the endless possibilities built up through the centuries. You will find yourself discarding formulas and moving into a new phase of living.

Step 2. Analyze Your Way of Life

AT FIRST, dreams may require a little disciplining; it doesn't pay to get lost in visions about castles on the River Nile. Begin by thinking about the life you would like your family to have, the aims and ambitions you cherish for the children. Try to visualize a room, a home, which would be an ideal background.

Take an honest look at yourself and your family. Are you a trail blazer or a follower? Do you like to do things which are a little different? Have you the self-confidence to use blue-and-white ticking edged with red ball fringe or burlap bound with velvet for a luncheon tablecloth when you entertain the club, when most of the crowd go in for lace cloths and so-called elegance? Have you the nerve to use a centerpiece of weeds and grasses, or a blue bowl full of white eggs, instead of flowers? Do you love to entertain or is it a task? Are you a shorts-and-slacks family with a paper-napkin, plastic-plate approach to dining, or are candlelight and flowers a more than once a year ritual? Are you a family who do things? Must provision be made for special activities? Are you content with the status quo or do you want to expand your circle of friends, your experience, your horizon?

Now study the room itself; let it talk to you. Are there gaping blank walls or is it all doors and windows? Has it architectural distinction, an interesting fireplace or bay window, or is it just a box, waiting to be filled? Is it large or small? Is it a dark, light or a bright room? Must adjoining spaces be considered? What goes on outside the windows? Should the view—or lack of view—have special consideration?

Don't guess what you and your family will do in the room. Instead, make three lists: Things done every day; things done occasionally; things done three or four times a year. Have a family conference. Discuss the project with your husband and the children.

Step 3. Learn to See

FURNITURE, CARPETS, FABRICS, lamps and accessories are used to make rooms, just as lumber, nails, bricks and concrete make a house. To acquire confidence, develop the ability to translate the character of things into the mood they create. Smooth silks and satins, fine finishes on delicate furniture, soft colors and minimum patterns will make a formal room. Textured fabrics, tweeds, strong colors, sturdy furniture and bold patterns are the factors that make an informal room. In between these two extremes are endless nuances which can be developed by the sensitive use of just the right textures, colors and patterns.

Learn to see what you are looking at. Start a scrapbook. Collect clippings from magazines. Visit museums, browse through decorating books. Get acquainted with styles in furniture and accessories. Take the mystery out of period design by learning all there is to know on the subject. Develop confidence in your taste and feeling about what looks good with what.

Step 4. Know What is Available

SCOUT STORES and shops, discover what local sources offer. Familiarize yourself with sizes, qualities and prices. As you go from wallpaper store to fabric department to carpet shop, a specific color scheme should start forming in your mind. Get samples to guide you in developing the final plan.

Scouting trips should also include visits to galleries, auctions and antique shops. This is where you will find the sweeteners, the individual touches, the objects with flair that will make the room you are planning really *yours*.

Step 5. Plan on Paper

DEVELOP THE HABIT of putting your ideas on paper. Anyone can learn to make diagrams, charts, plans. Getting it all down relieves the mind, simplifies visualization, makes it easier to make changes and perfect a plan. Others working with you can see what you have in mind even though the sketch is simple and diagrammatic.

One-fourth inch to the foot is a good scale to work with for room plans. This makes a chart which will fit in a folder. Work out the furniture arrangement, locate large pieces of furniture, then fit in the smaller supporting pieces around them. Check the traffic lanes—how will you move through the room? Next, put your pencil at the entrance, consider the view of the room from there. Visualize the family spending an evening at home. Consider where you would sit if several friends dropped in. Are seating units pleasantly grouped?

Next, work out the color scheme using actual paint, fabric and wallpaper samples so that there can be no mistake in the mind of the painter, carpet dealer or upholsterer. Play with your plan, live with it for days, for weeks; change it here, change it there, get used to it.

Step 6. Estimate the Cost

PROFESSIONAL OR AMATEUR, it is important to face the budget realistically. In fact, no orders should be placed before you balance the cost of your plan against what you have to spend. Peace of mind comes from staying within a budget, and delightful results can be had with very little as well as a lot. Moreover, rooms can be achieved a step at a time over several years.

There are two ways to stretch or manipulate a budget—both have points in their favor. Plan One requires everything in a room to be about the same quality—low, medium, or expensive. This will produce a harmonious whole. Plan Two permits you to withhold from Peter in order to pay Paul. In other words, you may invest in the world's most beautiful sofa and use make-do's for the rest of the room until you gradually replace them with the perfect pieces. This latter method may produce an uneven room, but it will have character.

Step 7. Enjoy Your Work

THERE IS A thrill in seeing paper plans turn into real rooms. You can be justifiably proud if you have persevered and everything comes out just as you planned it. Admire your work, but remember that a room is not just to look at—it's to use, to soothe, to serve as a background for family activities and interests. What is disarranged with use can be rearranged in a trice, and what the family has seen created lovingly before their eyes will be appreciated and respected.

The chapters that follow will elaborate.

FIRST THINGS FIRST

1

THE FOUR BASIC STYLES

IN DESIGN, as in other fields, it is helpful to develop some appreciation of the subject before going into its more complicated aspects. A baby crawls before it walks. One can enjoy music before becoming a serious student; or divide trees into needle-leaved and broad-leaved before delving into precise identification.

In interior design, a good first step is to train your eye in the nuances of style. Learn to recognize quickly the character of a piece of furniture, a fabric, a room. Be able to classify it as formal or informal, conventional or unconventional, as serene, dignified, simple, graceful, severe, plain, sturdy, quaint, sophisticated or modern.

While learning to translate the meaning of design, determine also the spirit, the mood or character which gives you the greatest satisfaction. A professional decorator or student should be conversant with all styles, but an amateur may specialize, become an expert in the design area which gives him the greatest satisfaction. Once you have established such a preference, it is possible to shop for and find the thing that is truly yours and that you will always enjoy, regardless of fashion changes.

Women who are well dressed discover *their* style early in life. The woman who likes sports and the outdoor life will almost automatically collect gay sweaters and skirts, separates and slacks, tweeds and homespuns in fresh, hearty colors. Conservative women who always manage to be perfectly groomed collect suits and trim dresses in basic black, gray, blue and beige. They eschew ruffles and frills and are never overdressed. Still other women yearn to be supremely elegant and sophisticated. They are innovators, experimenters, dramatic romanticists; they revel in the unexpected. They always know how to tie a scarf or do their hair; they favor simple sheath-type dresses which give them height and grace. They like unusual colors: coral, turquoise, gold, chartreuse. Finally, there are women who lean to the grandiose, who like rich fabrics, furs, jewels and a general feeling of luxury and opulence. They feel their best in elaborate evening gowns made of sumptuous fabrics.

If you have discovered your personal style in clothes and your favorite color range, it is most likely that the same general mood will please you in interiors. Furnishings are not quite as intimate as clothes, so you may not have resolved this style problem yet. Study and close observation will help you discover the one style, or the combination of styles, in interiors that gives you the greatest sense of satisfaction.

To develop your powers of observation, study a collection of photographs of rooms. Try your hand at analyzing them. Select the perfect adjective to describe each room, such as elegant, graceful, conservative, strong, powerful, bold, flamboyant, dramatic, simple, plain, dignified, playful, amusing, whimsical, youthful, luxurious, off-beat, common, ordinary, dull, ostentatious and grandiose. From among this great variety of moods it is desirable to determine the one or the combination of several that will give you the greatest pleasure. This discovery is invaluable; it not only will bring you deeper enjoyment in the things around you but it will channel all your purchases in the right direction. You will cease making costly mistakes, stop worrying about whether this or that is correct. Who can be a greater expert in the thing you like than *you*?

After all, this is what a designer does. Through questions and observation of your clothes and house, she classifies you before proceeding with the design of a room in your home.

Roughly speaking, all colors, all periods, all design can be divided into four classifications which parallel the four clothes types.

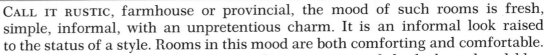

Style 1: The Country Look

CALL IT RUSTIC, farmhouse or provincial, the mood of such rooms is fresh, simple, informal, with an unpretentious charm. It is an informal look raised to the status of a style. Rooms in this mood are both comforting and comfortable.

Clear, strong, undiluted morning colors are a part of the look: red and blue and grass green, yellow and lively brown. Fabrics range through linens, cottons, plain woven wools, chintzes, calicos and tweeds, as well as a galaxy of hand woven fabrics. Such rooms are neither sleek nor grossly rustic.

There is a wide latitude in furniture. It may be modestly priced or expensive; it may be Early American pine, maple and cherry; it may be a blend of country furniture from around the world—French, Mexican, Italian or Austrian; or it may have seventeenth-century overtones. In part, the pleasure of such rooms is the fun of collecting fascinating but unorthodox accessories which may range from fine old glass to weathervanes, pickle jars, cast-iron matchboxes and wooden decoys.

Daisies, zinnias, cosmos, sweet William, geraniums and wildflowers tucked into a bean pot or white ironstone jug seem exactly right against such a background.

The country look is easy to understand; it may be sophisticated or primitive. It's a style that has warmth, it's bred in our bones, it's easy to create and it holds up under hard family use. Excellent reproductions are available which blend beautifully with old or new accessories. For the sincere Early American buffs, there are books, museums and "open house" tours that offer endless opportunities for study; for the truly persistent, there are old attics to raid and barns, carriage houses and even chicken coops to remodel.

The country look may even be modern. Old barns and buildings with enormous wall space and huge exposed timbers make wonderful backgrounds for plain or rustic modern furniture. Such furniture is often adapted from Shaker or Early American styles. The same colors, textures and even accessories and flowers fall comfortably into place.

Style 2: The Gracious Look

THE GRACIOUS MOOD in room design is the most difficult to define because it is not related to any one style of furniture, and the range of possibilities is tremendous. Such rooms are conservative and comfortable, with a pleasant consistency in furniture styles, woods and finish. The degree of formality may vary widely, but whether the room is small or large it will have a teacup-in-hand, gentle-voiced graciousness.

This mood can be developed with either conservative modern furniture (no molded chairs or hanging mobiles) or traditional furniture: English late eighteenth century, early nineteenth century, or so-called Italian Classic furniture with its simple straight lines, gently tapering legs and soft brown fruitwood finish. There will be the comfort of a carpet underfoot.

2

Rich red felt walls studded with brass nail heads, a red carpet, the handsome old table, black leather upholstered bench and the fine oil painting combine to give an air of elegance and formality to this room.

Fabrics will be smooth and fine and may range through satin, damask, chintz, linen and cotton. In a modern room, either the curtains at the window wall or the sofa might be a floral and other areas plain. Patterns in traditional rooms may be classic florals, stripes or plaids. The color values will be softer than those in rooms with a country look. Imagine pure colors diluted by the midday sun, and they will be right.

Gracious rooms are not the place for whimsical or off-beat accessories. Portraits, old masters, steel engravings are the classic choice for pictures; however, because of their wide acceptance today, an occasional abstract painting may appear in a traditional room just as an old master might appear in a conservative modern room. The small comforts are also always provided:

The latest book within easy reach.

The just-right light for reading.

Ashtrays and cigarettes where you want them.

Chairs which are comfortable as well as handsome.

Fresh flowers, growing plants, the evidence of loving hands.

Books and bric-a-brac which express the interests and personality of the owner.

Style 3: The Sophisticated Look

THE ELEGANT, sophisticated mood of today is blithe, young and gay. It is achieved through a delicate disregard for rules and convention and usually is a knowing blend of modern and traditional design and elegant textures.

Travel, broad cultural interests, the heart, mind and eyes of a collector and true confidence in one's taste are needed to assemble such rooms. They blend old, new, exotic and classic forms of architecture, furnishings and art. At first glance, such a room may appear to be another handsome, conventional room—but beneath the outward conformity there will appear traces of irreverence, a sharp critical feeling and a mood of intractable independence. In one such room Venetian, French Directoire and Italian baroque furniture and objects were used with delicate satin, taffeta and damask fabrics—the color scheme was pink, lavender and light brown.

For examples of such rooms, look at the photographs of the homes of young designers in all fields; they may be product or fashion designers, architects, art directors, decorators. Regardless of their specialty this group is immersed in the creative arts, and some of it rubs off on their homes. They have a spark, a flair for combining miscellany, furniture, styles, color that you can never find priced and packaged in a store. Such collections can be used together successfully only by those with understanding eyes, those who know and can translate the language of design as though it were their own second language. Specific details may vary widely as they reflect the owner's personal taste. Many ideas first tried in a designer's apartment later turn up as important fashions.

Furniture may range through Louis XV and XVI, Directoire, Venetian, Italian and Biedermeier; there may be a modern piece, a Teddy Roosevelt chair made of cattle horns, a folding director's chair with a velvet seat and tassels. There may be a split-peel fan chair or a huge French Provincial armoire, a stack of Korean chests or a skirted table. Colors will be clear and high-keyed, those associated with the late afternoon: coral, bright blue, bright green or sharp black and white. These colors will not be used in masses, but as staccato surprise touches.

The room may have a certain sparse look, thanks to the plain walls and polished floor which may have only an area rug, a zebra or bearskin to break its gleaming surface.

This is a New England "keeping room" reproduced in a new house in the middle west. Note the horizontal board wainscoating, the exposed window frames and the old barn beams used for the ceiling. The settle and cupboard with chalk figures are old.

Style 4: The Opulent Look

THE OPULENT LOOK today in our heavily taxed, rushing democracy is hard to achieve. True grandeur seems to be associated primarily with a more leisurely society. The great European houses built in the seventeenth, eighteenth and nineteenth centuries and those built in this country along similar lines qualify. Now many of these houses are open to the public. Grandeur on a shoestring and without finesse in the architectural background is a poor thing. Nevertheless, the luxurious look can be achieved if you are guided by a designer with impeccable taste. However, even one unfortunate table, a too ornate lampshade or too heavily fringed draperies may upset the balance and make the room gaudy and pretentious rather than handsome.

Traditional rooms in this category may be developed around Louis XIV and XV furniture, fine old paneling, beautiful accessories. Modern rooms will have big sofas upholstered in quilted fabrics, deep pile carpeting, lavishly tufted chairs, enormous lamps, and may verge on the mood often referred to as the "Hollywood style."

If you yearn for grandeur, move gently; a little gilt and marquetry go a long way. In fact, one *bureau plat* (flat-top desk) with gilded bronze mounts may have enough *éclat* to carry a whole roomful of lesser pieces. Use fine velvets, brocades, silks and tapestries, rich Renaissance colors; use marble and gilt only if you dream of the grand style and have the house, the taste and the bank account to do it justice.

After you have sorted out the four basic styles discussed here and have tried them on for size, study again the room illustrations you have already labeled and see how many times one of these moods appears to dominate. In many rooms several forms may be found; in fact, there may be thousands of blends and variations of these four basic styles.

Next, check your own reaction. See if you can decide which style gives you the greatest satisfaction—which you would be most at home with. Which, if any, gives you a visceral feeling? Which makes you smile? Which brings ideas surging into your mind?

Learn to understand your own personal response to style. An even clearer knowledge will develop from a study of the theories of design and period design.

THE ABC'S OF DESIGN

IT IS POSSIBLE to speak without much knowledge of grammar, but you can't read or write without study. You can bake a cake without knowing anything about flour, eggs and milk, if you use a mix and follow the directions. In the same way, it's possible to furnish a room without much basic knowledge about materials and design if you duplicate something you have seen; but such an approach does not give much delight or satisfaction. These come only from understanding the potentials of the materials you are handling and from adapting them to your requirements.

The meat-and-potatoes cook seldom enjoys cooking, does not surprise the family with unique dishes, and seldom is rated a great hostess; whereas the gourmet cook, who knows the cuts of meat available and how to cook each one, and has a repertoire of favorite menus, loves to cook and entertain. She has discovered that knowledge offers the road to a happier way of living through knowing.

Henry Cecil, in an article in *Holiday*, tells about how he learned to enjoy pictures. He considers himself a cultured man. He reads good books, is fond of music and the theater, but he got no pleasure from pictures. A friend convinced him it was because he knew nothing about them, so they arranged a museum trip.

The first excursion was a failure. They studied only six pictures, discussing subject, composition and paint techniques. Mr. Cecil found interest in small details such as the trace of red used in all the pictures to heighten values, but he felt no mental or physical response to correspond with his conscious enjoyment of a good book or concert. "What I wanted," he writes, "was to feel the actual direct pleasure one gets when one eats good food, drinks good wine, reads a good book or hears good music."

The next time he visited a picture gallery, he went alone. A landscape caught his attention and he went back and looked at it several times. He began to read about artists, then to study their pictures. Soon he became absorbed in the subject. Paintings by Bonnard and Vuillard gave him his first deep "visceral" enjoyment.

As Mr. Cecil came to understand pictures, so must interior design, furniture, carpets, fabrics, color, accessories, be studied and understood before they can be used with ease.

There are dozens of paths to take in the study of decorating, ranging through the basic elements of design, the history of design and materials, and their application and use. But one of the first things to do is to learn to see what you are looking at. As someone has said, "It isn't the dark place that hinders, it's the dim eye."

What's in a Line

FURNITURE STYLES, architecture, and design are constantly changing and evolving under the influence of social and economic factors, scientific developments,

trends in the arts, world exploration and archeological discoveries. It adds enormously to the pleasure of interior design to be familiar with the historic styles, but before launching into that inexhaustible realm it is helpful to have some understanding of the elements of pure design.

Line, form and composition are the elements of interior design—the ingredients that together make a chair, the surface pattern on a fabric, or affect the choice and arrangement of the elements of a single room.

The easiest of these to understand is line. It is the beginning point of all form and composition. You are already familiar with coarse and delicate lines, heavy and fanciful ones; but only when you see and feel the uncompromising masculine strength of a straight vertical line, feel the lilt of a controlled curve and the freedom in a flowing line are you progressing.

Lines are said to have movement because the eye moves the length of the line. Horizontal lines create a feeling of relaxation and informality and are associated with modern styles. Vertical lines are associated with the soaring Gothic cathedrals and the trimness of Sheraton designs. Straight lines used in opposition as vertical and supporting lines are strong and classic in feeling. Diagonal lines offer weak support unless they are balanced by lines pushing in the opposite direction, as in a roof; then a diagonal is strong and satisfying. Used as a surface pattern, left and right diagonals form a herringbone pattern or a chevron.

Controlled curved lines are gay and romantic and are associated with the period of Louis XIV and XV, but free-form curves are the lines of nature made by the waves on the shore or clouds in the sky. Free-form curves are the basis of oriental art.

Lines also establish shape or form and are a factor in composition. Whether flat or three-dimensional, the influence of lines is the same. With a little study you will be able to see and feel the static quality of round and square shapes, as well as patterns like stars and snowflakes which fit inside round and square shapes. Compare them with the movement of rectangles, ovals and shield forms.

Only when lines and shapes begin to mean something to you are you ready to think in terms of composition.

Composition

COMPOSITION IS inseparable from interior design. It refers to the grouping of different parts of a work to achieve a unified whole, and expresses man's yearning for order. It applies to furniture, wallpaper, and fabric design, to the arrangement of furniture in a room or to the grouping of objects on a mantel or pictures on a wall.

The elements of composition are harmony, rhythm, emphasis, scale, proportion and balance. Understand these terms. They are the subject, verb, object, infinitives and participles of design. When you can parse a design (take it apart, as you do a sentence), you are making progress.

The elements of design are simple and are a part of your basic knowledge. All that is necessary is to find them, dust them off and put them into use.

Harmony in a design is just what you would expect; it calls for a pleasing and orderly arrangement of parts with no discordant notes. Consistency in mood, line and color in the parts of a design or in the composition of a room give harmony.

Rhythm in design and decorating has endless application and is used in reference to surface pattern as well as to the arrangement or composition of objects. When effectively used, it is like the coupling in a freight train—it helps hold the varied elements of a composition together.

Repetition offers a simple way of developing rhythm. Repeat a color, a line, a design motif or an object more than once in a composition and a sense of design or purpose in the arrangement develops. One plate standing on a shelf is static; a pair appears to have purpose. But line up

This informal living room is a knowing blend of moods. The blue-on-blue fabric on the sofa and the simulated wood wallpaper have a country look but the velvet table cover, the shiny black leather chair, the white textured brick-patterned rug, the handsome painting, and the palm lend an air of sophistication.

More Than a Place to Sleep

three, five or seven plates on a shelf and the eye is carried along and the resulting composition is interesting. Repetition is the key to the design of borders.

In room composition, if a round rug is the only curved line in a room, it seems out of place, but add a round table and a scalloped valance and the round rug settles down comfortably. In a more subtle way, the repetition of an idea can contribute rhythm to a room. A duck painting over the sofa, for instance, may launch an idea that leads to duck decoys on the mantel and perhaps a gun case in the corner. In the parlor of an old plantation house on the James River, a collection of old flower prints hangs over the sofa. The mahogany side chairs have seats of petit point with a floral motif, draperies are a floral chintz and the tea service is flower-spattered Spode. By staying within reasonable bounds of one idea or period, repetition of line and color is almost guaranteed.

Graded sizes offer a second technique of developing rhythm. Imagine an all black and white room with one red wing chair. Now, in your mind's eye, add a painting with a dash of red and a bunch of red carnations on a table. The eye is carried around the room through repetition of the red, and through masses of different size, and the sensation is pleasant. Line up a row of pewter tankards from large to small and the eye responds. Use too many big upholstered chairs in a room and the effect is dull. Mix in some smaller chairs and open-arm chairs, and at once the composition is more interesting.

The use of continuous lines offers a third method of obtaining rhythm. In classic design this was seen in the fluting of columns, in the concentric rings on medallions, in the banding or borders on togas. In modern design, the theory of continuous line is called streamlining and has resulted in smoothing out the irregularities and erratic forms of objects. This is a helpful theory to remember in making architectural changes. Wherever possible, carry lines evenly around a room.

Emphasis—also called "center of interest"—is another factor that is important in design and in decorating. Emphasis is important in all art—in painting, furniture design and room arrangement. It makes the difference between calm and confusion. It is the strong, clear voice of authority. It is the principal feature, the commanding note, in a design, and can be achieved in a variety of ways: converging lines, contrast in size, color, masses of dark and light, plain and patterned surfaces.

For instance, if the fireplace grouping is to be the center of interest in a room, it should be given importance with a fine overmantel composition, good lamps and interesting furniture. The sofa opposite should concede importance to the fireplace and not compete for attention.

If a foyer is dull and seems to be all doors, paint all doors and walls but one white; paint that one wall red or emerald green. Place a console and mirror there and it will be the focus of attention, the center of interest. In a bedroom, a canopied bed will command attention; whereas an understated studio bed with matching bedspread and headboard will relinquish attention to a bookcase wall and desk grouping.

In the average-size room, one center of interest is enough, but in a large room there may be several centers. Even then, however, one grouping should dominate.

Scale is related to weight and size. Furniture should be in scale with the room. Too large furniture in a small room will overwhelm it. A very small table beside a huge chair looks out of place. Pattern, too, should be scaled to the size of the room.

Proportion applies to space relationships within a design. For instance, you say that the proportions of a room or a window or a fireplace are pleasing or that a chest or a chair or a picture has good proportions. In both cases, you are referring to the relationship of dimensions within a space or an object.

Exact division of spaces like a half, a third, or a fourth, and objects of identical size used together intrigue the eye less than divisions which are close to basic dimensions, but far enough off for the eye not to catch the relationship at once.

The Greeks discovered that the most pleasing rectangles were those in which the length could not be evenly divided by the width. In mathematical terms, the most pleasing relations are two to three, three to five, five to eight, and eight to thirteen, etc. In each case, the sum of the two parts creates a whole that bears the same relationship to the larger part that the larger part bears to the smaller. This is sometimes called the Greek law of proportion, and can be applied in many ways: to determine the amount of pattern to plain surface in a room, for instance, or determine the most pleasing dimension of objects.

The gracious, conservative character of this room is timeless. The Lawson button-back sofa, the pair of pier cabinets, the mahogany tea tables with removable tray tops and the arrangement of architectural pictures are 18th century in character.

Balance is related to poise, equilibrium. It is admired because it creates an air of stability. There are two types of balance: formal or symmetrical balance, and informal or asymmetrical balance.

Formal balance is achieved when the two halves of a composition are exactly the same. Identical chairs flanking a chest, a pair of candlesticks equidistant on each side of a bowl of flowers, or the two halves of a medallion all represent formal balance. The balance is clearly established and easy to see but is somewhat static and conservative. However, almost every room will benefit from the use of several pairs of objects used in balanced groupings.

Informal or asymmetrical balance is some-times called occult balance, because the eye alone is the scale and determines whether the two halves of a composition balance when they are not identical. The weight of a design is not always physical weight. A red box will have more weight than a gray one; a weirdly shaped object will catch the eye and have more weight than a smooth, simple one—so that a trained eye and experience are needed to arrange informal groups.

Compositions using informal balance may be light, gay and exuberant. Such design is particularly associated with French Regency, Rococo and Louis XV design. Chinese design and Japanese flower arrangement are also keyed to asymmetrical balance.

Practice in Making Compositions

To UNDERSTAND THE theories of design is not enough—practice is necessary. It is a fallacy to suppose that you can get great results with a minimum of effort. There is no such thing as getting out of anything more than you put into it. The laws of design apply to all the arts, dress design, landscaping, to everything you do to beautify your home.

Setting the table, arranging flowers, grouping accessories on the mantel are all lessons in line and composition. By consciously doing these things, you train your eye and develop a feeling for association of sizes, textures and objects.

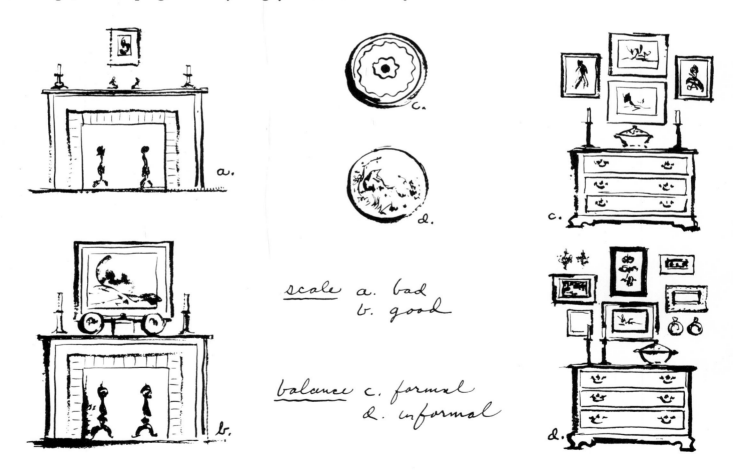

scale a. bad
b. good

balance c. formal
d. informal

14

This room has an international look, blending as it does: a French provincial cupboard, English and German blue-and-white plates, Mexican chairs, a New England maple table and Spanish hand-woven rug. Textures and colors are sturdy.

THE LANGUAGE
OF COLOR

Do YOU UNDERSTAND the language of color? Can your eye read the messages that colors send you? Do you practice color reception and perception daily to develop keenness and facility in the use of color?

To become an expert in color takes no extra time; you can cultivate and develop your eye's cunning as you feed the baby, shop for groceries or clean the house. Learning to see color is not greatly different from learning the meaning of what you hear, learning to read or even to speak.

Understanding the language of color is worthwhile because it can bring you endless delight and pleasure, not only in decorating, but in viewing the whole wide world. All but the blind see light-color, but unless you have practiced, you see it with a limited understanding comparable to a four-year-old's comprehension of the language of music. He hears but he doesn't understand.

You can see color, even see that a color is basically blue, red or violet, but you may not be able to separate its melody of hues, to sense fully its emotional factors or trace its style significance.

Color is not a thing that you can touch and feel in the sense that you can touch and feel a table or a fabric—green damask feels exactly like red damask. Color is like sound—a matter of wavelengths. The only difference is that color wavelengths are shorter. The ear cannot hear them; the eye is the receiver. Each hue has a different wavelength. All colors mixed make white light, daylight, the light of the sun. Shatter white light by passing it through raindrops or a prism, and you see a rainbow or the full color band. Because there are impurities in dyes and pigments, when they are mixed together, gray, not white, results.

An object appears to be the color that is rejected, or not absorbed, by the pigments in the object. For instance, a pillow appears to be red because the dye in the fabric absorbs all of the wavelengths in white light but the red ones. These waves move on through the air to be received by the eye, which says to us, "That's red." The expert immediately wants to know what type of red. Is it a pure red or is there some yellow in it, some blue?

Hundreds of different hues and millions of variations of them are discernible by the human eye. The basic six for which there are specific color names are red, yellow, blue, orange, green, and violet. A convenient color wheel for studying color includes six intermediate colors or twelve hues. Reading around the circle they are:

Red	Green
Red-orange	Blue-green
Orange	Blue
Yellow-orange	Blue-violet
Yellow	Violet
Yellow-green	Red-violet

If you graduated from an accredited high school, or if you have ever taken an art course, you have probably mixed paints and made a color wheel. With practice your eye will catch the subtle differences in colors and identify the hues which are blended and those which are pure. Your color vocabulary should include the following terms.

16

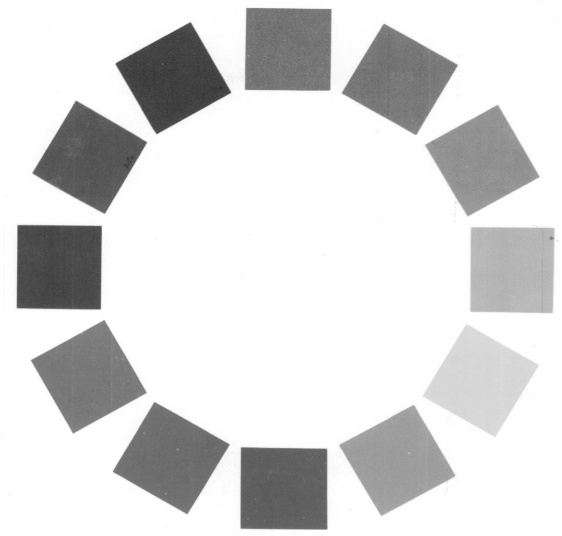

HUE: A term often used interchangeably with color. It is the distinguishing difference between colors. It is the redness of red, the greenness of green. Hues are pure, undiluted colors.

VALUE: The lightness or darkness of a color. The amount of difference may be reckoned by comparison with a scale of ten equal steps between black and white. Yellow has, naturally, a higher value than violet. Mixed with black, yellow turns brown, but yellow is an airy color when mixed with white. Violet becomes almost black when black is added, but becomes a light, clear orchid when diluted with white.

INTENSITY: Also called chroma, it is the degree or strength of a color. Weak intensities are close to neutral gray, but strong intensities are pure. Imagine two reds, one strong, pure color and the other with a weak, grayish cast. The difference between these two reds is one of intensity.

All so-called grayed colors, the popular off-beat or "dirty" colors, are softer than the light or dark values of the same hues, and are useful in decorating large areas and for achieving unusual color effects.

Terms commonly used to describe variations in value and chroma include the following:

    Tints are hues with white added.
    Tones are hues with gray added.
    Shades are hues with black added.

Color Confidence

CORRECT TERMINOLOGY is important because it develops color confidence. It is even more important to build up your own color responses until every hue, tint, shade, and value have meaning for you. Develop your personal reactions. Don't just look at color—experience it, hear, taste, smell, feel it. As you peel an orange, smell its pungency, taste its sharp sweetness and relate it in your mind to the color orange. As you cut and eat a melon, trace the color from the gray-green hue at the skin line through the lime tint of the flesh to the flash of coral at the center. Now close your eyes and feel a sunset.

Learning to "see" and "feel" color covers only a part of color understanding. To handle color successfully you need to be conscious of emotional responses, to be familiar with basic color associations and color as it has been used through the ages.

To "see" red and "feel" blue are only two of the many well-known reactions to color. Everyone knows the expressions "green with envy," "purple with rage," "pink of condition," "in a brown study," "yellow streak." Such colorful and frequently used phrases, which have become part of everyday speech, are proof that colors cause psychological reactions.

Response to color is all mixed up with body chemistry. Some people rise and shine in the early morning— their preference, no doubt, will be for clear, challenging colors. Others begin to feel like themselves only by noon and very likely will respond to more conservative colors which are diluted slightly with white and lightened to correspond to a sun-soaked garden at midday. A third type may begin to shine by late afternoon. They will like strong tints and slightly grayed colors: turquoise, coral, chartreuse. Finally, there is the late-evening person, who purrs when surrounded by dark, dramatic colors, luxurious fabrics and an air of opulence.

Study paintings and it becomes clear that all artists have a favorite palette. Think of paintings by Van Gogh, Matisse and Dufy. These are clear morning colors. Then observe Utrillo's dusty midday hues, Turner's and Bonnard's high-keyed, rosy, late-afternoon tints, and Gauguin's and Rubens' rich, dark values.

The hide-a-bed corner of a studio apartment with a happy yellow color scheme developed around the shades in the chintz. The accessories are good.

To have color confidence, discover the hues, the values, the intensities that lift your spirit. Discover the colors enjoyed by each member of your family. Learn to see colors in the world around you and see how they change through the day. Become familiar with:

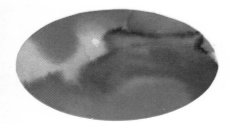

COLORS IN THE GARDEN, where you can study the fascinating range through red to pink in roses, peonies, phlox, azaleas and zinnias; where delphiniums give lessons in blue, chrysanthemums, nasturtiums, and gaillardias tell a matchless yellow story, and foliage offers a choice of hundreds of tints, shades and values in green.

COLORS IN THE SEA, which give a master lesson in blues, grays, greens and white. Follow a wave from its crest to its valley, see the turquoise, deep violets and blues, and how they break into a white froth. See the pale greens and grays of the ocean on cloudy days and the deep blues of late evening. See how the water changes as it comes in over the sand flats and as it reflects the sunset.

COLORS IN THE FOREST, which will make you an expert in the green family. Any artist knows that the glint and shadow of the sun on leaves creates dozens of greens on a single tree, from pale yellow and gray-green clear through to black moss green. There is the tender green of willows in the spring and the black-green of yews, the rich leatherlike green of summer oak and the unique red-greens of swamp maple in the fall.

COLORS OF THE SUN, which range through all the reds and yellows, with many degrees of orange and orange-red and yellow. See them in sunbeams, see them in sunlight white, sun gold, sunsets and sunrises.

COLORS OF THE ATMOSPHERE are clouded, grayed, subtle but delightful—morning mist, pale beige smoke, airborne silver fog, silver evening hues, mauve shadows on the snow.

By studying color you will learn to think in color terms and see it in all its infinite variety. Seeing color accurately is the first step in using color successfully and in combining hues in color schemes.

Further help and understanding come from familiarity with the colors associated with geographic areas or nationalities. White, gray and middle blues are linked with the Scandinavian countries. Hot red, orange, pink have a Latin connotation. Temple rites and festivals in Asia bring visions of brilliant reds, sharp greens, royal blues, screaming pinks and rich yellows, picked out with gold and tinsel.

There is also the relation of color to a period. The hues used express the character of furniture just as they reflect the social and economic climate. Who would use subtle Louis XV fabrics and colors, the grayed blues and pinks, mauve and yellow, on dark heavy Tudor furniture? Who would use hearty red, blue, and green Early American colors in a dainty Louis

20

The green-and-blue color scheme was developed from the chintz window shades which are hung over, not under, the full sheer floor-length glass curtains. The shaggy rug, the black wire chairs and the palm tree contribute to the garden atmosphere.

XVI room? Who would disturb a calm English eighteenth-century room with clashing Spanish colors?

During depressions, colors are drab and serious, but let times be prosperous, and gay, light, frivolous and elegant hues take front and center.

The subject of color doesn't fall exclusively into fashion, economic, technical, social, and psychic realms. Its active relation to light and air vibrations gives color a demanding nature, makes it a factor in the architectural aspect of a room.

Clashing colors used in a small room can create as much commotions as a jostling crowd of people. Colors with short wavelengths, the violets and blues, make a room serene and cool; longer yellow wavelengths are warm and active. Red fills a room with long wavelengths; it is an actual presence. The correct use of color can make a room seem larger or smaller, warmer or cooler, active or passive.

Guides to Color Schemes

DEALING WITH COLOR—assembling colors, selecting colors, combining colors—is probably the most satisfying part of decorating. With a few basic guides, anyone can develop delightful color schemes. It isn't a mysterious business; there is no hocus-pocus. All you have to do is learn to see color and understand the few key methods of combining colors. These methods, in a sense, correspond to building chords in music or phrases in language.

There are five basic methods for combining colors, all quite simple, like scales in music—you can forget them after you have mastered them.

THE NO-COLOR SCHEME is a twentieth-century phenomenon. Walls, draperies, carpet and even the upholstery may be white or off-white. A Stockholm designer even rubbed white paint into oak floors before waxing them—a handsome background for a shaggy Rya rug woven with a range of white yarns in varied textures. Usually one major accent color is used—in a dramatic painting, an important chair, or cushions. Add some handsome green plants and soft fruitwood tables and the "no-color" room develops a feeling of color. White gives maximum reflection, and each texture and surface will modify the color it reflects, so that far from being a colorless room, the no-color room may hum with reflected greens, with beige, with accent notes that change through the day as the light changes.

The no-color room may not be the answer for the family with children, but this type of color scheme is worth remembering and using when a luxurious effect is wanted.

ONE-COLOR SCHEMES, also called monochromatic, are built around the tints, shades, and variations of one hue used with white or black. A one-color room might have light-blue walls and draperies, a medium-blue carpet, midnight blue sofa, a tweed mixture of light and dark blue-and-white upholstery on several chairs and perhaps one white leather wing chair. Add green plants, flowers, pictures and wood tones and it is a lovely room which is far from dull. The same type of color scheme can be made with changes in the lightness, darkness and saturation of greens or reds or yellows. Popular beige-to-brown schemes fall into this classification. Beige is a grayed, diluted yellow, and brown is yellow with black which may also be grayed. These are easy color schemes to achieve and are easy to live with.

ANALOGOUS COLOR SCHEMES, also called related hue harmonies, are groups of colors which are related in hue, or neighbors on the color wheel. If all the colors used share one hue, the scheme has a close harmony. For example, green, yellow-green, green-yellow and yellow are closely related because they all have yellow in their

22

composition. Interest is created by introducing variations in lightness, darkness and saturation. In working out these variations, remember that grayed colors and pure colors tend to neutralize each other. A more pleasing harmony can be made with light and dark grayed colors or light and dark pure colors.

COMPLEMENTARY COLOR SCHEMES are strong, bold and useful when selecting accent colors and making flower arrangements. However, since complementary colors, when used side by side, seem stronger, complementary colors have to be combined with judgment, with variations in value and intensity and a consideration of the area to be covered.

Complements are those colors which are directly opposite on the color wheel:

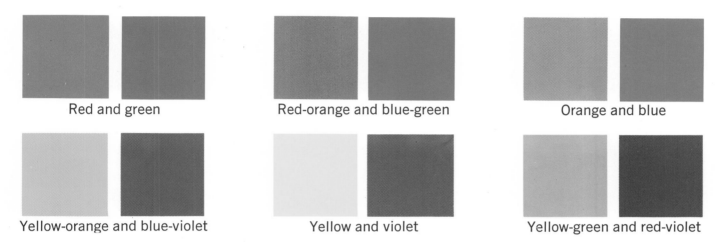

Red and green	Red-orange and blue-green	Orange and blue
Yellow-orange and blue-violet	Yellow and violet	Yellow-green and red-violet

If an all-blue room seems a bit tiresome, introduce a few orange pillows or a bunch of orange zinnias and see what happens.

In a room with white walls, green carpet and draperies and green-and-white chintz upholstery, introduce a big bunch of red roses and the whole room seems more interesting.

TRIADIC HUE harmonies are developed by using three hues equally spaced around the color wheel. In a twelve-hue wheel the triads are:

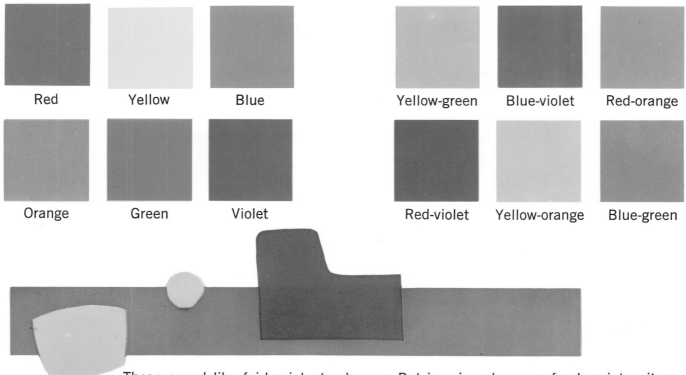

| Red | Yellow | Blue | | Yellow-green | Blue-violet | Red-orange |
| Orange | Green | Violet | | Red-violet | Yellow-orange | Blue-green |

These sound like fairly violent schemes. But imagine changes of value, intensity, and their unique nature appears. A room with blue walls, a white carpet, red and white upholstery and gold (yellow) accents would be charming.

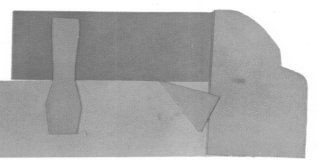

Or imagine a room with grayed yellow-green (bronze) walls, a lighter carpet of the same color, red-orange upholstery and blue-violet accents. Lovely!

Creative Color Schemes

THE FIVE BASIC methods for developing color schemes outlined in the foregoing will help you in the beginning; but until you are able to master them and then put them out of your mind and follow your own inspiration you will be a novice at handling color and an I.B.M. machine could produce color schemes as effective as yours.

In decorating, the simplest and often the most satisfying color schemes are built up around a picture, a fabric or a carpet. This is easy to do—just select from a key fabric the two or three most interesting colors. Plot the areas each is to occupy and you have a guide, a control for the rest of the room and possibly a satisfying color scheme quite different from one derived from a scientific formula.

Before you have to cope with color problem in decorating, experiment with color, learn the scales, the alphabet of color. Here are some games to play. Collect a box of fabric clippings, a folder of colored papers, colored advertisements and fashion pictures. Play games with the clippings. Plan imaginary room schemes.

Keyed to red with large masses of black and white, the color scheme acquires a certain magic from the subtle red violet and blue printed linen table cover and the bunch of anemones.

Assemble gay, lighthearted schemes, dramatic, unusual effects, placid homey ones. Start with a picture, select colors from it—let it launch a color scheme. Play with the clippings until you begin to really see them and can interpret what the colors have to say. Once you have done this, you have mastered the ABC's, the language of color, and you'll never have any further problems.

Shopping for the furnishings of a room will be less haphazard if you have a color plan worked out and carry a sample card of color swatches with you. This is the way to avoid errors, to take advantage of sales and accidental discoveries.

The home-fashion color cycle is not as hectic as the clothes cycle, and it never makes a clean sweep; rather, there are cycles within cycles.

Over a ten-year spread, colors will move from light to dark. Whirling along inside the big fashion wheel will be a changing series of colors which may be at their peak only two or three years at a time. Pink may be everywhere, then turquoise, followed by violet and then perhaps green, and so on through the rainbow.

Never take up a fashion color just because it's fashionable, but if yours is a yellow room and moss green is the fashion color, it may be fun to use it as an accent color in pillows or slipcovers—whatever note that can be easily changed. Recognizing and using current colors before they are everywhere is the way to develop a color reputation.

26   **The same room as the one on page 24 in summer dress. Blue ticking is stretched over the walls and slipcovers the sofa, the print has been removed from the table and paintings replace the mirror. Green accents reflect the new cool color mood.**

Violets Are Soothing

A BRIEF
ON BUDGETS

EVERYTHING TODAY but the sky, air, clouds, rain, sunshine, joy and a deep true sense of appreciation costs money. Furnishing a house that will make you proud and happy is one of the costly things of life, but the price varies widely. What you spend may amount to a small fortune or be less than a thousand dollars, depending on your circumstances. But even with a minimum budget your home can say, "Nice people live here."

Some women will leaf through this book and, instead of getting a lift, a feeling of excitement and pleasure out of the pictures, colors, ideas and accessories, will feel unhappy and discontented with their lot. They will believe that it is only lack of money that stands between them and a charming home—whereas the real barrier is their own attitude—that "world owes me a living" syndrome. The only way to get the life, the house, the furnishings, the joy you want is to make the best of what you have at every step of your life. Wield a paint brush and a hammer and use imagination if your cash is limited. Sometimes a minimum of money and a maximum of ingenuity produce the most exciting results. A beautiful home does not happen overnight; there is no Aladdin's lamp approach. It takes years of knowing, dreaming and collecting to arrive at perfection.

Houses to suit various family requirements can be roughly divided into four main types: the economy house, the comfortable or family house, the "personal" house and the "prestige" house. The shopping pattern and the desired effect are different for each one. The first three types of houses can be achieved even on a limited budget if there is a will and ambition.

How Much is Enough

THERE ARE CONVENTIONAL guides which are worth reviewing before listing ways and means of spending what you have, or planning to decorate with a small budget. There are no rigid rules to go by: investments, future job potentials, family contributions and background may affect the amount you can afford to spend. However, studies of family income and outgo show that, if hidden reverses are not encountered, the house you buy may cost approximately twice your annual income. If your income is ten thousand dollars, you can manage to buy a twenty-thousand-dollar house.

Furnishings may cost one fourth the cost of the house, or half your annual income. This allots the modest sum of $5,000 for the furnishings of a $20,000 house, and this is hardly enough.

The way to stretch a home-furnishings budget is to give some of your own time and skills to the furnishing project and to operate on a long-term basis. Start with necessities only and gradually, year by year, make additions. In a five-room house or apartment it would be reasonable to distribute your funds in the following way:

Living room and foyer: sofa, two upholstered chairs, a desk or chest, a coffee table and two lamp tables, lamps, draperies, rug 40%

Dining area: table, six chairs, a buffet, chest or serving table 20%

Two bedrooms: two beds, three chests, three bedside tables, two chairs, rug, draperies, three lamps 30%

Kitchen: 10%

Of course, being reasonable and consistent isn't always the way to get the most exciting results. There are several ways of stretching a small home-furnishings budget, and the course you select will depend on your circumstances, temperament and abilities. All methods begin with an over-all decorating plan, a picture in your mind as well as on paper of what you need and want. From this point procedure varies.

METHOD 1 If you have had no decorating experience or training and have no confidence, you may go to a furniture store and spread your funds thinly over inexpensive suites of furniture for every room. You may even let the salesmen influence your choice. Even though you resort to installment terms to get everything you think you need, the results will probably be average—with no excitement, long-term investment value or true quality.

The average family can assume an installment obligation of up to 12 per cent of its basic monthly income with 1 per cent deducted for each dependent. This limit applies not to furniture alone, but to over-all credit obligations. Of course, furniture bought on the installment plan costs more than a cash purchase—the true price is the base price plus as much as 20 per cent interest. If you do buy furniture or carpets on the installment plan, don't be misled by the small amount you pay each month. Get two quotations: (a) the cash price; (b) the cash price plus the total carrying charges for a time-payment program. Then make your decision with your eyes open.

METHOD 2 This plan requires a husband who is a cabinetmaker at heart, a real handyman, with a workshop. The cash reserve can be put into good upholstered pieces and bedding. Chests, all smaller pieces, can gradually be produced in the workshop. These makeshift pieces will tide you over until the budget permits the purchase of investment-quality casegoods (wood furniture).

METHOD 3 The way of young sophisticates who want a "personal" house, who have an awareness of living and confidence in themselves, is to tolerate empty spaces until they find just the right thing and can pay for it. Wonderful results can be had with almost nothing at all by combining Methods 2 and 3.

In all three methods of buying, bedding should have top priority. It should be new and the best you can afford. A good double box spring and mattress of standard size is the least expensive. Extra-large beds and twin beds cost more and require a larger investment in sheets, blankets and bedspreads. Laundering costs are higher, too. A sofa and upholstered chair should be the next purchase. These may cost as much as you can afford and may be a proud lifetime investment.

To stretch your sofa and chair money, for quality as well as years of service, select simple straight-line models of standard dimensions. Curved lines, unusual proportions and details sell in less volume, may be passing fashions, require more handwork and cost more. For example: Two sofas are the same price. One has a curved, exposed wood frame and bisquit tufting; the other is a simple, straight-line Lawson. The chances are that the straight-line one will be of better quality.

After buying the mattress, sofa and chair, the handyman may head for the lumber yard, and our young sophisticates will start scouring the family attics, going to rummage sales, Salvation Army stores, and secondhand shops. With ingenuity in selection, perseverance in refinishing and painting, and the alchemy of imagination, striking interiors can be achieved with inexpensive odds and ends collected from here and there.

31

Scavenging is an art as practiced in New York by college students and young career people. Discards from apartments are put out on the street for the city garbage collector, and many first apartments are furnished by grabbing the cast-off pieces before they are hauled away. Some of the finds are very handsome and are far from being "just any old junk." Even in this field one develops a certain connoisseurship. One young couple was offered two hundred dollars for a Victorian Morris chair with a ratchet back and book holder, which they found, rebuilt and re-covered in a remnant bought at an outlet store.

Also remember that off-season sales of summer furniture may offer real bargains. Peel tub chairs, deck chairs, directors' chairs, old Bar Harbor chairs and ladderback Southern mountaineer chairs are frequently in the less-than-ten-dollars category. Yards and yards of inexpensive cotton, even cheesecloth hung full and put up with a staple gun, are prettier than skimpy, pretentious draperies.

I recall the first apartment of a young married couple who had a meager free-lance writer's income. They rented a loft space with two windows and a skylight. Scrub brushes and a good all-purpose detergent were their first investment, paint their second. One wall was painted coral, the other walls and the floor were painted white. Paul built a box about twenty-four inches wide and six inches deep—the width of the coral wall under the skylight—and lined it with polyethylene. Each weekend they brought back from Long Island bags of white pebbles until the box was full. In it they established a jungle pot garden. A ladder up to the skylight, which was shielded with split-bamboo porch shades from Sears, Roebuck, was painted coral. A big white Mexican hammock was slung across one corner of the room and a huge white bubble lantern was hung from the ceiling to within thirty inches of the floor. Also hung from the ceiling was a forty-inch-long coral, white and black Japanese paper kite fish. Two black director's chairs and a miscellany of colorful floor cushions constituted the rest of the furnishings.

For the bed, box spring and mattress rested on the floor. The spread was an old blue patchwork quilt. Brick-and-plank shelves and covered baskets were substitutes for chests, and all sorts of things were hung on the walls—driftwood, bunches of dried grasses, the bleached bony skeleton of a fish (a Picasso touch), and some

Small scale furniture and the yellow-and-white color scheme give amazing spaciousness to this small room. The cupboard was made from an old door, and the furniture was bought at auctions.

dashing red wash paintings. An old chest painted antique red, with heavy black strap hinges, and two bright-blue ladderback chairs completed this highly individual room.

When the time comes to replace some of the "junk" which has tided you over, don't worry about combining good pieces, new or antique, with the refinished, painted miscellany you started with. If the room has plan and pattern, fine additions will improve it and make everything look better. If you have one fine lamp, don't hesitate to use plain inexpensive white classic shapes with it. Plain white ironstone saucers make good ashtrays and fade into the background better than more elaborate and almost-good ashtrays. A coffee table cut from an old pedestal dining table and painted black will quietly serve while the eye is engaged by a beautiful chest which may have cost several hundred dollars more than the table. As William Allan White has pointed out, "Consistency is a paste jewel that only cheap men cherish."

It's Not What You Spend

BEGIN A PICTURE collection with at least one original, even if it is a pencil sketch. Get a "thing" too that symbolizes your dreams and build your room around it: a bit of carved wood, an ironstone pitcher, an old lute or Japanese silk tapestry. Grow your own plants. With patience, an avocado seed will turn into a fine substitute for a palm and a schefflera bought for a few dollars will fill a corner.

Furnishing this way creates an evolving home with continuing projects the whole family can work on. There's the fun and excitement of new finds, new things to show when friends call. It is the opposite of yearning for extravagant things you may never own, of frittering your life away on aimless wishing. The positive approach leads to knowledge and experience.

Even with a reasonable budget it is sometimes difficult to know how and on what to spend. Through your own lifetime the focus will change. The person who rents has different problems from an owner. If your property is old, the approach will be different, or if you have valuable pictures or family furniture your budget takes a different turn.

For example, two couples bought cooperative apartments in the same building at the same time. One family had put up with a shabby apartment for years, saving on clothes, on food, on travel, assembling a fund against the time when they could own property. They wanted their new apartment to be gorgeous but practical and they had the money to make it so. They reconditioned their better pieces of furniture; the other pieces were passed on to a married daughter. Their capital was spent on carpets, curtains, draperies, wall coverings and medium-priced but classic furniture. The apartment draws "ah's" and "oh's" from everyone who sees it.

The other couple had some fine family furniture but no lump sum for furnishing. Their plan was to spend a little each year out of income until the apartment was completed. Since they had many books, they first spent several thousand dollars putting built-in shelves across one wall of the living room and around the bed in one of the bedrooms. Their curtains were ready-made, the rug old. The apartment is comfortable and in time can be handsome, but now it causes no exclamations.

Still another couple haunt picture galleries, have developed an acquaintance with many young artists around the country and, using a time-payment plan, have acquired some really fine paintings. Their house is simple; the walls are all painted white, bamboo shades shield the windows, upholstery is black and white with brilliant dashes of color. Their major investment is in their pictures. Their house is a pleasure to visit.

Finally, there is a couple on Long Island who own their own home and have children in their teens. Their house is pleasant but up to now they have not had any furniture of any worth. Mrs. S. has enlisted the help of a decorator. When he finds the perfect piece of furniture, it is bought. Eventually some walls will be wood-paneled, some damask-covered; cornices will be added in the dining room, carpeting and fine pictures where appropriate.

To overspend on furnishing your house can be tragic; not to spend what you can afford is an affront to your family. But to want an attractive home and then not do anything about it suggests that you haven't the confidence to do it yourself. You need a decorator.

34 **Inexpensive furniture handled with imagination requires no excuses. From the smartly painted black floor and the white-and-black plaid rug to the snappy red plank shutters, this room gives pleasure.**

WHY USE A DECORATOR?

MECHANICS, EVEN excellent mechanics, do not build their own automobiles. If you are ill, you call a doctor; on legal matters you consult a lawyer; when building a house you engage an architect or a builder. If your husband's hobby is baseball, he doesn't expect to play with the pros—he is content to watch them. But only now, after years of obscure labor, are decorators being recognized as useful and essential professionals offering valuable aid even on budget projects.

Decorating involves a tremendous amount of headwork, footwork and organization and is a fairly costly undertaking. It means being an expert in a dozen different fields: lighting, space division, traffic flow, color, man-made fibers, furniture construction, finishes and styles—to name only a few.

You may know just how you want your home to look; but the market is complex, and it might take days of shopping to locate just the right drapery fabric, the exact lamp, the perfect table. Sometimes you can shop your locality from end to end and come up with nothing you really want. In such a situation, professional help can save you time, money and worry. Once your decorator has a clear understanding of what you need, experience, market knowledge, another head and another pair of feet go into action. You save hours and are spared possibly costly mistakes.

The experience of working with a decorator can be both educational and fascinating. A friend of mine who has just finished furnishing her apartment found the project so stimulating that she urges all her friends to do likewise. In fact, she can hardly wait to get a larger apartment so that she can continue to work with her decorator. She contends that interior design is a more personal pleasure than going to the theater and much more entertaining.

Some women find doing their own decorating a shattering experience, but still are reluctant to call in an expert. They seem to be embarrassed if they have a decorator; they take it as an admission of failure. However, there is a growing group who have mastered this psychological quirk and talk about "my decorator" just as they talk about "my psychiatrist."

How to Select a Decorator

As IN ANY profession, there are decorators and decorators. Someone has lightly divided them into charm-gatherers, designers and innovators. Certainly, among the 10,000 decorators listed in the 1960 United States Census, there are both qualified and unqualified individuals who range all the way from mere shoppers to competent professionals. Decorators fall into four classifications:

- Decorators who are just shoppers.
- Decorators associated with department and furniture stores.
- Decorators who offer consultation and supply floor plans, fabrics and draperies.

Only a decorator would have the courage to use this large-scale mural wallpaper in such a small room. The light metal furniture used with it seems to take up almost no space and is the secret of the success of this dramatic small bedroom.

- Decorators who take over the whole project, submit architectural and furniture plans and perspectives on a completely professional basis.

Since the range of services is wide, you can select help according to your needs and budget. If you are reasonably knowledgeable, you may want advice only on carpets and draperies. Perhaps you like the work of a department or furniture store in your community. You may then find it feasible to use its decorating service, and there will probably be no fee, or at most a minimum one. But if you want a complete interior-design service you may want other help.

There are two professional societies, the American Institute of Interior Designers (A.I.D.) whose national headquarters are at 673 Fifth Avenue, New York, N. Y. 10022, and the National Society of Interior Designers (N.S.I.D.), 157 West 57th Street, New York, N.Y. 10019. Although there are qualified interior designers who are not members of either group, membership indicates training and experience. About 15 per cent of all listed decorators are members of one or the other, and the national headquarters of both organizations or the local chapter will give you a list of dependable members in your locality. Your request should include a brief statement of the job you have in mind so that designers specializing in your needs can be recommended.

Before selecting a designer, if possible look at some of his completed projects. If this is not possible, ask to see photographs or sketches. To get the kind of room you want, you must have a certain kinship with your decorator. A designer specializing in modern work will not execute the ideal eighteenth-century room, and the decorator who does highly sophisticated interiors will not be happy developing a country look, though there are some versatile designers who can and will produce up to "57 varieties."

Throughout this discussion, the terms "decorator" and "interior designer" have been used interchangeably. The original term was "interior decorator." This phrase was used by so many people, many of them unqualified, that the two professional interior design organizations have substituted and promoted the use of the preferred designation, "interior designer."

According to the A.I.D. Bulletin, "an interior designer is a person qualified by training and experience to plan and supervise the design and execution of interiors and their furnishings . . . to organize the various arts and crafts essential to their completion."

About Decorators' Fees

FIND OUT EXACTLY what the basis for fees are, and how, when and in what form bills will be submitted and whether a contract form will be used. It is always better to understand financial matters at the beginning than to be surprised at the end. Fees are handled in several ways: straight retail with a deductible retainer; an hourly design, shopping or consultation commission; cost-plus; retail sales commission only; or a combination of these methods. It is quite natural to use a different method of charging for a $75,000 job than for a $1,000 one; and for a $1,000 project than for the purchase of a single chair.

STRAIGHT RETAIL WITH A DEDUCTIBLE RETAINER is probably the most common method. An estimate is made of the cost of the project and after plans and sketches have been submitted, a 10 to 15 per cent advance or retainer is paid by the client as a guarantee that the designer will be allowed to execute the plans. This retainer is deducted from the final bill.

The interior designer's profit is in the difference between the wholesale price and the price he charges the client. If important architectural changes are made or special built-in furnishings are a part of the project, an additional design fee may be asked, based either on an hourly fee or 10 per cent of the cost of the job.

HOURLY DESIGN COMMISSION is a method of charging used by both large and small firms. A record of the total time spent is kept and the design fee is based

This is the living room of an average house built in the 20's. The decorator paneled one wall, framed the fireplace in a bolection molding, painted the walls white and the floor blue and was off to a flying start toward an updated, charming room.

on the salary outlay involved plus a profit; this may run as high as 30 per cent of the total cost of the job. If carried through in its entirety, this program of charges calls for no rebate to the designer on furniture or fabric purchases. Selections are suggested, but the client can make the purchases wherever he wants. If these are ordered by the designer, the wholesale price may even be passed on to the client, depending on the base fee already charged.

An hourly consultation commission is often used by clients with modest budgets. If the client knows in advance what the hourly rate is, she is less apt to waste time in idle talk. The minimum hourly fee may be twenty-five dollars. A full day's consultation may be a hundred dollars. In a day a decorator can supply a fairly exact decorating plan for one or several rooms, which the client herself can then work out. If, however, the client wants furniture, fabrics or other things ordered, the decorator may take a sales commission. Charming rooms—but rarely remarkable ones—can be developed this way.

COST-PLUS refers to the designer's fee, based on a fixed percentage of the total cost of a job. This is a standard method used by architects and industrial designers. When a great deal of special designing is involved, charges are apt to be a straight percentage of the net cost, but on a smaller job, charges may be made on an hourly basis, plus a 10 or 15 per cent commission on purchases. Some designers have established minimum fees as protection against time wasted on jobs that do not materialize.

RETAIL SALES COMMISSION, as used by interior designers, is the difference between the wholesale price of furniture, fabrics, and rugs which the decorator pays and the retail price he charges the client. This is the key to the operation of the decorator-shopper—who may not be a designer but who has an established credit rating and access to decorator showrooms that are closed to the public. These showrooms and shops, as a rule, have a card on the door that reads, "To the Trade Only."

FREE CONSULTATION is offered by some stores. However, the free service is often so misused that many stores with large decorating departments now make a minimum charge. They have found that women take hours conferring with decorators, permit a home call or even ask for floor plans and then pass up the store merchandise and buy elsewhere, using the store plan. Now it is usual for a store to make a moderate charge for simple plans, deductible from the first purchase. The rates vary with different stores.

MANY DECORATORS will only make minor changes in their initial presentation. "We find," one decorator explained, "that too many changes can ruin a scheme. We give clients what we think is best and insist that the spirit of the job be retained if we do it." This is the dream of all designers, but the majority are willing to modify a plan to please the client even if the change does not improve it.

All but minimum jobs should be covered with a contract, drawn up by the decorator. The client should expect to have the following points covered in the contract:
- Plans and specifications for design or architectural alterations must be submitted by the decorator and agreed to in writing by the client before work begins.
- All delivery and freight charges are paid by the client.
- All sales taxes are paid by the client.
- All guarantees by the manufacturers are passed along to the client. The decorator should offer no guarantees beyond the maker's claim.
- Nothing should be ordered by the decorator before the signed confirmation order is received. This form should contain a description of the merchandise, its price, any fee or service applicable, any sales tax or delivery charge.

Standard practice between a decorator and his client usually calls for a deposit of one third to one half the estimate at the time the client confirms the order. On delivery, the final billing for individual items will be made and the full amount due paid promptly.

Blue violet flower-strewn wallpaper launched this simple bedroom. Instead of draperies, wallpaper-covered plywood frames the window. An inexpensive maple chest was enriched with white china knobs and blue violet paint with green trim.

THE BACKGROUND

2

INTERIOR ARCHITECTURE

START A DECORATING project by studying the bare room or area to be furnished. Often minor changes in the architectural features of the room can make a major contribution. These may only involve putting in a bolder cornice at the ceiling line, the addition of several electric outlets; or they could mean the installation of a window wall or a case for the air conditioner.

If the room in question is one you are familiar with, it may take real concentration to take it apart in your mind to see what changes should be made. Review each area individually. Study the ceiling; examine the walls, windows, wood trim, lighting, hardware; finally, consider the floors and adjoining rooms. Ask yourself how each could be improved or what simple change could be made to better establish the mood you want to develop.

If you are going to be a short-term occupant of the room—in other words, if you rent or have a short lease—throttle any impulse to make major architectural changes. Work out ways and means of remodeling with paint, wallpaper and fabrics—teamed, they can work wonders in minimizing or even eliminating background flaws. Invest in good furniture and pictures you can take with you.

However, if you own the property or have a long lease, correcting background faults before painting, papering or resurfacing walls and ceiling may bring more satisfaction than any other expenditure. In time, a faulty architectural feature can get on your nerves as much as a squeak in a car; and on the other hand, the addition of even one correct detail, such as a colonial mantel in a room that is to reflect that period, can make a major contribution.

Consciousness of the space in the room and adjoining areas should parallel your study of the background. After all, the space is intended for people, chairs, tables and lamps. Only after the space is occupied in your mind's eye, only after you see people moving through the rooms, the furniture in place and the lights and shadows cast on the walls and floors, is it time to consider changes.

To get the feeling of the room, wander around and study it from every angle. Also look at the room while you are seated. If no chairs are available, put a box or a barrel where the sofa will be placed. Then move it over by the fireplace and visualize the family grouped around it as you pour tea on a Sunday afternoon. Look out the windows, consider the view and the exposure. Walk through all doors both out and in and consider the vista in both directions.

Rid yourself of the tyranny of the room as it now appears. You may want to modify the size, make it larger or smaller. It is quite simple to remove partitions but expensive to shift supporting walls. Often a room can be reshaped by removing closets or by adding storage walls. Irregularities can be smoothed out by adding bookshelves or closets. A room can be optically reshaped by paneling one wall. Paneling on the end wall of a narrow room makes it seem wider. If the paneling is applied to the long side wall, the room will appear narrower and longer. The type of paneling, the wood and finish, also make, a major style contribution, and this must be carefully balanced with other decorating elements.

Vertical paneling, whether plank or plywood,

connotes informality, has a country look. Smooth plywood paneling without accented joints establishes a modern feeling, and wood paneling with applied wood moldings develops a period atmosphere. Paint and wallpaper that contrast in color with the other walls offer a less expensive, if not so distinguished, method of reshaping a room.

Windows can also be used to apparently change dimensions. By the addition of a window wall or even a stock six- or eight-foot sliding glass door or a bay window, a room can be made to appear larger. If, by chance, the new windowed area has a grand view or opens onto a terrace, a new dimension to living has been added.

Ways with Woodwork

Now LOOK at the woodwork: the door and window trim, the baseboard, the molding or cornice around the ceiling. In a new house or apartment, you will find yourself examining a clean, unadorned box, without moldings or cornice to cast interesting shadows. If the house is old and was "good in its day," the weight and detail of the woodwork may be overwhelming. In the first case, you may want to build up interest; in the second, the problem may be to remove excessive detail before painting or perhaps bleaching what remains. What you do may depend on the mood you want to develop.

If detail is needed, it is quite simple to add a molding at the ceiling line and perhaps a narrower one four inches below it and in this way create an eight-inch cornice. In a dining room or hall the effect of a dado can be had inexpensively by simply adding a molding or chair rail thirty to thirty-six inches from the floor. The area below may be painted or papered to contrast with the upper portion.

Archways and door openings deserve attention. In houses with open planning, with entry, living and dining area combined in one open space, consider introducing barriers such as fin walls held in place at floor and ceiling, or actual hinged paneled screens. Tall, leafy plants, furniture dividers or portieres are alternatives.

In old and traditional houses there may be gaping archways, often with clumsily shaped tops. These can be easily squared off and columns can be removed. It might even be worthwhile to install, in the opening, handsome double doors painted the wall color, or a contrasting color or wood tone.

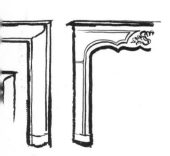

IF THERE IS a fireplace, consider it carefully. Eighteenth and early nineteenth-century fireplaces in this country were excellent. They were beautifully proportioned and scaled to the size of the wall and the room where they were used. They still remain in thousands of old houses, and measured drawings are available. Still, about nine tenths of the fireplace mantels seen in new houses are almost embarrassingly ugly.

Many are easy to change. Just rip off the wood framework and replace it with a heavy bolection molding. If you are on the Eastern seaboard, you may even be able to find an old mantel. If the facing is gaudy, paint both hearth and facing black or resurface them with slate. Early nineteenth-century marble mantels, often with arched openings, may be charming and can even be assimilated in rooms with modern furniture because of their simplicity. In modern and ranch-style houses, the fireplace may be just an opening in a brick, stone or masonry wall. Such fireplaces give a room a rugged, masculine air. Textures, colors, mood should cater to it.

Houses built between 1900 and 1930 may have plain brick fireplaces flanked by built-in bookcases squared off at mantel height. The wall will be much better-looking if the bookcases are continued up to the ceiling and the area over the fireplace is wood-paneled. If the fireplace is a deep one, closets flush with the face of the fireplace may be built on each side.

Carnation-strewn wallpaper with matching sheer white curtains give this room its air of freshness. By adding a simple half-round molding four inches below the existing molding the effect of a wide cornice was achieved.

Consider the Wiring

SINCE REWIRING involves wall damage, it, too, must be studied. Consider the present location of all fixtures and convenience outlets as well as the style and quality of the present fixtures. In a house or apartment, built within the past ten years, wiring may be adequate, but houses built during the forties or earlier may need more wiring and new fixtures. Locate the position of all electric outlets:

- Is there a ceiling fixture or chandelier?
- Should it be removed, replaced or relocated?
- Are there wall brackets? Should they be removed or replaced?
- Are there enough electric outlets for all purposes?

Double convenience outlets every six feet are considered adequate for living areas. Strip outlets or a power center are kitchen requirements.

In a bedroom, if you allow yourself all the comforts available, the usual two double convenience outlets are not enough for a bed wall. Check your requirements against this list:

Two lamps

An electric clock
One electric blanket (two for twin beds)
Electric shaver
Electric vibrator
Coffeemaker
Radio
Telephone
Intercom

The bathroom may also require special wiring. Outlets for an electric clock, a small night light, an electric shaver, a hair dryer and toothbrushes may be needed.

In a dining room with a sloping ceiling, actually place the table to be used under it before installing a drop fixture. The center of the ceiling is not the center of the floor space, and it is often difficult to locate the correct position for the ceiling outlet.

In remodeling an old house, consider an illuminated ceiling in bathroom and kitchen. They are simple to install, the lighting is superior and the effect good. Even in a traditional setting, don't overlook the value of spot lighting on pictures or the dining table. Such spots may even be used with a crystal chandelier.

The Heating System

IF ANY MAJOR changes are being made in the heating system, consider them in your survey. Perhaps bulky old radiators are being replaced by baseboard units; or, for a forced air system, smaller registers are replacing the old ones. Either of these changes may affect walls and floors.

Smooth or soft-surface floors are the last of the background projects. They should go in before draperies are hung so that the length of the curtains can be perfectly gauged. Brick, ceramic tile or flagstone floors should be installed before painting, as baseboards for such floors are usually installed after the floors are laid.

Hardwood floors may be bleached, painted, stenciled or elaborated with metal inserts, but the usual method of reconditioning them is to sand, stain them a dark or antique walnut. shellac and wax them.

Parquet Floor Patterns

Versailles

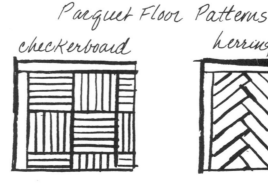

checkerboard

herringbone

butterfly wedges

46

An authentic New England fireplace in a house built in 1779. The wide floor boards and the flagstone hearth have been left, the firebricks were rechinked and a damper installed. Wallpaper with all-over pattern hides the roughness of the walls.

Simplicity is Elegance

A built-in bunk bed in this eight-by-eight bedroom saves space. Chintz is used for walls, curtain and bedspread.

Pennsylvania Dutch style is this simple brick-frame fireplace with bracket shelf. Cupboard conceals TV, Hi Fi.

A mantel was replaced by a wide molding which was also used for the bracket. Note the animal theme throughout.

The fine finish on the Hi Fi and TV cabinet contrasts with the wood-paneled wall and its interesting pictures.

By remodeling the door and adding beams this ordinary room was converted into a pleasant background for the Early American furniture. The rug is hand-hooked.

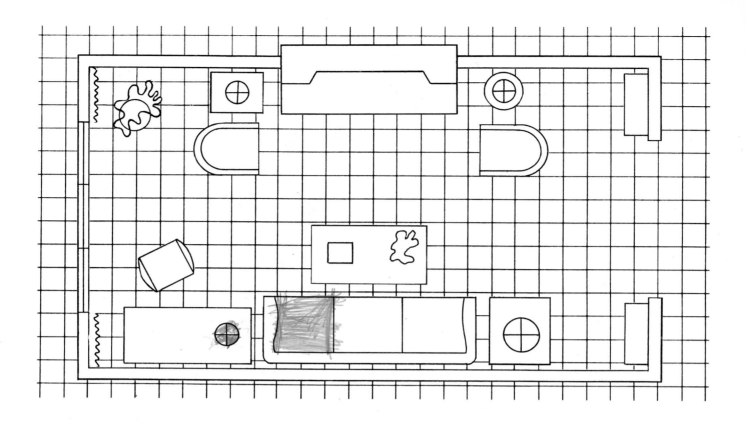

Room Chart

Now THAT ALL carpentry and electrical changes have been determined, it's time to make an exact room chart. Use a steel tape and record the following:

Size of room
Height of ceiling
Size of alcove or other room irregularities
Location of windows on each wall
Window sizes
Radiators
Location of doors on each wall
Door sizes
Location of fireplace or other architectural
    details
Over-all dimensions of fireplace
Over-all dimensions of hearth
Width of mantel top
Width of mantel
Width and length of wall space over mantel
Width of baseboard
Width of trim on windows and doors
Height of dado
Diagram of door paneling
Diagram of windows
Width of window trim

Distance from window top to ceiling
Height of window from floor
Sketches of unusual features

While the architectural features of the room are fresh in your mind, make a diagram using graph paper and allowing one-fourth inch to the foot. Scale paper makes this a simple job. It is interesting, but not necessary, to make wall plans. However, if you are drafting bookcases, fireplaces or other important features, work with a one-inch scale. If you are developing plans for built-in bookcases or cabinets, either draft them full-scale on the wall or make full-scale drawings with chalk on heavy drafting paper and hold the paper against the wall so that you can check the proportions and the scale of the unit before it is built.

The room chart is your helpmate in developing the furniture arrangement, in working with floor-covering salesmen, in developing the window treatment, in estimating the amount of paint or wallpaper needed, in about everything you do to the room from now on. Such a chart, which you can carry with you when shopping and selecting, will reduce both worry and errors.

PAINT POINTERS

PAINT IS possibly the most valuable and least expensive transformer at an interior designer's disposal. Given a room with shabby walls, a scuffed floor, a beat-up piece of furniture, an off-color lamp, paint them, and in a few hours, for a minimum cost, they become bright and beautiful, rescued and restored to the company of cherished possessions.

Four things are involved in any painting project—the object or surface, the paint, the brush or roller, and the painter. His contributions are imagination, a plan, and coordination with the rest of the project.

Whatever you decide to paint, start by analyzing the job. Select a color, determine whether the surface should be dull or glossy and whether any special effects are needed such as marbelizing, stenciling or spatterwork. Be as creative, as imaginative, as original as you please during the planning stage.

One manufacturer has developed formulas for 1,300 colors. You can mix the paint yourself by recipe or use the mixing service offered by many paint stores. You will get better cooperation if you are reasonable in your color demands. It is interesting to build a color scheme around an object, but it is almost impossible to match a paint color exactly to the pink of a shell lining, the blue of a cornflower, the red of an old Chinese brocade. The pigments and texture are different. Be content with a reasonable facsimile.

Study paint colors by daylight and lamplight in the room where they are to be used. Try a patch on the wall; live with it a few days. Note how it changes in value in the morning, afternoon and evening light. Remember that a color seems darker when used in a large area than in a small one. It is darker, too, in shadow and when it is wet.

If you are using any paint other than white, give the painter half the color sample; you keep the other half. Designers may ask to have both client and painter initial both samples to avoid after-the-fact arguments.

The plan for a paint project is not complete until every part of the room to be painted has been analyzed: ceiling, four walls, woodwork, doors, windows, fireplace and perhaps floors. Below are quick pointers to help you make decisions:

- Ceilings when painted white make rooms look higher; dark ceilings reduce height. If ceilings are painted the same color as the walls, they will look darker. If you decide on white ceilings, mix in a little of the wall color to develop a rapport between them. Sharp-colored ceilings—blue, grass green or Persian pink—may be handsome with white walls and woodwork but they will absorb light. In a high-ceilinged old house with fine woodwork, the cornice may match the ceiling color. In a basement game room with pipes and flues exposed, paint the ceiling and all pipes and flues black, and they will seem to disappear.
- Woodwork may be painted to match or contrast with the walls. It should contrast only when it is handsome and invites inspection. If a special cornice has been added, it may be painted a contrasting color, or to match the doors while all other woodwork matches the walls.
- Doors have two sides and four edges. They

may be painted to match the walls or they may be painted a contrasting color. Handsome doors centered on a wall may be painted a contrasting color: grass green, golden yellow or red.

- If adjoining rooms have different wall colors, the two faces of the door should match the color of the corresponding room; the edges of the door are painted to match the walls of the room the door swings into. The door jamb is painted to match the edge of the door which rests against it when closed.
- Paneled doors may be dramatized by painting the frame and panels different colors with a display line around each panel.
- The moving parts of windows, like doors, may match or contrast. They are usually painted the color of the woodwork, but they may be painted white or black.
- Include the inside of closets in your painting plans.
- Fireplaces may offer special problems. The wood mantel may match or contrast with the woodwork. In a room with painted woodwork, the mantel may have a natural wood finish. It may be painted black or it may be marbelized. Brick facings and hearths that strike a discordant color note may be painted black. Ugly brick or concrete-block fireplaces may be improved if painted the wall color or white.
- Shabby wood floors may be revived inex-

pensively with a coat of paint. The regular floor paints offer only drab colors, but alkyd paints in white, shocking pink or grass green, plain or spattered, lend excitement and, if kept waxed, hold up remarkably well except in rooms with heavy traffic.

There is a special paint for almost every purpose. There are wall paints, paints for woodwork, masonry, wood floors, cement floors, metals, paints for indoor and outdoor use. Before buying paint, read advertisements, consult friends and discuss the project with a paint dealer. He will recommend the correct paint for the job and give valuable pointers for its use.

For interior walls and ceilings, quick-drying, easy-to-apply flat latex paints are a good choice for amateurs. They are water-thinned and easy to wipe up. Use semigloss alkyd-based enamel on woodwork and in kitchens and bathrooms, where water resistance is important. Professional painters may use alkyd paints throughout the house. For walls in poor condition there are latex paints that dry with a ripple or fine sand finish. There are paints that are fire- and rust-retardant, and paints in spray cans under pressure that give a spatter finish.

The link between the painter and the paint is a brush or roller. Brushes come in many sizes for use with paint, enamel, shellac and varnish. There are large ones for walls, medium ones for woodwork and small ones for window muntins. Rollers vary in size also. Take the dealer's advice on the right equipment for the job.

Get-Ready Rules

START BY READING the label on the paint can, and read it as seriously as you read a new cake recipe or an insurance policy. Follow each step in a careful, workmanlike way. Here are a few general rules that apply to many types of painting projects:

- Clean and repair all surfaces to be painted; remove wax, grease, stains. Fill nail holes and cracks with putty-like spackling compound. After the compound hardens, smooth repaired and glossy surfaces with sandpaper and see that all surfaces are clean and dry. Don't be surprised if it takes more time to get ready to paint than it does to put the paint on.
- Prepare for painting by moving all furni-

ture to the middle of the room, cover with old sheets or plastic drop cloths. Loosen lighting fixtures and cover them with paper or transparent plastic wrap. Doorknobs, escutcheons and other hardware can be protected with a coat of petroleum jelly. Mix the paint thoroughly. This is an important step; don't slight it. It is a good idea to pour about two thirds of the paint into a clean, disposable pail or can and stir the remainder with a paddle until it is thoroughly mixed. Then gradually add and blend in the poured-off paint.
- Work in a well-ventilated room, especially when using materials that produce strong and harmful fumes.

The crisp lines of the fireplace and the square white painted tables contrast pleasantly with the country character of this informal sitting room in a remodeled carriage house. The slate floor is an attractive practical feature.

- Take care of the brush and roller. If the work is to go on for several days, clean the brush thoroughly when you stop painting for the day. Remove the excess paint by stroking the brush on newspapers. If using an alkyd or linseed-oil paint, soak brush in turpentine or brush cleaner; if a latex paint, wash it in detergent and water. Work the solution right up to the bristle setting. Before storing brush for future use, comb and straighten the bristles and wrap the brush in foil or plastic wrap so that the bristles remain straight and moist.
- Wear old clothes that won't get in your way: comfortable low-heeled shoes and old cotton gloves, a short-sleeved shirt and slacks that can be thrown away. Professional painters dress for the job and make a point of neatness and comfort.
- Consider safety. Since the only thing you need to fear about a paint job is falling off the ladder (painting mistakes can always be corrected), make sure that the ladder isn't rickety. Be sure it is fully spread and that the metal arms of the spreader are locked open before you use it. Never place a ladder in front of a door without first locking the door, or placing someone on guard, or at least posting a large notice on the other side.

How to Paint Walls and Woodwork

To CALCULATE THE paint needed for walls and ceiling, figure in square feet. A room of, say, twelve by fifteen feet, will require one gallon of paint, but consult the paint salesman to be sure. To calculate:

Ceiling area: Multiply the length of the room by the width.

Walls: Multiply the distance around the room by the height from floor to ceiling. Don't substract for windows and doors.

For woodwork, window frames, chair rails, baseboards: Measure and allow one pint of paint per one hundred running feet.

Read the label on the paint can to be sure you understand the directions for that particular paint. If an alkyd paint is to be used, patched areas must first be primed as directed on the label.

Paint the ceiling first, using a long-handled roller; for a neat job, first paint a twelve-inch strip around the sides, next to the wall, using a brush. Start to paint with the roller in a corner and roll the first stroke away from you, rolling into the painted strip. Always work from an unpainted area into a wet area. As you roll along, work backward into the edge of the previous strip and crisscross strokes to cover the area completely.

Paint walls from ceiling to baseboard, working your way to the left. Use vertical strokes, lifting the brush gradually at the end of each stroke to avoid depositing a thick edge of paint. Always paint from a dry area into a wet one. When you have covered an area about two feet wide by three feet long with up-and-down strokes, go over it with horizontal strokes. Be careful not to spin the roller at the end of a stroke as this action may spatter the paint. Protect ceiling, baseboard and all woodwork with a piece of cardboard or, if you prefer to have your hand free, use masking tape.

How to Paint Floors

THIS IS AN easy job, once the floor is rid of wax and dirt. Paint is a good way to treat floors that have become badly scarred or that have no particular beauty worth preserving. It is an authentic treatment for Early American rooms. If you are repainting an old floor, touch up the worn spots with enamel thinned with turpentine, fill cracks and sand when dry. Deep, wide cracks can be filled more successfully if they are given a thin layer of the filler first. When this has dried, fill the crack. A roller makes a quick job of floor painting; but first, using a brush, paint a strip around the baseboard, where it is difficult to use a roller without spotting the woodwork. New wood requires a minimum of three coats, the first one thinned with turpentine. Tough deck enamel and alkyd paint especially recommended for floors give the most lasting finish.

To paint concrete floors, use paint especially

The white louvered doors open into the living room. To give the old dining room furniture a little gaiety in keeping with the new house, the chairs were painted. The hat rack and ivy are real, but the bird, the nest and the green ribbon are painted.

made for this purpose which will not be damaged by the alkali in the concrete. If the floor is below grade, use a latex paint made for such floors.

How to Spatter Floors

SPATTERWORK DATES back to Colonial days. It is said to have developed in Cape Cod to hide the sand which was inevitably tracked in from the beach. It is usually used on floors, but walls, furniture and accessories may be spattered. The results are not as interesting as hand spattering, but the easiest way to spatter paint today is to use special spray paint under pressure. All you do is to roll on the base coat, then spray on a lacquer spatter. Finish with a coat of clear varnish. For accessories, trays and bathroom walls, use a spray which gives a gold or silver tracery. Marbelized effects can also be sprayed from a can.

To hand spatter, first paint floor. When dry, apply spatter coat with a very coarse paint brush or long-handled whisk broom. Fill the brush with paint. Hold twelve to twenty inches from the floor and rap the handle sharply. Let the spatters dry before applying a second or third color. (Practice on paper before spattering the floor.) The size of the spatters will vary with the force of the rap and the distance from the floor.

The sponge method is easier and quicker, but not as attractive. Rough surfaces are cut into the face of bricklike cellulose sponges. These are lightly touched over the already painted floor, using a different sponge for each color. (One handsome white painted concrete floor in a white-walled basement recreation room was sponged with pink, red and black.) For added interest, stencil patterns may be added to both spatter and sponged floors.

How to Stencil

IN THE EARLY days of the nineteenth century, stenciling on plaster walls took the place of wallpaper, and ambitious housewives decorated entire rooms in this fashion or hired itinerant artists to do the work. Today, stenciled patterns are used effectively on floors and furniture, walls, screens and small accessories. Stencil designs can be bought at art-supply shops or traced from any pattern that lends itself to this technique. To make your own design, transfer the tracing to heavy brown paper or cardboard and cut it out with a razor. Sharp, clean edges are important.

The stencil should be held firmly in position for painting. Double mastic tape does a good job. The consistency of the paint is important in stenciling. If it is too thin, it will run outside the edges of the pattern; if too thick, it may stick to the pattern and make uneven edges. This technique requires practice.

Painted Furniture

OLD FURNITURE should be thoroughly cleaned with paint thinner and sanded lightly before painting or enameling. If it is in bad condition, the old finish should be taken off completely with a paint remover. Since the aged look is often wanted, it may not be necessary to overdo restoration. Use judgment in reconditioning the surface. Gouges, cracks and dents may lend character to the piece, and may even be added to new pieces to make them look old. On such pieces, you won't want the glossy sheen of enamel. A flat, chalky effect, accented by antiquing, will result in a mellow look. The type of paint you use depends, too, on how the piece is to be used and how necessary it is to protect the surface from accidents. Remember that lacquer applied over paint or enamel acts as a paint remover and will spoil your work. Remove handles and pulls from chests before painting. One flat coat and a finish coat are usually sufficient.

Unpainted furniture usually comes factory-

The painted antiqued cabinet and the stenciled oak floor are the eye-catching features of this foyer. The window reflected in the mirror is in the living room.

sanded, but it is worthwhile to sand it lightly once more before putting on the undercoat. For new furniture, a three-coat job is best—a prime coat, an undercoat which is a mixture of the primer and the enamel, and an enamel top coat. Sand between coats.

Don't overlook the enamels that come in spray cans. The spray-can method is excellent for refinishing rattan and wicker furniture. Metal furniture should be cleaned, rust removed with steel wool, and a rust-control primer used before applying enamel.

How to Glaze Furniture

MELLOW ANTIQUED furniture has a luxury look that is not hard to come by. Antiquing can make a prima donna out of a shabby old piece and turn a new piece into a star boarder. Old furniture should be cleaned and repaired. First, look at hinges, pulls or brasses and insides of drawers. If the finish is in bad condition or a new color is desired, a base finish should be used and lightly sanded before applying the final coat of flat paint. Unpainted furniture requires a prime coat of shellac or a flat undercoat before the top coat is applied.

You can make your own glazing fluid—the material used to produce the effect—by mixing one part varnish and three parts paint thinner. But it is a lot easier to buy prepared glazing liquid and add oil color to it to suit yourself. Experiment with raw sienna or burnt umber or

perhaps a little green paint. Or use white paint thinned with turpentine over a blue or green painted surface. If you have never glazed furniture, experiment on a piece of plywood.

Brush the glaze on one area at a time and make sure that it goes into all corners and depressions, and into the crevices of carving. After several minutes, wipe with a clean lint-free cloth, following the grain of the wood. Leave the glaze in indentations and around edges. Remember that the purpose in using the glaze is to simulate the effect of years of wear. Wipe it off at points of natural wear. On carved surfaces, wipe the glaze from high points. If the job doesn't suit you the first time, wipe the glaze off with paint thinner and try again. When the project is finished, protect the antiquing with a coat of clear, flat varnish.

60

WALLPAPER WORLD

WALLPAPER IS NO Willy-come-lately. It originated in the Middle Ages, probably in Italy, where squares of paper called "domino" were used to imitate marble. It has been acquiring prestige, variety and associations ever since. Panels of old paper, carefully removed from their walls and mounted on canvas, may cost thousands of dollars; but you can buy a good copy for a few dollars a single roll. Because of its long history, wallpaper lays the whole story of design at your feet. In fact, wallpaper offers the quickest, least expensive way of establishing a mood or feeling of a period.

Wallpaper can also compensate for lack of architectural distinction; it can camouflage irregularities and defects and can be used in every room in the house. It has warmth and it improves surface texture. The price of wallpaper may range from fifty-nine cents to fifteen dollars or more a single roll. Some of the more costly hand-printed papers may not be as serviceable as less expensive ones, which may offer color-fastness and washability and may even have adhesive backing for easy application.

If you have a limited budget, get an estimate on the cost of hanging paper before you buy it. In some states paperhangers base their fee on the price of the paper, not the size of the room and the labor. Such a fee is called the "roll price."

The rules for color on walls when using paint also apply to wallpaper and other coverings. Since paper usually has pattern, it may be more difficult to determine its dominant hue and value. If you have any doubt, cut out a disk of the paper, slip it over a top and spin it. The mixture produced will determine the lightness or darkness and the dominant hue.

Wallpaper Patterns

PLAIN PAPERS ARE available, but the papers that make the greatest contribution to a room are patterned. Instead of facing this fascinating aspect, the average person selects dull, conservative, wishy-washy, so-called "safe" colors and patterns that add little or no zest.

The over-all rules for using pattern are quite simple. Unless some special effect is wanted, the size of a design should be scaled to the size of a room. In other words, use small patterns in small rooms and large patterns in large rooms.

The decorator with flair may ignore these rules completely. For instance, a paper with big bunches of violets twelve inches in diameter could be beautiful when used in back of a bed in a white-walled, medium-sized room. A panel of paper with one huge green leaf twenty-four inches across may be used with telling effect in a small white-walled bathroom with the leaf divided between wall and ceiling. In a hall with a stairwell sixteen to twenty feet high, patterns with a

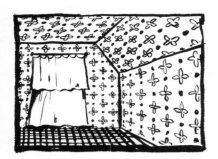

large thirty- to forty-inch repeat are not out of order even though the floor space may be small.

The type of pattern can affect the proportion of a room. Vertical stripes make ceilings look higher; however, wide vertical stripes in a lower ceilinged room will have the reverse effect, whereas a pin stripe will have practically no dimensional effect.

Horizontal stripes, sprawling, all-over floral or leafy patterns and patterned paper on the ceiling all appear to lower the ceiling. The darker the value and the heavier the pattern, the more striking the optical illusion will be. Some scenic patterns with perspective may expand room size.

Checks, polka dots, snowflake patterns have no directional movement. They are identical upside down or right side up. Such patterns are excellent when used on ceilings and walls of rooms with sloping dormers. They tend to camouflage irregularities. If you have a large chest, grand piano or wardrobe that you have tried for years to make inconspicuous, paper it to match the walls. Like the irregular gabled ceiling, it will seem to disappear!

A dull, small bedroom can be turned into a conversation piece, even a showplace, by covering all background surface—doors, ceiling, walls and floors—with the same paper, say a moss green scattered with roses. Match an area rug and curtains to the flower color and upholstery or bedspreads to the moss green, and the room will be as fresh as a garden.

Avoid using too many different patterned surfaces in one room. One should dominate, the others be subordinate in scale. If a strong pattern is used on the wall, floors, draperies and upholstery should, as a rule, be plain or have a textured pattern. However, happy combinations can be made with patterns and geometricals. The basic formula is: A patterned plus a geometrical plus a plain surface equals peace. Even with this combination, either the pattern or the geometric should dominate. Many wallpapers with matching curtain and drapery fabrics are now available. These are useful in creating the one-pattern look, which parallels the one-color look. But they are possibly most useful in establishing a period look. Moreover, papers are available representing practically every period and every theme anyone could dream up.

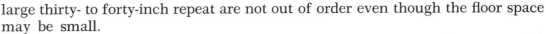

Pattern Classifications

WALLPAPER PATTERNS fall into twelve classifications or design types.

Plain or textured papers: There are dozens of plain colored papers ranging from pink to purple and white to black. Use plain papers instead of paint if you aren't sure your painter can mix the right color; if your plan calls for a combination of plain and patterned walls; if you want a plain surface, but the finished look that paper gives.

Textured patterns give more depth to walls than plain, and come in great variety. The term applies to any paper with a self-toned crosshatched, linen-like or small all-over pattern, a paper which at a distance appears to be without pattern.

Florals: By actual count, florals may be the largest classification. They offer a horticultural directory of large and small flowers, of desert, garden and jungle blooms. Some are fantastic, others quaint. There are papers featuring lilacs, carnations, violets, sunflowers, mimosa, roses, daisies, anemones, cornflowers, primroses, wisteria, magnolia, camellias, water lilies, apple blossoms, iris and tulips. There are splashy Victorian rose patterns, Queen Anne garden bouquets, ribbon-entwined Marie Antoinette florals, conventionalized damask-type Renaissance patterns, as well as gay and bold modern ones. The motifs may be scattered loosely or placed in orderly clusters or rows.

Fruits and vegetables: Apples, cherries, strawberries and blackberries make handsome motifs. There are also papers featuring watermelons and other fruits. Vegetable patterns are more unusual, but there are some gay ones for

Grass cloth, because of its texture, gives depth and richness to the walls of this room. The low-keyed beige, brown and orange color scheme gets a lift from the copper and brass accessories and lamp bases. The open arm chair is a fine piece.

kitchen use featuring squash and eggplant.

Leaf and verdure: These patterns have always been popular and come in a wide variety, including ivy, pine branches, ferns, palms, bamboo, herbs, maple leaves and grasses.

Chintz and calico: These constitute a special class, even though they are miniatures of the three previous categories. They are, as a rule, tight, prim patterns with an Early American or provincial look. Many are copies of old patterns. They are frequently the key to the success of rooms in which pine, maple and cherry furniture are used.

Birds, insects, fish and animals: These offer wide zoological possibilities ranging from zebras to dragonflies. Ducks, geese and seagulls have a following, as well as polo ponies and hunters. There is period fare, too—eagles for Federal rooms, Napoleon Bonaparte bees, oriental dragons and chinoiserie types featuring monkeys.

Geometrics: These are the familiar stripes, plaids, checks, polka dots, as well as a modern collection which may include rhomboids, prisms and trapezoids right out of your high-school geometry book.

Scenics: These timeless and useful all-over patterns often have a fine feeling of perspective. They come both in one-color effects, such as the toile de Jouy types, and in multicolors. They are often used in hall and dining room, although they are correct in any room. Subjects range from English hunting prints to French pastorals and chinoiserie conceits. They are easy to live with.

Trompe l'oeil *papers, panels and borders:* These "fool-the-eye" patterns look like something they aren't and offer wonderful possibilities for invention. In this group are marbelized and brick-patterned papers, Spanish tiles, moires, flock papers, imitations of cork and board, louvered shutters and latticework. One paper creates the illusion of a well-stocked library; still another appears to be a wall hung with framed pictures—this would look especially effective above a dado in a small hall.

Panels and borders are used for trimmings with plain papers or painted walls. There are classic figures, jardinieres spilling over with flowers and fruits, topiary and espaliered trees —to use in niches or to spot strategically like pictures over long stretches of plain, unbroken walls. There are sets of *trompe l'oeil* architectural designs with fluted columns, cornice moldings, door frames and wainscoting that

This French provincial living room has a black, white and grass-green color scheme. The combination of the scenic wallpaper and the hounds tooth checked upholstery is dramatic, but the room has charm and comfort.

are sold in strips by the yard. Some can give plain plaster walls the look of having been designed by Sir Christopher Wren. There is a fine collection of authentic stencil borders for Early American interiors and a Victorian rose-garlanded border series which sweeps along the ceiling in a spectacular fashion.

Murals: These are usually scaled for use above a dado. They may be used in any room, but are seen most frequently in halls and dining rooms. The subject matter is almost endless, ranging from scenes of early New York to ancient Venice, graceful branches of pine arranged in the Japanese manner and Pennsylvania Dutch heart-and-flower stencils, as well as sailing ships and woodland views.

Murals are usually sold in sets that make up a complete scene; however, sometimes sets are broken and the panels sold individually.

Children's papers: These gay and delightful papers are available in increasing number. They feature clowns, circuses, characters from Mother Goose stories, Alice in Wonderland and strings of paper dolls. There are also delightful patterns by Saul Steinberg—one consists entirely of birds—which would arouse any child's imagination. Another sophisticated paper is called "Spencerian Zoo." Lions, elephants, deer, swans, chickens, owls and cows are all developed in pen-and-ink scrolls.

There are also paste-on motifs for children's rooms—picket fences, ducks, sunflowers, cows and rain, which can be placed to suit your fancy or the furniture arrangement.

Whimsical and miscellaneous motifs: These form a wide classification which has been broadening. Such papers are used in dens, bars, recreation and hobby rooms. Subjects include old automobiles and locomotives, musical instruments, revolvers, ships, the flags of the United Nations, old woodenware, wagon wheels, old whiskey bottles. In fact, it is difficult to think of a motif which is not represented on wallpaper.

If you have the ambition, you can use a wide assortment of oddments for wallpaper ranging from sheets of old music or pages from the *New Yorker* to a collection of restaurant menus. One delightful powder room is papered with the pages from an old shoe catalogue. A bathroom is "papered" with old playing cards. The sloping ceiling of a big country kitchen in Michigan sports old flower prints bought for almost nothing on a Canadian vacation. A bedroom hall in a house furnished in country antiques is papered with pages from a turn-of-the-century Sears, Roebuck catalogue.

Wall Coverings

PAINT AND WALLPAPER are only half the story of wall surfaces. There is an almost endless and unclassifiable collection of other possibilities, some very new and others older than either paint or paper. Among these coverings are vinyl-coated fabrics, fabrics—including felt—with and without paper backing, foils, fabric-backed wood veneers, ceramic tiles, marble and vinyl tile, leather, cork, mirror glass and a wide range of grasscloths. Most of these coverings may be applied with adhesives.

Vinyl-coated fabrics are possibly the most versatile and practical. They offer the greatest range of color and pattern. They simulate wallpaper and many other types of surfaces including moire, taffeta, shiki silk, grasscloth, linen, leather, wood paneling and damask. They are waterproof, so they can be scrubbed; they resist soil, abrasion, and scuffing, and are stainproof. For use in bathrooms, corridors, kitchens and children's rooms, they are ideal; however, they are handsome enough to use in any room. They are hung like wallpaper.

Oriental rugs and tapestries, no doubt, were the first wall hangings. However, damask- and velvet-hung walls became popular in the seventeenth and eighteenth centuries, continued into the early nineteenth century, and are again popular. A wide variety of fabrics is available, with paper backing for easy hanging. These include burlap, canvas, mattress ticking, felt and an assortment of other fabrics. It is possible to have paper laminated to almost any fabric to simplify hanging. Velvets, damasks and silks may be stretched and tacked to a lath frame screwed to the wall.

Grasscloth, a Japanese import which has been used for hundreds of years, has a paper backing. It comes in all colors. Grasses pressed into the surface range from quite fine to coarse. Since grasscloth is largely handmade from roll

66 **Blue-and-white wallpaper and matching chintz draperies create a relaxed feeling in this small room. The old formula—a pattern and a plain surface and a geometric— is extremely well illustrated in the room.**

to roll, there may be wide discrepancies in color and texture. Before the first roll is hung, all those needed should be examined and corrections and exchanges made if necessary.

How to Hang Wallpaper and Wall Coverings

IN GENERAL, the rules used for hanging wallpaper apply to hanging most wall surfacings.

First, recondition the walls. Wallpaper will not hold a cracked, crumbling wall together or keep out dampness. The source of dampness should be traced and corrected. New plaster walls should be dry and all hot spots should be shellacked. Cracks, nail holes and gouges in old plaster walls should be filled with spackling compound. Cracks and seams in wallboards should be first dabbed with spackle, then perforated tape applied, followed by more spackle. When thoroughly dry, smooth all spackled areas with sandpaper. Size plaster walls before applying paper.

Next, collect all tools: wallpaper paste, paste-brush and bucket, a good pair of shears, a razor blade, a yardstick (preferably a metal one), smoothing brushes, clean cloths, acetate sponges, seam rollers and a plumb line, a steady stepladder, and a big flat-topped surface for cutting paper—unless you plan to use the floor.

A good paste should be selected and the weight of the paper checked. Thicker paste should be used for heavy, unruly papers. However, thin paste does not ooze as much at the seams as thick paste. Dry weather and a well-ventilated room promote fast drying and reduce the possibility of the paper's staining.

If paper is not pretrimmed, cut off the edges using either shears or razor blade. Measure the ceiling height and cut off the first strip of paper at least three inches longer. Unroll and match the pattern of the next strip before cutting. Repeat until enough strips are cut to cover one wall.

If there are any electric switch plates or wall brackets, *turn off the current* at the fuse box. Unscrew the plate so that the paper can run underneath. Also remove all hooks or nails.

The first strip, which acts as the control, is usually hung by a door or window. It must hang straight even if the ceiling or floor line are not. Measure over from the door or window the width of the paper and drop the plumb line from the ceiling as a guideline.

Now lay the first strip of paper face down, and apply paste to the lower two-thirds. Fold the pasted area over on itself, paste to paste, and do the remaining third. Lift the strip, still folded, by the top; apply, starting at the ceiling line and working down along the plumb line. Let it overlap the ceiling line—this can be trimmed later. Smooth the top third, then unfold the bottom two-thirds. When strip is adjusted, smooth out all air bubbles, using a clean cloth. Before paper dries, trim off the excess length at ceiling and baseboard, using a razor; then remove any excess paste on the surface with a dampened sponge.

Repeat, using the previous strip as a guideline and matching the pattern carefully. The seams should be butted, not overlapped. Let the paste set ten or fifteen minutes, then smooth seams with the roller.

At corners, cut strips that will extend around the corner one inch. Firm the wallpaper into the corner and match the next strip to the overlapping edge. Use small pieces to fill in above doors and windows. Fill in with neatly matching patterns and trim along woodwork with the razor.

Wash waterfast and washable papers with a soft sponge and plenty of lather, using a circular movement. The lather between sponge and paper loosens soil and prevents friction.

There should be few complaints on the paper itself. Four are justifiable. These are misprinting, shading, variations in color between rolls and poor registration of design.

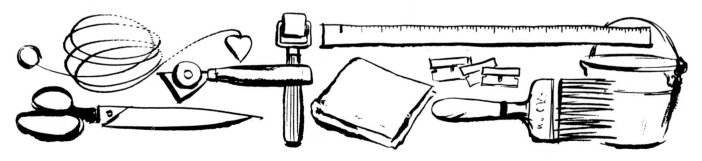

The bed is covered in a classic blue print, the onion pattern. The motifs are repeated in white on the one blue wall. The other walls and the draperies are white.

TERMS YOU SHOULD KNOW

BUTTED SEAMS: Made by bringing the edge of a panel of paper up to the other at the seams with no lap. Usually the edges of the paper have to be trimmed. This makes a neat, flat joint.

CHINOISERIE: French scenic designs done in the Chinese manner and characteristic of the gay, playful, Louis XV period. They often featured monkeys in ribbon swings, fanciful Chinese figures and palm trees.

DOUBLE AND SINGLE ROLLS: Terms used in measuring quantities of wallpaper. A single roll is approximately eight yards or enough to cover thirty square feet. A double roll is twice as long as a single roll. Many stores sell only double rolls and will only accept the return of unopened double rolls.

FLOCK PAPER: Made by printing a pattern on paper with glue or adhesive instead of with paint. While still wet, the paper is sprinkled with finely chopped fibers that stick to the glue, creating a soft velvetlike pattern. The process was introduced in the seventeenth century as an imitation of Italian cut velvet.

HOT SPOTS: When wall plaster is not perfectly mixed, concentrated spots of lime make so-called "hot spots" on a wall to which wallpaper paste will not stick. A new plaster wall should be checked carefully and spot-shellacked before papering.

PLUMB LINE: The term applied to a weighted string dropped from the ceiling used by carpenters and paperhangers to get a straight line when working on walls.

TROMPE L'OEIL, literally translated, means "fool the eye" and is applied to painted or applied devices that look like the real thing. For instance, a hat could be painted so realistically on the back of a door that it would be mistaken for a real hat.

The ceiling paper was cut out and used as a border. Nothing is extravagant, but furniture and accessories are well arranged.

Green-and-white wallpaper was cut out in a window effect over the blue buffet. Butterflies were strewn over the opening.

The wallpaper which simulates whitewashed boards contributes to the airy garden atmosphere. The headboard was contrived from scrolls in a garden gate.

SMOOTH-SURFACE FLOORING

AFTER A HUNDRED years, smooth-surface or resilent floorings have broken through all social barriers and are now used happily throughout the house. They have graduated from kitchen, laundry and bath into the foyer, living and dining room, den and family room. The vinyls can take the credit for this new status.

Smooth-surface flooring comes in two basic forms: sheet goods and tiles. Six-foot-wide sheet goods is available in linoleum, vinyl and rotogravure vinyl. It can be laid with a minimum of seams and labor if the room has no irregularities.

Tiles come in asphalt, cork, linoleum, rubber, vinyl asbestos, vinyl and vinyl cork. Standard tiles are six inches square, but nine- and twelve-inch squares are available and they may be ordered in almost any size and shape for an additional charge. Price is based on the material used, the thickness, the intricacy of the pattern and the color. Clear, light colors require ingredients of greater purity and as a rule cost more than darker ones.

Tiles are easy to install. There is less waste, they are easier to fit around irregularities, and worn areas can be more easily replaced. Moreover, tiles offer maximum individuality with the use of bands and inserts.

ASPHALT TILE is the least expensive tile. It can be laid on concrete, on grade or below grade, because of its resistance to dampness and the alkalis in concrete. For this reason it is popular for use in basements and recreation rooms. It is not recommended for other service areas because it is hard to maintain. Grease stains soften it and harsh cleansers, detergents and solvent waxes rough up the surface. If you own your house it is better to pay a little more and get **vinyl asbestos tile,** which has all the advantages of asphalt tile without its disadvantages.

LINOLEUM is an excellent product and because of its resilience and grease-resistant properties has acquired a fine reputation for kitchen installations. However, it cannot be laid on grade or on concrete as it is affected by alkalis. Colors are not as clear as in vinyls and the range of pattern possibilities is limited. If laid on a smooth underfloor it wears well.

LINOLITE is related to linoleum and was developed for maximum resistance to wear. It is used principally for contract work and is two-and-a-half times as thick as linoleum.

RUBBER TILE has handsome clear colors, is resistant to grease and deadens sound, which makes it ideal for corridors. Like inlaid linoleum and solid vinyl, the colors go through to the back. These tiles come in standard sizes. This flooring is also

This was a practically useless sunporch. Painted white with a new cork floor, a built-in cupboard closing off an unnecessary door, it has become one of the most popular rooms in the house and is used extensively by the whole family.

available in 18 x 36-inch units, in 4 x 36-inch plank form and in sheet goods 36 and 45 inches wide. Rubber flooring is easily damaged by cleaning fluids and strong detergents. Rubber tile is slippery when wet and may not be the best choice for bathrooms.

CORK floors are handsome and soft underfoot, and have the greatest sound absorption of all the resilient floor coverings. Cork should not be used in kitchens and service rooms as it does not hold up well under grease, moisture, sand or grit. It is seldom a good choice for entry halls. The grit wears down its porous surface.

VINYL comes in both tile and sheet form, with a wide range of qualities and styles.

All About Vinyl Floorings

VINYL HAS REVOLUTIONIZED the resilient-floor industry. Now there are so many types and variations of vinyl flooring that careful questioning should precede purchase. Cost variation in vinyl floors is as wide as that between an agate and a diamond ring.

Basically, vinyl is a mixture of vinyl resin, plasticizers, pigments and fillers and is formed under pressure while hot. It comes in tile form, sheet goods, rotogravure sheet goods and the dramatic laminates. It has unlimited color possibilities and a lustrous, easy-to-care-for surface.

Solid or homogenous vinyl tile has no backing; it ranges from one-eighth to one-sixteenth inch. It is tough, pliable and resilient. It is easy to care for and has excellent resistance to alkalis, food spills and grease. Even tougher types of floorings are now available for contract jobs. They employ Hypalon, a polymer. There are two on the market. One is called Vistelle Corlon, and the other is Robblon. They are resistant to burns, chemicals, abrasions and weather, and recover better from dents than vinyls.

Standard solid vinyl tiles come in nine- and twelve-inch squares but they can be custom cut in any size or form and the edges can be beveled. There are vinyls that simulate marble, terrazzo, travertine and wood. Terra-cotta-colored vinyl, hexagonal-cut and laid with a display strip, simulates ceramic tile. Cut in three- by six-inch blocks, it looks like brick and can be laid in herringbone or other classic brick patterns with mortarlike stripping. There are rough-surfaced gray vinyl tiles which have the look of slate, and rough pebble-surfaced ones which simulate pebble concrete.

Vinyl sheet goods has a layer of vinyl overlaid on a backing which is usually alkali-resistant so that it can be used in basements and on grade. The range of patterns is enormous, the price less than the solid vinyl tiles.

Rotogravure vinyl has an asphalt-saturated felt backing on which a pattern is printed. Clear vinyl is applied to form a wearing surface. It looks like sheet vinyl but is modest in price. It comes by the yard in six-, nine- and twelve-foot widths as well as in rug form.

Vinyl laminates are the most exotic and costly development in the vinyl field. A sturdy laminate of crystal clear vinyl is laid over any backing from printed chiffon to a Picasso painting to give it "walkability." On order, any drapery fabric, wallpaper or other material may be processed this way. Laminated flooring comes one-eighth inch thick, so that it is compatible in wear with other vinyl floors and can be used in combination with them. Therefore the laminated area need not cover the whole area. Floors of this type have been made of ocelot and zebra furs, of woven cane, of Japanese tatami matting, of sliced riverstones and marble and of stenciled wood veneers.

Design and Color for Smooth-Surface Floors

WITH SUCH A smorgasbord of choices it is often hard to decide which material to use as well as what color and pattern. This problem is quickly solved if you visualize the floor not as a floor, but as a part of the total room design. It is important to keep in mind the size of the room, style or period, furniture arrangement, color of walls and draperies, location of the ceiling fixture, and floorings used in adjoining rooms. The floor is a large and dominant area, and if it is not pleasing in design and color, it can be very disturbing.

A woman I know bought an old house in Connecticut. On the walls of the wonderful big kitchen she used a quaint herb wallpaper, and the cabinets were maple. Then she ruined the whole effect by laying a crisp white vinyl floor with orange diagonal bands. The floor was handsome and would have been fine in a modern room, but its sharp lines fought with the

The stars flashing in the floor of this foyer were easily achieved and make a major contribution. Also notice the fine damask-patterned wallpaper, the black-framed portrait and the comb-backed bench.

provincial background. Her decorator convinced her that the new floor should be replaced with vinyl simulating slate. This was done, and immediately the room assumed a quaint, delightfully integrated air.

There are three basic ways of developing individual effects with tile floors: a center motif, over-all design and borders.

CENTER MOTIFS are particularly effective in dining rooms and foyers with a centered ceiling chandelier. The tie between the ceiling and the floor is at once obvious. In the dining room the furniture, too, is centered; but in the foyer, the furniture placed against the wall frames the floor design.

OVER-ALL DESIGNS for smooth-surface floors are the simplest, and they give a sense of spaciousness. Checkerboard black-and-white floors and their many variations develop a feeling of size through repetition. Over-all designs can be used to hold irregular spaces together and as a background for heavy, uninteresting furniture.

BORDERS may be used to frame unusual patterned tiles, to reduce the size of a room and give a finished feeling to a space. But borders will be wasted if they are hidden by furniture.

Installation

To LOOK ITS best and to wear as it should, proper installation of smooth-surface flooring is important. The perfect base is a good plywood floor. In old houses with worn floors, plywood should always be laid before the smooth surface flooring is installed.

Concrete floors should be sanded until they are as smooth as glass. If the concrete floor is in contact with the ground, it is wise to use a polyethylene moisture barrier under the concrete before it is laid, to check all moisture.

Seepage through concrete releases alkaline salts which cause deterioration of some floorings and loosens others. Solid vinyls and asphalt tile may be laid where moisture exists; however, special waterproof adhesive should be used. This adds considerably to the installation cost. Litmus-paper tests determine alkalinity.

If you have a do-it-yourself urge, don't start in a large room, using expensive vinyl tile. Test your talent with asphalt tile in a closet or the doghouse before you tackle a major room.

Care of Smooth-Surface Flooring

PLAIN, LIGHT COLORS are hard to maintain because they show every speck of dust. Spatter, marbelized, terrazzo and other patterned surfaces conceal soil. A matte finish also tends to camouflage soil more than a high-luster finish. Use the maintenance method recommended by the manufacturer of your particular floor covering. If your dealer can't supply a leaflet giving directions, write directly to the manufacturer for one.

In general, follow these rules: Go over the floor daily with a dry mop, broom or vacuum cleaner. Wipe up spills as soon as they occur. Regular cleaning and light waxing keep dirt from being ground in. Wax fills small scratches and takes the wear and soil. Remember, too, that warm water softens wax and should be used only for thorough cleaning before waxing. Cold water hardens wax and should be used to wipe up occasional spills.

- Don't use a harsh cleaner, such as all-purpose detergent or ammonia, or very hot water. Such treatment may fade or discolor floors or make them brittle.
- Don't use an oil mop on your floor. It will streak wax and injure rubber and asphalt tile.
- Don't wax your floors too heavily or too

The hexagonal vinyl tiles in this Spanish room simulate ceramic terra cotta. The red plaid draperies are fiberglass. The bench is a fine seventeenth-century piece.

An Indoor Patio

often. Two thin coats are better than one heavy coat that stays soft under the surface and collects dirt.

- Don't fail to remove the old wax before rewaxing.
- Don't neglect your floor covering, but give it only the necessary care to keep the surface clean and protected.

Traditional Hard-Surface Flooring

IN ADDITION TO the resilient floorings already discussed, there are many hard-surface floorings which have been used for hundreds of years. Although nonresilient, they are fireproof and almost maintenance-free. They can extend from the inside of the house out onto a terrace, and they make handsome backgrounds for furniture and area rugs.

Nonresilient floorings include flagstone, marble, slate, brick, terrazzo and cement.

In cold climates, heating coils may be laid in a concrete slab beneath the flooring so that the whole floor is warm.

TERMS YOU SHOULD KNOW

ON GRADE: A concrete slab laid at ground level is a typical on-grade floor. The slab may be placed directly on the earth or on a gravel fill.

BELOW GRADE: A concrete basement floor is a typical example, but the floor of any room below ground level presents the same problem.

ABOVE GRADE: Wood or concrete floors suspended or above a full or partial basement.

GAUGE: The thickness of tiles and sheet goods which may vary from one-eighth to one-fourth inch. A so-called "standard" gauge or thickness is generally used in homes where traffic is light and a heavier gauge for public installations with heavy traffic. The gauge affects the price.

TERRAZZO: Flooring which is a mixture of colored broken stone and cement, highly polished. Stones of two or three colors are used and many color effects are possible. It is commonly used in Florida. Terrazzo is hard to maintain in kitchens and is also hard on the feet.

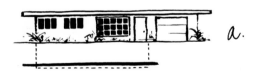

a.

b.

a. Below grade
b. above grade
c. on grade

c.

RUGS AND CARPETS

SOFT-SURFACE floor coverings—rugs and carpets—are one of the oldest and still one of the most important elements in home furnishings. Primitive man made rugs before he thought of furniture. They were used for wall coverings, doors, floors; to sit on, sleep on, and wear.

There are many books on the fascinating history and lore of Oriental rugs, the highest peak of the rug-making art. American Indians wove rugs before the advent of Columbus, using mixed yarns of dog and mountain-goat hair; they sheared the animals with a sharpened shell. Early pioneer women yearned for the warmth and beauty of rugs on the floor. At first they used fur rugs of bear, buffalo and deer. Later, when there was more leisure and a reserve of old cloth, they began weaving and hooking rugs and carpets. The crude products were the perfect background for simple pine and maple furniture of early America.

Sizes and Shapes

RUGS AND CARPETS, like walls, are background, and take up one of the largest areas in a room. To paraphrase that old State of Maine political slogan: "As the floor goes, so goes the room." The market provides a wide choice. If you are buying a rug or carpet, think about it, plan, study prices and materials. Consider the style of the room, its relation to other rooms and decide whether to use a carpet, a room-size rug or a smaller area rug.

There are appropriate rugs or carpets for all periods and styles. The "country look" may call for a woven rag carpet, although oval braided or hooked rugs or coarse-textured pile carpets are also suitable. A luxurious wall-to-wall carpet might be considered first for a modern room; but area rugs are increasingly used. They are in effect pictures on the floor and give drama as well as comfort under foot.

The wall-to-wall carpet, as it is used now, is a reflection of our affluent society; but, though a carpeted room is a luxury, it is also a practical choice. A one-color floor without a floor border tends to make a room seem larger, gives a feeling of spaciousness and is comfortable underfoot. It seems to hold the furniture together and permits greater freedom in placing it. In rooms with irregular shapes or with open planning where one room flows into another, a carpet helps develop a look of unity. The safety factor is another plus, especially for older people. In a carpeted house there is greater comfort underfoot, more warmth, less danger of falling—and it's quieter. Wall-to-wall carpeting should be at least of standard quality, and installation and upkeep should be calculated in the cost.

Rugs are room-size when they leave exposed a three- to twelve-inch floor border. For renters who foresee frequent moves, room-size rugs are the solution. There is no installation charge, and wear can be distributed by turning the rug. Room-size rugs may be patterned or plain, with or without a border.

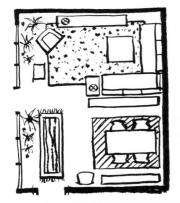

Area rugs, or accent rugs, as they are sometimes called, are smaller than room-size rugs, usually more dramatic in color, pattern and texture, and are used to focus attention and give comfort underfoot in one area of a room—in front of a sofa, before a fireplace, under a table, beside a bed. The term "area rug" is most often applied to a medium-size rug four by five feet, six by six, or even nine by twelve feet. Rugs three by four feet and smaller may be referred to as throw rugs. An area rug may be any shape: round, oval, octagonal; it may be fringed or bordered, or may have an all-over abstract design—may be, in effect, a floor painting.

Color, Pattern, Texture

COLOR IS THE second major consideration in selecting a rug or carpet. The floor covering may account for 20 per cent of a room budget, and strongly affects its character. When selecting a carpet, study color photographs of rooms, look at advertisements, visit friends' houses. The right color on the floor will take a lot of dither out of developing the color scheme.

The average and dull choice is a tame go-with-everything neutral color in the beige family. But carpets come in mouth-watering hues: lavender, mauve and heliotrope, plum, grape, melon, pumpkin, apricot, raspberry, cocoa, sandalwood, walnut, burnt olive, copper, chocolate, azalea, jade, celadon green, mocha, russet, cadet blue, fired gold, bronze, avocado, tartan red, ivory, maple, caramel and cinnamon. High colors, brilliant colors, singing green, clear bright red, shining blue, give a marvelous lift to a color scheme. Used with white or neutral walls, black-and-white upholstery, such high-keyed carpets make the same contribution to a room that a red coat does to a wardrobe.

Always check actual samples of the wall and sofa color with the rug or carpet. These are big areas and their colors should be compatible. Probably monochromatic and analogous color relationships between walls and floors are easiest to work with, though complimentary combinations can be handsome. Colors that match exactly are unnecessary. In fact, a half-note or more of difference in value between sofa and carpet or carpet and wall may be more subtle than an exact match.

Two-tone or tweed effects made by blending two or more colors in the yarn are good-looking and practical because they do not show footmarks or soil as quickly as solids. Handsome tweed combinations are red and orange, blue and green, blue and violet and black and white.

When the two colors are mixed in the yarn, the carpet is often referred to as a Moresque carpet.

There are patterned rugs and carpets characteristic of all periods—eighteenth and nineteenth centuries, Early American, modern, Oriental, French and Spanish. The choice includes self-toned and multicolored effects. Some patterns are bold, some are muted.

In eighteenth-century English rooms, Orientals, *mille-fleur* patterns and formal medallion types are appropriate. In French eighteenth-century rooms, delicate florals, Aubusson and Savonnerie patterns accent the period.

Dramatic florals have a Victorian flavor while all-over leaf patterns and geometrics suggest contemporary interiors. Bold stripes, hexagonal tilelike patterns sound a Spanish note, while quaint hooked rug motifs shout Early American.

Figured carpets and rugs are practical because they do not show soil or footprints. If a strong pattern is used on the floor, it *should* dominate; walls and upholstery should be plain or have only a small texturelike pattern. Scale the size of the pattern to the size of the room. Patterned floors tend to subtract from the size of the room in direct ratio to the size and boldness of the design. Most patterned carpets are woven on Jacquard-type looms; however, printed patterns are appearing.

Texture, possibly the most used descriptive term applied to rugs and carpets, is the field in which twentieth-century designers have made the greatest contribution. Textures range from a smooth, lustrous velvet to rough, nubby and shag effects with two- or three-inch pile. There are plushes, twists, loops or combinations of cut and uncut yarns. Textures may be unpatterned, have a border, or have a self-toned pattern which is either sculptured or a combination of cut and uncut pile, or is carved

A white wall and a white
sofa, a blue wall and a
blue rug push out the walls
of this small room and
appear to double its size.

after weaving. Use sculptured textures and tone-on-tone patterns as though they were solid colors. The effect of pattern is so subtle that other patterns can be used without confusion.

Construction, Fiber, Quality

AT ONE TIME, weave was the first subject brought up in discussing carpets. It affected the design, the quality and the price. Thirty years ago a chenille or Oriental almost automatically would have been selected for the living room, an Axminster for the library, a Wilton for the foyer and stairway, a Brussels for the dining room and velvets for the bedrooms. Today the problem is both easier and more complicated— the term "construction" should be used instead of "weave," because carpets are tufted and knitted as well as woven, and the standard old carpet looms have been taught to do so many new tricks that only a dyed-in-the-wool carpet man would venture a guess on construction.

One type of construction is not necessarily better than another and there is no such thing as a characteristic design associated with any particular construction. With few exceptions carpets are tufted, woven or knitted. At a casual glance, they all look alike. To judge quality, I was taught to look at the back. These days, however, all tufted and knitted carpets and many woven carpets have a coating of latex, a so-called "patent" back to anchor the pile and prevent stretching, shrinking and buckling. Better-quality rugs have an additional scrim or fine burlap backing covering the latex, so that nothing can be learned about the construction from looking at the back.

You will learn more by folding a sample and looking down into the surface pile. The closer the rows of pile and the heavier the fabric, the better it will wear. There are exceptions, however, that outlaw arbitrary rules. Shaggy long pile, for instance, is never as closely packed as that of a Wilton; still, some shaggy rugs wear remarkably well.

Traditionally, carpets were once either wool or cotton, and identification of the fiber was simple. Now man-made fibers have invaded the field and it's advisable to read the label required by law before buying, because identification of the fiber or fibers is daily becoming more difficult, even for experts.

The man-made fibers fall into four main categories: acrylics, rayon, nylon and polypropylene. Under each of these classifications are brand names used by different manufacturers:

Categories	Brand Names
Acrylics, modacrylics:	Acrilan, Creslan, Dynel, Orlon, Verel, Zefran
Rayon:	Avicron, Avisco, Coloray, Corval, Topel, Skyloft, Super-L
Nylons:	Caprolan, Cumuloft, Enkaloft, Nyloft, Tycora and Du Pont
Polypropylene:	Herculon

These chemical fibers have several unquestionable advantages. They are mothproof, mildew resistant, relatively inexpensive, and offer great color brilliance.

They have been developed specifically for carpet use and are tougher than the synthetic fibers used in dress fabrics. Many yarns are blends. If there is only 5% of one fiber and 95% of the other, the trace fiber will not modify the carpet performance in any way; the fiber having 51% or more will always establish the character of the yarn and carpet performance.

Carpet padding, also called rug lining, cushion or underlay, is a worthwhile investment. It reduces wear by smoothing out irregularities in a floor and by minimizing the shock of traffic. It provides insulation and reduces noise. It gives an inexpensive rug a luxurious feeling underfoot and provides a nonskidding surface which will also keep a lightweight rug from wrinkling.

There are three types of padding: waffled rubber, waffled cattle hair (or a blend of jute and hair), and urethane, a chemically produced foam sheet which has great resilience and is the most inert of the three. It will not rot or mildew and can be easily cut with a scissors or joined with staples.

A rug pad should be three or four inches smaller than the rug so that there is no danger of its showing. Doors may have to be rehung to swing over a deep pad and carpet.

Deep texture and the glowing color combination give this carpet the strength needed to balance the heavily-carved seventeenth-century chest and the massive accessories.

Carpet Costs

CARPETS AND RUGS have a tremendous price range, and usually you get what you pay for in quality and durability. Your choice will depend on your personal needs, temperament and bank balance. There are handsome colors and textures at all prices, but durability varies.

If you think of a rug or carpet as a long-term investment, an item of furnishing that you can rely on for twenty years or more, select a good quality that has body and a conservative color. But if yours is a young family, if you rent, live in an apartment or have young children, and if you see frequent moves ahead, you may want to buy a less expensive carpet in an unusual color; then it can be discarded in five or ten years when it gets shabby.

Another element in the price-quality discussion is the amount of daily wear the floor covering must take. The traffic plan of your house will be your guide. Halls, stairways and living room are much-used areas where good quality pays off in more years of wear and less care. Bedrooms have much less traffic and less expensive rugs will give adequate wear.

Carpet prices are quoted by the square yard. To make a quick estimate of how much a carpet will cost, first multiply the width of the room in feet by the length. Convert this to square yards by dividing by nine. Multiply the resulting figure by the cost of the carpet.

Example: The room is fifteen feet by twenty feet: 15′ x 20′ = 300 square feet; 300 divided by 9 = 33 1/3 square yards. If the carpet costs $15.00 a yard, 33 1/3 x $15.00 = $500.

Don't forget to add the cost of the padding and the installation to your final figure. The left-over yardage, as in laying carpet in an L-shaped room, is yours.

Always buy a carpet from a reputable dealer in your locality. A guarantee should state who is behind it, the dealer or the manufacturer, or how it is prorated if it is divided between them; the time period; against what hazard; and whether the offer is for replacement or repair.

Ask to have the contract or invoice you receive confirming the sale state the following:

Name of manufacturer of carpet

Trade name of fabric

Fiber content

Identifying number

Color (get a sample to check against delivered carpet)

Price per yard

Type of padding

Number of yards

Total cost of carpet, padding and installation

If purchase is financed, the statement should include the charge, the number and the amount of weekly or monthly payments, as well as the amount of the down payment.

Rug and Carpet Care

RUGS ARE WALKED on. They are the victims of spills and a variety of accidents: fire, water, dogs, cats and stiletto heels. A schedule of continuing care will help maintain a rug's appearance and prolong its usefulness. If practical aspects are especially important to you, when selecting the color of a carpet consider the color of the dust in your community as well as the color of the family pet's hair, if it has the run of the house.

When a carpet or rug is first laid there will be extra fluff—short fibers not caught into the fabric or left over from shearing or clipping the surface. Let these work in or out a couple of days before vacuuming. If there are loose

threads, cut them off with a scissors—do not pull them. The basic theory of rug care is to keep dust and dirt off the surface so that it does not get buried in the pile and cut the fibers. This calls for a daily going over with a hand or electric carpet sweeper to remove surface soil. At least once a week give a carpet a slow, thorough going over with a vacuum cleaner to remove deep dirt.

Twice a year apply a surface brightener which will remove any dulling film. Use an absorbent powder, then vacuum thoroughly, following directions on the package carefully. Periodically, a professional cleaning is essential.

Elegance and restraint are the chief characteristics of this handsome room. Because walls and furniture are understated, the unusual rug assumes control.

Pattern is beautifully handled here. The bold oriental rug has close kinship not only with the geometric pattern of the paper but also with the oriental motif featured. The accessories, though lavishly used, are linked to the seascape.

Mop up spots and stains while they are still damp, before they have set and before they are absorbed. A clean, dry cloth stored in a nearby drawer is advisable in a household with pets. Also have a can of dry cleaner such as Frost-Spot for emergencies.

TERMS YOU SHOULD KNOW

AXMINSTER: A classic rug weave made on a special loom which permits almost unlimited design and color, distinguished by a heavily ribbed back. Axminsters can only be rolled lengthwise.

BOUCLE: A rough yarn with a loose thread which produces a knotted texture.

BROADLOOM: A term used to indicate that the carpet is woven in six-foot widths or more. It does not apply to the weave, construction or quality. Broadlooms are woven six, nine, twelve, fifteen, and eighteen feet wide.

CHENILLE: Rugs and carpets woven with a chenille yarn which is like a furry caterpillar. The best qualities have deep pile and are custom made, often by hand, in any shape up to thirty feet wide. Chenille weave is also used for very inexpensive machine-made rugs which are reversible.

CONTINUOUS FILAMENT: Yarns spun from long unbroken fibers such as silk and some manufactured fibers such as nylon.

FRIEZE: Not a weave, but a tightly twisted yarn which gives a rough, nubby look when woven. These yarns are often used in one-color carpets to develop engraved effects.

JACQUARD: A loom that weaves complicated patterns, named for the man who invented it.

JASPE OR STRIA: Patterns which have a fine, irregular horizontal-striped effect.

SHADING: The change in the appearance of the rug caused by the pressing down of pile in different directions. As the light catches the pressed-down pile the color seems to have a slightly different value. The pile simply needs to be brushed in the direction in which it was woven. Running the sweeper in the direction of the pile restores it. Shading may make an interesting effect in rugs in a solid color.

SPROUTING: Occasionally a newly laid carpet or rug may show a tuft that has risen above the surface. When this occurs, the tuft should be cut off even with the rest of the tufts. It should not be pulled out. If a bare spot should appear in the pile, don't think your rug is ruined. The manufacturer can replace such spots by retufting.

STAPLE: Textile fibers such as cotton and wool, with reference to their length and fineness. Filament staple applies to man-made fibers cut into short lengths and spun into yarns.

TUFTING: A pile surface sewn into a wide fabric backing with multiple-needled machines.

VELVET: Simplest of all standard carpet weaves, usually in solid colors, but now made in a variety of textures.

WILTON: Woven on a Jacquard loom, traditionally a firm, heavy, low-pile, long-wearing fabric with the surface yarns showing through on the back. Patterns are neat and small. Now made in cut and uncut combinations and carved effects.

HOW TO SELECT FABRICS

DOZENS OF YARDS of fabrics may be used in a room today. The average room is so starved for architectural interest that fabrics are used to soften, shape, lend grace and beauty. They are used for curtains and draperies, for upholstery, slipcovers, portieres and pillows, for bedspreads and even for wall covering.

Today's room is literally painted with fabric. In one charming small apartment, the walls in the alcove bedroom, the day bed and the windows are all covered with the same paisley-patterned linen. In a bedroom, walls, doors, door frames, bedspreads and draperies are all one floral fabric. The carpet and chair covering are plain. A young New Jersey woman put in a ceiling track for curtains between the living room and dining room. Now each room has complete privacy and the curtains can be dramatically opened when dinner is served. In a Chicago apartment, a similar separation was achieved with narrow red felt-covered screens, also hung from a ceiling track.

When the many uses for fabric in a room are added together, and the cost is counted, fabrics account for a fairly large percentage of a room budget. To figure the actual cost of curtains, draperies, upholstery and slipcovers, count in the "make-up" charge, which may be more than double the cost of the yardage. However, if you have made a wise selection of fabrics, the cost may be amortized over the five to eight years they will be used.

The choice of fabrics should be keyed carefully to the use of the room. Delicate colors and fabrics are delightful and require little maintenance in rooms which do not receive hard use, but in a family room fragile fabrics would be shabby before you turned around. I recall a young couple and their first apartment. It was all white: white rugs, white walls, white damask on the sofa; only the fruitwood of the furniture and a collection of blue glass supplied color. Then came the baby, and in three months the white damask sofa was a sight and the pristine beauty of the white, white room was gone forever.

Fabrics Should Age Gracefully

FABRICS, WHETHER used for upholstery or draperies, should age gracefully, not suddenly. In fact, there is charm in carefully cleaned and mended bits of old fabric, which seem to tell a story just as do the patinas of old furniture and silver.

With today's less complicated color schemes, fabric selection is easier in some ways than when every chair had to be a different color and pattern. Now there are only a few general rules to remember.

- Don't use too many patterned surfaces in a room; it's confusing. Let one pattern dominate, keep others modest in character and texture.
- Don't use too many colors; let one or two colors dominate, let the others be accents.
- Be cautious in the use of bold designs in

90   **Deeply fringed white fiberglass draperies are hung underneath an arch-shaped plywood cornice. The window shade fabric matches the material used above the dado.**

strong colors on upholstery fabrics. They are apt to become tiresome, and appear to fill up too much space and make a room seem smaller. If you want strong colors for upholstery, use plain fabrics or shadow patterns.

- Use large and boldly patterned fabrics for draperies. The folds obscure the design and cast lights and shadows on the pattern that reduce its vigor.
- Look at boldly patterned drapery fabrics in folds; the effect is quite different when they are flat.
- If you want durability and performance, select firmly woven fabrics with a color and cleaning guarantee. Check upholstery fabrics for threads that tend to pull. If you have dogs or cats, select upholstery with a latex backing that anchors fibers.
- Fabrics with an all-over pattern are easier to cut for upholstery and slipcovers than patterns with large repeats or motifs which have to be centered on backs and cushions.

Both drapery fabrics and sheer curtains should have stability to light and weather conditions. If a fabric absorbs moisture, it will stretch in humid weather and shrink in dry weather. If the dye used or the fabric itself is susceptible to the sun, it will fade or rot. The sun is fabric's worst enemy and is especially harmful to wool, silk and nylon.

Of all the aspects of fabric, color is the most important, and the ideal plan is to select all of the fabrics for a room at one time so that they will all be happy together.

Increasingly, manufacturers are studying old documents: fabrics, wallpapers, snips of dress fabrics and the linings of hatboxes. From these, designers develop patterns scaled and colored for use today.

Learn the language of fabric design and pattern; it is an aid to good selection and adds to your enjoyment of fabrics. With the most superficial study, you will be able to recognize eighteenth-century French patterns, small-patterned calicos and handwoven textures, as well as classic Empire designs, stripes, snowflakes, bees and fleur-de-lis. You'll also become familiar with crewel-work designs that copy wool needlework motifs of good Queen Anne, acanthus leaves and pomegranate-patterned damasks of the sixteenth and seventeenth centuries. Add to these Egyptian lotus-blossom motifs, Oriental frets, figures and chrysanthemums, Indian paisley patterns and good Scotch plaids. Next spend an afternoon in the textile room of a museum, or sit at home some evening and leaf through art books looking only at the fabrics in the pictures. There is an amazing amount of detail and inspiration especially in Dutch, Flemish and Italian paintings. Follow this program and you will be on the way to becoming an expert.

Man-Made and Marvelous

THERE HAS BEEN a tremendous break-through in textiles since World War II. The question is still whether to look on the vast array of new textile fibers as a bonanza or a headache.

Fibers now include not only time-tested cotton, linen, silk and wool, but a dozen additional fibers, used alone or in blends, that never came close to a farmer's field or a silkworm. Moreover, the parade of new fibers issuing from chemical plants has not ended.

Each fiber has a generic name and three to a dozen brand names given them by manufacturers. Briefly classified, acetates and solution-dyed acetates are variously called Arnel, Celaire, Celaperm, Celanese acetate and Chrom-

spun. Acrylics and modacrylics include Dynel, Orlon and Verel. Glass fibers are made by several companies and may be referred to as Fiberglas or fiber glass. Nylons include Chemstrand nylon, DuPont nylon and Antron. Polyesters include Dacron, Kodel, Vycron and Fortel. Rayon and solution-dyed rayons include, among others, Avisco rayon, Coloray, Enka rayon, Fortisan, Topel and Bemberg. Saran includes Rovana and Saranspun. Blends are becoming increasingly common and introduce another long parade of fabrics and textures.

Manufacturers of these fibers include the great chemical plants of the country. With vast resources at hand and with constant research,

Fringed portieres shaped to fit the archway separate front and back parlors. Across the room and up two steps is a breakfast room with table and splat-backed chairs.

Green Framed Mesh Screens

it is not surprising that one or two new fibers appear annually. The manufacturers' names include—American Enka, American Viscose, Celanese, Chemstrand, Courtaulds, DuPont, Eastman Chemical, Hercules Powder Company, Owens-Corning Fiberglas, Pittsburgh Plate Glass, Union Carbide, Dow Chemical and others.

Since fibers are woven in sheer and heavy fabrics and blends appear in all the classic weaves—plain weaves, tweeds, twills, damasks, piles, satins, etc.—and every effort is made to fool the eye, it is practically impossible for the amateur to identify fibers. Even textile chemists sometimes cannot identify them, with the exception of fiber glass, without a microscope.

It is increasingly important to ask about fibers when buying fabrics. Develop a basic understanding of the differences in their use and performance and you can dive into this new world with reasonable safety.

CHARACTERISTICS OF THE GENERIC MAN-MADE FIBERS

ACETATE AND SOLUTION-DYED ACETATE FABRICS are soft, lustrous and drape nicely. They have excellent sun resistance and average fastness and dyeability. They are mildew-, heat- and wrinkle-resistant. Dry cleaning is recommended generally.

ACRYLICS are soft to the touch, drape well and have easy-care features. Many are hand washable and dry rapidly, but dry cleaning is recommended for others. These fibers darken after long exposure to sunlight. Press with a cool iron.

MODACRYLICS retain whiteness in sunlight, are flame-resistant and resist spots and stains. They drape well and the fiber resists breakage, cracking and splintering.

FIBER-GLASS FABRICS wash easily, dry quickly, need no ironing. They are also resistant to moths, mildew, heat, sun and wrinkling and are fireproof. Color retention is fair. The fabric is hard to sew.

NYLON dyes well, cleans easily, is wrinkle resistant and fine for upholstery. It can be heat-set for dimensional stability. Prolonged exposure to sunlight weakens it.

POLYESTER FIBERS, when heat-set, have excellent dimensional stability, durability, crease retention and wrinkle resistance. The fabrics are washable and require little or no ironing, withstand sunlight well when protected by glass.

RAYONS AND SOLUTION-DYED RAYONS are soft, drape and dye well. Wrinkle resistance and dimensional stability are fair, as is the heat resistance, although these fibers will burn relatively fast. The durability and abrasion resistance are fair.

SARAN is easy to care for, is unaffected by sunlight and retains its strength for the life of the fabric. It is not flammable, may be hand washed or dry cleaned, is receptive to dyes and is wrinkle- and abrasion-resistant. It drapes well.

SPECIAL PROCESSES FOR FABRICS

MILIUM is a material used in linings of draperies which gives them insulation.

PERMANENT PLEATING is a process applied to polyester fabrics and high percentage blends which makes them shed wrinkles and retain pleats.

SCOTCHGARD is a process used on fabrics which makes them resist soil.

SOLUTION-DYED fabrics are woven from fibers that were dyed before the fibers were spun. The dye is a basic element in the fiber; it is not applied only to the surface.

URETHANE LAMINATES are made by backing fabrics with a thin layer (an eighth of an inch) of urethane foam. The urethane gives body to lightweight materials draperies and upholstery. The urethane also has excellent insulation qualities and may be used on walls.

ZE PEL is a "fabric fluoridizer" which resists oily and greasy stains and sheds water. The protection lasts through repeated washing and dry cleaning.

WINDOW SPECTACULARS

WINDOWS HAVE NEVER offered more of a challenge and greater interest than they do today. Not only do windows come in an infinite variety of sizes and shapes, but curtain and drapery fabrics and colors are unlimited. The only restrictions are your own imagination and the room's requirements.

The perfect window treatment does many things: it controls light and reduces daytime glare; it softens the harsh architectural lines of the window frame and gives a room a well-groomed look; it gives privacy day and night; it leaves a beautiful outlook unobstructed, but conceals a poor one. In addition, curtains, draperies and shades add to the sum of fabrics used in a room. They improve acoustics as well as insulation. Since these are part of the background, colors, textures, patterns and style should be carefully coordinated with the walls and floor coverings. In a small room, draperies that match the walls in color and pattern will make the room seem larger. In a large room, draperies with a contrasting color and bold pattern will give the room character. With patterned walls use plain draperies to avoid an atmosphere of confusion.

Before selecting fabrics or developing a plan for the windows, review the following questions:

Has the window a view? When the average window was only thirty-six inches wide, whether there was or wasn't a view didn't matter much. But with the noble size of windows today in both houses and apartments, views often become a part of the charm and interest of a room. The view may be an intimate garden, a grand gesture of nature or the impressive canyons and arteries of a city. If you are fortunate enough to own such a view, it should never be obstructed by too many curtains. Use draw curtains which can be easily manipulated or easy-to-operate decorative shades or blinds and no curtains.

Is it a daytime or nighttime room? Apartments of working couples and bedrooms offer a problem just the reverse of the window with a view. Colors and arrangement must look their best at night; this usually means completely shielding the glass area to cut out the blackness of night, which is seldom warm and friendly, and using colors and fabrics that are attractive in night light. These same points apply to any room that does not have a pleasant view, or that must afford privacy.

Do the window sizes and shapes present a problem? There are a greater variety of window types than ever before, including window walls, view windows, pairs of windows, single windows, high clerestory, corner, square, bowed and angled bay windows. There are jalousie, awing-type, casement and double-hung windows. In rooms with cathedral ceilings, there are glazed gable ends. There are skylights, kitchen and bathroom windows. Some open up, some out, others slide, have louvers or are fixed.

Sometimes several of these types are used in one room, and in areas with open planning it may be possible to see the windows in the dining and living room and the hall all at one time.

Work out a consistent and coordinated plan for the windows of an area, considering both the inside and outside effect. It would be ridiculous to hang widely varied window shapes with identical curtains and draperies. For instance, in a long room with exposures on the north and south, I used white linen draperies at the living room windows on the southern exposure and linen with wide yellow, gold and orange stripes on the northern exposure in the dining area. A window wall may have draperies with a large pattern which would be too large in scale for a row of high windows on another wall. Curtain them with fabric that matches the wall color. At clerestory windows, avoid fabric. If they must be covered, consider using fine bamboo curtains. Unless absolutely necessary, don't curtain the V area of a gable window—somehow curtains or shades at such windows always look fussy.

Are there obstructive architectural elements such as radiators, air conditioners, construction beams? These may even turn into an asset. In one apartment with a steel column on one side of a window and none on the other, a balancing column was added and one of equal size across the top of the window to create an interesting architectural effect. In another room, a steel beam across the top of the window was covered in the drapery fabric to serve as a valance.

Frequently café curtains are hung as much as twelve inches out from the window, at windowsill level, to conceal air conditioning and radiators. The advantage of café curtains lies in the ease with which they are opened when the air conditioner is in use, and the ease of cleaning.

Should the drapery or curtain treatment follow any particular style? Let the mood, the spirit of the room, be your chief guide. Consider the size of the room, the kind of furniture, whether the mood is informal or formal, and whether you are precisely following a period style or developing a free-wheeling circa '60 feeling to re-create the spirit of a period rather than a copy.

Should the windows look the same from the outside? Yes and no. Consider the exterior appearance, but be sensible in handling it. It's never necessary to coordinate the curtains on more than one façade, and in a two-story house the first floor need not exactly match the second floor. Finally, coordination of windows in a modern or ranch house with widely different windows is not as necessary as in a Georgian house with perfectly balanced façade and identical windows. In some modern apartments identical drapery treatments are required by the management. Matching linings for draperies and laminated shades or two sets of shades offer the solution for uniform exterior appearance.

In the end, the simplest method will be best. Windows today are not exactly wearing bikinis, but curtains and draperies are lighter and airier than they have ever been. The design elements which may be used in developing window treatments vary, but will consist of one or more of those listed below.

Draperies and/or Curtains	*Headings*
Draperies	Pinch pleats
Glass curtains	Box pleats
Ruffled tiebacks	Fluted
Casements	Shirred
Café curtains	Smocked
	Scalloped cafés

Top Treatments	*Shades and Blinds*
Valances: shirred	Roller shades
tailored	Venetian blinds
draped	Austrian shades
Lambrequins	Roman shades
Frames	Folding shutters
Canopies	Shoji sliding panels
Cornices	Bamboo and woven
Pelmets	shades

Draperies and Curtains

DRAPERIES, CURTAINS, casements or cafés, shades or blinds may be used singly or in combinations of two or more. Draperies or overdraperies, as they are sometimes called, are usually made of heavier, more handsome material than curtains, and they frame the window. They are most effective hung floor length from the top of the window or the ceiling. They should be lined to make them hang well and to protect them from the sun. At long window walls, to reduce the weight, fabrics which do not require lining may be used. Allow 100 per cent fullness, or twice the width of the windows, for one pair of draperies. Normally, 48-inch fabric will pleat to a finished 24 inches and a 36-inch material to 18 inches. For a little more fullness, allow one-and-a-half widths or pleat a 48-inch width of fabric to 20 inches.

Brown wooden hold-backs and the yellow lining are the featured elements of these white linen draperies in a white-walled, white-carpeted room. The settee, the tasseled steel ottoman and the pedestal table with its black lamp are worth study.

To calculate the quantity of material, allow about 12 inches for finishing top and bottom, and extra for fabrics with a large repeat which must fall in the same place on each side of the window. Draperies may be hung either to remain stationary or on traverse rods. The latter, of course, are preferred.

Glass or sash curtains are hung close to the window glass and are usually made of sheer scrim, marquisette, net, rayon, organdy or batiste. At sunny windows, fiber-glass fabrics will probably hold up best. Silk and nylon deteriorate rapidly. Glass curtains give privacy and soften the hard flat plane of the glass; they are never lined and are usually stationary. In formal rooms they may hang from the ceiling or top of the window to the floor. In informal rooms, they may end at the sill or the bottom of the apron beneath the sill. They are usually shirred on a rod, edges are double-hemmed to conceal the cut edge. Selvages are removed before hemming. Since the material is very soft, three-to-one fullness is advisable, that is, a forty-eight-inch width of material would be shirred to sixteen inches.

Ruffled tie-backs are the first cousins of tailored glass curtains. They are made of similar fabrics and may be short or long, but are finished with ruffles instead of hems. They may be hung under draperies. When used alone, they are more decorative than glass curtains and are looped back with bands of the material.

Casements curtains are often referred to as draw curtains because they are hung on a traverse rod and can be opened and closed. There are special casement-weight fabrics, heavier than those for glass curtains. They are opaque and are seldom lined. However, many fabrics such as chintz, sateen and similar textiles that look well with light shining through them may be used. Casement curtains are made sill or apron length. Draperies may be used with them but seldom are.

Café curtains or sash curtains may be made of fabric of any weight from sheer marquisette to heavy homespun. Their chief character is that they are short—not the full height of the window—and are hung with rings so that they can be easily moved by hand. One, two or three pairs may be used at a window. Study

Below. In this white-walled room, the bold red-and-blue linen dominates.

100   **Right. Tightly shirred striped silk was used for these Austrian shades operated with pulleys. They are used without draperies.**

photographs of windows—note the great variety of café curtains. Draperies may be used with them, but increasingly they are handled in such decorative ways that they carry their own glamour. Often poles of exaggerated size are used for emphasis.

Curtain and Drapery Headings

HEADINGS ARE needed to help assemble the fullness of fabric at a window. Draperies hung to draw are pleated at the top to window width plus a three- to four-inch overlap. If the rod has brackets, an additional six to eight inches must be added for the returns. Hooks are inserted into the traverse rings. Pinch pleats, box pleats, fluted headings, occasionally smocked headings, and exposed decorative rings are used.

Café curtains made of heavy fabric may have extra fullness controlled with a pleat at each ring. Lighter fabrics which are washable look better with a flat scalloped top and a ring sewed on the top of each scallop.

Glass curtains have a casing stitched at the top, with or without a heading, just large enough to run the rod through. When the rod is removed, the curtain is flat and easy to launder. Sometimes glass curtains are shirred on cords and hung with rings.

Shades and Blinds

SHADES AND BLINDS started life with a double mission: to cut out light and provide privacy; but this utilitarian role was not enough. Variations, novelties and fascinating developments of the original idea have brought shades and blinds out of their background role and into the limelight.

Shades or roller shades were traditionally white, cream or green; they were pulled down at night and rolled up during the day; the careful housewife made a precise alignment of all shades in a room. Now shades of standard shade cloth are available in two or three dozen different colors. They may be white on one side and on the other geranium pink, tangerine, lemon peel, curry, wood violet, Bristol blue or citrus green. But that's not all—it takes only a

Fiberglass curtains and draperies outlined with fringe gain depth and character from the easily made shirred valance with its self-made scalloped edge. Red draperies lend a dramatic touch.

few weeks to have laminated shades made of the fabric of your choice, to match walls, draperies or valances. Painted shades are coming back, too. Motifs may be picked up from wallpaper or fabrics. Used in the kitchen, shades are very attractive with just a valance across the top. They are gay and easy to care for. Shades may be shaped at the bottom, have handsome pulls and play the chief role in a window treatment. Popular, too, are shades of split bamboo, fabrics woven with plastic reeds, and other novelty materials.

Austrian shades and Roman shades are not operated on rollers; they are really dressmaker interpretations. Both types are pulled up with a cord, rings and pulley, like a porch shade. The Austrian shade is shirred and draped when lowered or raised, whereas the Roman shade pleats flat when it is raised. Both can be used with or without draperies.

Shutters of all kinds are used instead of glass curtains and cafés under draperies or as a substitute for draperies to frame curtains or cafés. Solid, louvered and fabric shutters all give an architectural look. There are also spindle, stretched wire and pierced hardboard shutters and screens used to frame windows. Possibly the most novel shutters I've seen are very narrow folding shutters of pierced tinwork, which were used in a country living room.

Venetian blinds are available in narrow and wide slats of wood, steel or aluminum. They may have different colors front and back, or be laminated with the drapery material. There is a wide choice of tapes, both plain and patterned. Vertical blinds are often used at large windows in modern rooms.

Top treatments are usually classified as valances or cornices. They give finish to a window treatment and can be used to change or improve the dimension of windows. Added height is gained by placing the valance at the ceiling line instead of the top of the window. Deep valances will lower the window and, if a wider look is wanted, the curtains and draperies may overlap the walls 12 to 15 inches and a valance at the top will establish a normal appearance. As a rule, valances are made about one-eighth the height of the draperies. For the average room, an eight-inch valance is satisfactory. Cornices are usually narrower.

Valances may be shirred, flat, shaped, straight or draped in a variety of ways. They may match or contrast with the draperies. Often the pattern of the fabric determines the shape of the valance bottom. Shirred valances are informal. Elaborate draped valances with swags and jabots are formal.

Cornices are also used for a top finish. The cornice may be an extension of the cornice of the room, brought out four to six inches so that the curtains and draperies can be hung under it.

TERMS YOU SHOULD KNOW

FLOOR PULLEY: A spring tension device used to take up the slack in the rope on a traverse track.

INSTALLATION: Mounting the rods and hanging the draperies.

MEASUREMENTS: Using a steel tape line, these must be taken for each window. Measure the space to be covered, add eight inches for returns, four inches for overlaps at center to get the finished drapery width.

OVERLAP: The center closing where the two drapery panels overlap each other.

PULL: The drawstring on a traverse drapery. Usually it is located on the right, but if that position is hard to reach, place the pull on the left.

REPEAT: The distance in inches on a patterned fabric for a motif to re-occur. It may be twelve, fifteen, twenty or more inches.

RETURNS: Four-inch brackets which hold cornices and rods out from the wall.

STATIONARY: Curtains or draperies which are hung in a fixed position.

TRAVERSE: Draperies hung from a traverse rod or track mounted at the top of the window or on the ceiling. By pulling a cord, the draperies open or close.

SLIPCOVER
SLEIGHT-OF-HAND

SLIPCOVERS ARE a magic wand, the inexpensive route to a new chair or sofa, a new headboard, a new table; an inexpensive way to change a color scheme, a new look for the whole room. They represent a way to spread the beauty of fine upholstery over more years by giving it a semiannual rest while they take over. Slipcovers are prestidigitators; they disguise, freshen and protect furniture.

For a new look, use one color and one fabric on all upholstered pieces. With dark green walls, white duck slipcovers are noteworthy; with white walls, grass green, bright blue or yellow for slipcovers can be dramatic. In fact, when one color and one fabric is used on all upholstered furniture the effect is so forceful that almost any color can be used. Attractive combinations of a plain and a floral, or a stripe or a plaid and a floral are more commonly used. When two or more fabrics are combined one should dominate.

Slipcover fabrics may be silk, cotton, linen, wool, nylon, acetate or any combination of these fibers. The fabric should be a tightly woven one that will not stretch. Welting of the slipcover material is most effective. On occasion, however, contrasting welting, cable cord or even fringe may be stitched into the seams. Year-round slipcovers that are not just summer dust protectors should be made with upholstery precision. Velvet, antique satin, damask, corduroy, chintz, linen may be used, as they all tailor beautifully.

When selecting fabrics, keep the scale of the furniture in mind. Large patterns will overpower small chairs. To camouflage badly proportioned furniture, use a small all-over pattern. Better still, use a plain fabric the color of the walls or carpet. All-over patterns cut better, with less waste of material, than patterns with large repeats which have to be centered on the backs of cushions and side arms. Plain fabrics which have no grain or stretch may be railroaded on a sofa. This means running them lengthwise on the sofa instead of crosswise.

Avoid human figures, horses, dogs or other figures that are objectionable when dismembered. Some people even object to sitting on chairs covered with highly stylized scenic patterns.

Stripes, plaids, harlequin patterns, polka dots and other geometrics present no such problems. However, stripes and plaids should be matched exactly at seams. Stripes of equal width are easier to use than graduated ones. If you have any doubt about the way a print, stripe or plaid will look on a chair or sofa, get a decorator-sample length or buy a full repeat and actually try it on the furniture. Figure out the total yardage and you will save yourself cash and disappointments. Very often the same pattern from two different bolts of fabric will have a marked variation in color, so buy all you need at one time.

Skirts on chairs and sofa may be tailored, shirred or pleated, or they may be omitted altogether. The style of the room, the chair and the fabric will guide your choice. Tailored skirts hang straight and have single or double inverted pleats at the corners. On a sofa, inverted pleats may be used at each leg to break the length and ease the fabric. Skirts keep a room from looking too leggy and give a softer, more hospitable look.

Stripes Are Always Favored

A neatly fitted white slip cover on a Lawson loveseat is combined with a black-and-white print used for draperies and on a club chair.

Plaid patterns are ideal for slip covers in informal rooms. Here a pair of old chairs do service by a fireplace in a family room.

Slipcover Anything

OTHER THINGS besides chairs and sofas may profit from a slipcover. Have you ever thought of slipcovering the front door? They do it in Bath, England. The famous Crescent town houses designed by the Adams brothers face west. Throughout the summer, the handsome painted doors all wear neat slipcovers to keep them from blistering. Holes for the knobs, the lock, the knocker and the letter drop are cut out and bound. The cover is tightly held by hooks and eyelets at the four corners.

Slipcovered walls can save a shabby rented house when the landlord says "no" to painting. A well-known designer completely transformed a bedroom in a summer cottage with white cheesecloth. She first screwed lath at the ceiling line and just above the baseboard. Then with a staple gun she stretched and pleated yards of cheesecloth around the whole room. Rug, painted furniture, fluffy Ottavia embroidered

curtains, tufted bedspread and flounce were also white. A collection of gold-framed flower prints and a grass-green chair supplied the only color. Result—wonderful!

Side chairs are easy to cover. For a new look, give them floor-length skirts. An unused chandelier can take on glamour if it is bagged with tarlatan, net or thin blue polyethylene film. Tie it first at the ceiling line, then pull it in at the bottom and tie with a velvet ribbon. It's even fun to hang a tassel or a few artificial flowers from the bottom. A piano bench looks less like an awkward adolescent under a neatly tailored velvet or damask slipcover with a scalloped skirt or a deep fringe. The slipcover can be tacked or held tightly at the corners to keep it from slipping.

Ugly stair balusters were made the feature of one London town house. The floor is a black-and white checkerboard vinyl, walls and woodwork are white, the ceiling grass green, the entrance door shiny black enamel. The balusters are covered with grass-green, white-fringed antique satin swags. Every thirty inches there is a pleat, which is tied to the handrail, giving the slipcover a scalloped line at the bottom.

Floor-length table covers are one of the greatest disguises in use today. They give a luxurious, *soigné* look to a room, and they don't even require a table. Any lumber yard will cut a piece of plywood the size you want; it can be placed on any support available. Once it is hidden behind a rippling skirt the underpinnings are forgotten.

YARDAGE CHART

These yardages for slipcovers are approximate and apply to average pieces and average patterns. If the fabric has a large repeat, an unusual drop repeat or is expensive, an accurate estimate based on the exact chair and fabric required is recommended.

Furniture	48″-Wide Fabric	36″-Wide Fabric	Welting
Sofa—6 to 7 feet 2 or 3 cushions	15 yards	23 yards	36 yards
Love Seat 2 cushions	12 yards	14 yards	24 yards
Club or Lounge Chair 1 cushion	8½ yards	12 yards	18 yards
Wing or Barrel Chair	9 yards	13½ yards	18 yards
Boudoir Chair	6½ yards	9 yards	15 yards
Sofa Bed 2 cushions	16 yards	21 yards	40 yards

Fitting and Cutting

- With seat cushion in place, center large designs on both inside and outside of back and arm, and top and bottom of seat cushion. Match design as nearly as possible at all seam lines.

- When a chair has shaped or rounded lines on arm or back, ease in fullness as for setting in a sleeve.

- Fit and cut slipcovers on the right side; chairs are seldom identical on both sides.

- Always place material with the grain or thread of the material running straight up and down, regardless of the shape of the piece.
- Never forget four- to five-inch tuck-in allowance on three sides of the inside seat.
- If you have never made slipcovers, use plain fabric for your first one.
- Smooth out deep creases; never stretch or pull material when fitting it. Use lots of pins.

Care and Laundering

IF YOU PLAN to launder your slipcovers, select a washable fabric and be sure that the trimming, tapes, braids and zippers are also preshrunk and color fast. Don't let slipcovers get too soiled. If the arms or the back are grease-stained, rub the areas lightly with soap, or presoak in cold water with one-half cup of Borax for fifteen or twenty minutes. Then wash carefully or put through the washer on medium speed. Whether dried naturally or in a dryer, do not dry completely. While still damp, touch up only the skirt with a steam iron and carefully adjust the still-damp, unironed slipcover on the chair.

109

FOREGROUNDS

3

WOOD FURNITURE

FABRICS, PAINT, accessories, draperies may be changed every five or six years, but chances are that when you make a furniture purchase it's going to be in your life for a long time. Making the right selection is both an exciting adventure and a challenge. If you have done your homework you will not make a mistake in this important area. Furniture bought by hunch and not because you understand it may lead to disappointment. It's the difference between living blindly and with a seeing eye.

Paul Signac wrote of Pierre Bonnard, the French painter: "He understands and loves everything: the pie for dessert, the eye of his dog, a ray of sunshine coming through his window, the sponge in his bathtub. He walked or drove through the countryside at the slowest possible pace, drinking in the smallest details."

Observant trips through museums and furniture stores and careful study of room photographs will gradually bring an understanding of furniture: its design, construction, wood, finish. And once acquired, the pleasure is permanent.

The furniture world is a large one and cannot be taken in one gulp; but it will be simplified if it is divided into two parts: wood furniture and upholstered furniture.

Design

DESIGN IS THE most important element in furniture selection. Like color, it carries no special price tag. For the same price, as a rule, you can get either good, bad, or indifferent design. Good design in furniture is a blue-chip investment, to borrow a Wall Street phrase, and will pay dividends. It will even have growth potentials.

Bad design does not deserve discussion, but because a vast amount of the furniture bought comes under this classification it's hard to ignore it. Such furniture is poorly proportioned, has conflicting design elements, a crude finish, or ostentatious hardware. It may be too spindly and thin to please the eye, or too bulky, overornate, gilded, gaudy. It is often cursed with pseudo-elegance.

Most furniture falls between good and bad design—it is in a gray zone of uninspired design.

It may even be stylish for a time, but in twenty or thirty years furniture in this category will have no significance. Much of this gray-zone furniture has a period flavor. In fact, it may be a blend of several styles. But because it is not handled in a strong manner it has no distinction.

When design details of the past are combined with functional features of today, we are repeating in the twentieth century what has gone on throughout design history. The Romans picked up ideas from the Greeks, the seventeenth-century sea captains saw wonders in the Orient and passed them on to designers back home. Thomas Chippendale liked and borrowed Louis XV motifs. Our own Duncan Phyfe adapted designs from Sheraton and Hepplewhite. The past is still a rich and wonderful

111

source of inspiration, and practically all design today, from an Eames chair to a space missile, has its roots in the past. To a creative designer the past is merely a starting point, but the ordinary designer uses it as a tiresome and often misinterpreted repetition, a mixing and blending of motifs. Like a mongrel dog, some of this crossbreed furniture is friendly—but it has little charm, meaning, or permanent value, and it is always better to avoid passing fashions.

Modern and Period Design

THERE ARE TWO main design classifications: traditional and modern. In both, the range of design is enormous. Modern design is also referred to as contemporary design. The two terms have the same meaning although the term "modern" usually refers to the more intellectual forms of pure design, while "contemporary" refers to the commercial, popular interpretations. Modern design grew out of a demand for less ornateness and greater simplicity, and is a part of the whole movement that has affected literature, art, music, over the last fifty or seventy-five years. With modern furniture, you can start a tradition in your family—you can buy furniture by name designers that will be the fine antiques of tomorrow.

Good modern furniture adheres closely to the tenets of good design. It is simple and has no tricky elements to grow tired of; it is graceful in proportion and has a feeling of innate harmony.

If you like modern things, become an authority. After all, the modern movement has had general acceptance for less than twenty-five years, so it isn't too difficult to trace origins. Learn the names of leading designers, study their work, become familiar with their museum-quality pieces. Your furniture will mean more to you, and even more in fifty years, if it was designed by one of the leaders in the field— a Paul McCobb, George Nelson, Edward Wormley, Harvey Probber or Jens Risom. There are great Scandinavian designers, too. To own a Hans J. Wegner, Bruno Mathsson, or Count Sigvard Bernadotte piece in the twentieth century is equivalent to owning furniture in the eighteenth century made by Chippendale or Hepplewhite. It is furniture worth keeping and noting in your household records.

You can enjoy the excitement of blazing a trail and the pleasure of encouraging the inventiveness of present-day designers and craftsmen. Bad modern design is crude, harsh and meaningless. Good modern design is calm and beautiful.

Good traditional design will relate to one of the great style periods and will carry the stamp of authenticity. Whether it is an antique or a reproduction, it will have weathered the test and taste of time.

The great traditional or period styles in use today are principally those of the seventeenth, eighteenth and early nineteenth centuries and are French, English and American in origin. Important, too, are styles from the Mediterranean countries—Spain and Italy—as well as furniture originating in Austria, Germany and the Low Countries.

Traditional furniture or period furniture— the two terms are interchangeable—may be correctly referred to in any one of four ways. You may identify it by the time in which it was made, the name of the reigning monarch, the name of the designer, or simply the wood and the country of origin. Thus a splat-back chair of particular design may be referred to as an eighteenth-century piece, a Georgian chair, a Chippendale chair, or an English mahogany piece. American pieces may be associated with one of the famous restorations or an important Colonial town or person. Available now are reproductions carrying the names Williamsburg, Deerfield Village, Newport (Rhode Island), and the James River Valley.

Traditional furniture can be subdivided for convenient identification once again. In all centuries and all countries, there are both formal and informal styles. The formal styles were developed and used by court circles and wealthy patrons, and they represent the finest styling and expressions of the day in which they were made. Reproductions are often slightly simplified but in essence they are the same.

The informal styles are generally referred to as "provincial." The country folk and the colonials far from London, Rome and Paris were also interested in the latest fashion, so country carpenters, using local woods, solid wood rather than veneers, and cruder tools, produced similar but less sophisticated and

112

Reproductions of Early American furniture have the charm of the originals. They are easy to use and make friendly rooms. The furniture here gains from the sprinkling of old accessories, the paisley shawl, the big copper kettle and the trivet.

often more delightful furniture. Country furniture differed from province to province and state to state, but changed less from one century to the next than the formal styles. Moreover, the provincial or country furniture of all nations looks well together.

The most noteworthy provincial furniture is our own American Colonial or Early American furniture. French and Spanish Provincial are first cousins, as are Spanish and native Mexican furniture. Less seen, but equally appealing, are provincial pieces from Austria, Switzerland and Holland.

The study of period design requires special reading and study. The Portfolio of Period Styles at the end of this book is a capsule course, included to arouse your interest and launch you into deeper, wider channels of research.

As Henry James said: "We are Americans born, an excellent preparation for culture. We have exquisite qualities of grace and, it seems to me, that we are ahead of European races in the fact that more than any of them, we can deal freely with forms of civilizations not our own, can pick and choose and assimilate and, in short, claim our property wherever we find it."

Woods

CHESTS, DESKS, BUFFETS and other such pieces of wood furniture are called case goods. After function and comfort are considered, the construction and woods used are of first importance. Many studies show that the average woman has only the haziest idea about furniture woods. She can name two or three but cannot be specific about the wood of her own dining table.

Today no one wood is used, but the great periods of furniture design are often identified by the most-used wood of the time. Thus there is:

The Age of Oak: identified with English furniture, fifteenth and sixteenth centuries
The Age of Walnut: identified with late seventeenth century and Queen Anne furniture
The Age of Mahogany: English eighteenth century, Colonial and Federal
The Age of Pine, Maple and Cherry: Early American

Not to know which wood a chest or table is made of is to miss some of its romance and glamour. The principal woods used in cabinetwork today include:

Mahogany

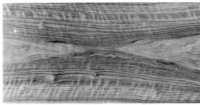
Walnut

Cherry

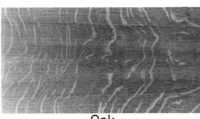
Oak

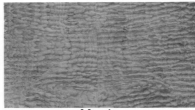
Maple

Teak

Much talked about fruitwoods often used in French and Italian Provincial pieces are apple or pear wood. In commercial furniture, so-called fruitwoods are often walnut or mahogany with a light-brown finish that simulates fruitwood. Woods used for drawers, backs and other concealed portions of chests are usually the less expensive gumwood, yellow poplar or magnolia. Moreover, solid wood and veneers appear in the same piece since veneers are used only for table tops, drawer fronts and display.

Veneer is wood cut paper-thin and applied

114

Veneered mahogany clearly seen in the grain of the end panels accounts for much of the beauty of this secretary desk. The reeded corner pilasters and simple brasses are also good. The square-backed, straight-lined chair is a Thomas Sheraton type.

with adhesives to a core under pressure. The core may be birch, poplar, alder or gumwood; the veneered surface, an exotic wood or a fancifully patterned conventional wood, may have swirls or wild graining. Veneers are also used for inlays and marquetry. There is a common belief that veneered furniture is not as good as solid wood. This is not true. The art of veneering is at least two hundred years old. Veneers may be stronger than solid wood and may offer the only method of achieving the beautifully patterned table and drawer fronts of unusual

woods which are in themselves not suitable for cabinetwork. Veneers also offer almost the only method of keeping large table tops from warping and cracking.

Good veneered furniture stock has a five-ply or even seven-ply core. Less expensive furniture may have only a three-ply core which is really plywood. The grain of each successive layer runs opposite to its neighbor to give stability and check warping and splitting. Selecting and matching veneers is an art in itself, and many of the finest ones are imported. In fine cabinetwork, when the design of the piece permits, the grain of the veneers may run across the top and down the ends without a break. In fine chests, drawer fronts and table tops, fascinating effects can be achieved with veneers. Among the special veneers you may have heard of are crotch, oyster shell, ribbon stripe, rope figures, mottle and burls. Train your eye to analyze veneers and the way they are matched on table tops and drawer fronts. It's a world in itself and a fascinating one.

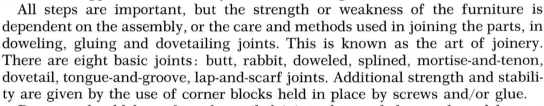

Case Goods Construction

corner block

dowel joint

dovetail

mortise and tenon

THERE ARE MANY variations in construction and finish of furniture, but even though you may know little about the subjects, there are guides to quality. After considering the reputation of the store, the name of the manufacturer and the price, and after reading the labels or tags on the piece, your fingers and eyes can tell you a lot. Feel, push, shake and lift case pieces. Look in drawers, open all of them, not just the top one. Study the back and sides of a chest, focus your eyes on the hardware, and intuitively you will begin to feel the worth of the piece.

Construction of furniture is most easily understood by taking a trip through a factory. There you will see the wood being dried in kilns; cut and shaped and the veneers applied; the assembly and the finishing.

All steps are important, but the strength or weakness of the furniture is dependent on the assembly, or the care and methods used in joining the parts, in doweling, gluing and dovetailing joints. This is known as the art of joinery. There are eight basic joints: butt, rabbit, doweled, splined, mortise-and-tenon, dovetail, tongue-and-groove, lap-and-scarf joints. Additional strength and stability are given by the use of corner blocks held in place by screws and/or glue.

Drawers should have four dovetailed joints, be sanded smooth and have a protective finish to keep them from swelling and shrinking. Remove a drawer, look at the bottom. Are small wooden blocks glued in each corner? Is there a center track or glide on the sides? (Metal slides are the most expensive.) Is there a dust panel between each drawer, and is the bottom strong enough not to sag? Some drawers will have pressed nylon rollers to insure easy operation and others a patented molded plastic drawer construction which does not affect the outside appearance. They have easy-to-clean corners and guarantee lifetime operation.

Drawer pulls should be carefully attached, convenient to use, have a permanent finish and an appearance consistent with the design of the piece.

Doors in cupboards and buffets should all be opened and examined. Do they fit well? Open and close easily? Are the hinges strong enough and perfectly aligned? Are there magnetic latches? In fine furniture each pane of glass will be set in the wood frame. In less expensive furniture small paned glass doors will be simulated by a wood or metal grille overlay.

Table tops should be examined and the operation of draw-top tables checked. Table leaves should match the table top perfectly in wood and finish.

Check the legs for study construction, for grain, attachment and bracing. Are the bottoms smooth? Are there glides or self-leveling swivel casters? Large pieces should be mounted on concealed casters for handling.

Simplified American versions of English eighteenth-century furniture have a special sturdy charm. All mahogany, the splat-backed chairs with H stretchers, the double pedestal table with a knife edge and oval draw top are all in the best tradition.

Furniture Finishes

FINISHING IS THE final treatment. It is the cosmetic touch, the powder, rouge, lipstick and eye shadow, that brings out the beauty of the wood. Finishing fine casework is an art and the craftsmen who do this are, as a rule, the most temperamental in the shop.

Inexpensive furniture may be sprayed, dipped or coated in one process. Better grades may be rubbed by hand and sprayed several times. The finish on really fine furniture is gradually built up through as many as twenty or twenty-five steps. Six to ten of these steps may be sanding, which may be done between each process. Other operations may include staining, glazing, patching, distressing, hand padding or shading, rubbing and polishing.

Because the style choice is so broad today, many types of finishes are used and many woods are given a wholly new look through their finish. We usually think of mahogany as a dark reddish wood. With the new finishes, it can be given a soft brown color to resemble walnut or fruitwood. Woods are also bleached and stained, given blond, glossy, or dull finishes. Varnish and, increasingly, lacquer are the principal ingredients of most finishes today; however, in fine work oils, waxes and gums are still used for special effects.

Scandinavian teak is usually given an oil finish. This is simply boiled linseed oil, which is applied, allowed to soak in and then rubbed. (Linseed oil is available both boiled and raw.) It takes repeated treatments to build up a fine hard surface. The effect is soft, with a dull lustre. It is not as permanent a finish as lacquer but it can be easily patched or removed or redone at home.

"Distressing" is another process employed increasingly. At one time, this process was used only on the most meticulously made reproductions that often went into the antique market from the cabinet shop. Distressed finishes have a shaded look, with mars, scratches, paint splotches and occasionally worm holes made to simulate those in old furniture. Sometimes the furniture may actually be made of old woods—or new wood first spread out on the floor and walked on. Edges may be softened and marred by beating them with chains and

Wood has warmth here. The primly handsome maple highboy with its fan carving and brass pulls gives character to a simple whimsical room. The bedspread is a quilted linen.

hammers. If not overdone or obvious, distressed finishes give new furniture the mellow, soft look of old pieces. Such pieces are, in effect, instant antiques.

Highlighted or French pad finishes are obtained by applying stain, then wiping it off the carved parts and in the center where the greatest wear comes.

Care of Furniture

FINE FURNITURE should not be exposed to the direct rays of the sun, which will bleach it. Contact with a register or radiator will dry out the wood and may even cause cracking and warping. Furniture which is frequently dusted with a soft cloth stroked with the grain of the wood, never in a swirling motion, will, like silver, develop a patina, a hand-tended look. Frequent attention is better than a mighty effort once a year. If allowed to go too long, furniture may have to be wiped with a damp cloth before polishing. In a dry atmosphere wood may dry out and have a starved look. Feeding with wax or oil, depending on the finish, is all that's needed.

Furniture that has been overwaxed may become sticky or blurred. When this happens, wash it with this brew: Into a quart of warm water put one tablespoon of turpentine and one tablespoon of olive oil or lemon oil. Swirl a soft cheesecloth in the mixture and wring it out.

Rub down the furniture briskly. Repeat as often as necessary until excess wax is removed and the surface is clear and satiny. Dry with a soft cloth.

When the furniture is thoroughly dry, apply a thin coat of paste wax. The wax should be buffed well for lustre.

White spots on varnished table tops caused by a hot pad or water can be removed by rubbing with a soft cloth dampened with spirits of camphor or essence of peppermint. Polish when dry. White spots on a waxed finish may be removed by wiping with turpentine followed by fresh wax.

Scratches on dark wood can be touched up with an eyebrow pencil, a walnut meat or iodine. Deep gouges should be filled. First remove splinters, brush in stain, then gradually fill in the hole with white shellac, using a brush. Do not touch the surrounding finish or let the shellac overflow the hole.

TERMS YOU SHOULD KNOW

BLOND: Light finishes which range from eggshell white through beige and light brown, achieved by bleaching dark woods before finishing them with a transparent, rubbed finish that brings out the grain. Mahogany and walnut are often finished this way.

KILN DRIED: A term applied to lumber which has had moisture extracted in a heated chamber. When wood is slowly dried, its natural contraction and expansion is reduced to a minimum and warping and crazing are prevented.

INLAY: Designs made on the surface of furniture by inserting bits of contrasting wood, metal or ivory. Borders, medallions, flowers and other motifs are used.

MARQUETRY: Inlays, when the entire surface, such as a table top, creates the pattern. Usually the design is not intricate and may only be herringbone veneering.

GRAIN: The figuration of the wood itself and the pattern made when it was sliced from the log. All woods can be identified by their grain.

HARDWARE DEFINITIONS

BAIL HANDLE: A loop drawer pull.

BRASSES: The general name for cabinet hardware; also called mounts.

DROP HANDLE: A pear- or teardrop-shaped drawer pull.

ESCUTCHEON: A metal shield framing keyhole to protect wood from scratches.

Red and green used in large areas make a strong background for the imposing cherry grandfather clock, the ladder-back chair and the portrait. Even though the two-tone buffet is moden, its basic integrity makes it an integral part of the room.

UPHOLSTERED FURNITURE

THE SOFA AND upholstered chairs are the royal family of the living room and should be credited with the look of comfort and the deep-seated ease of the twentieth-century living room.

Upholstered furniture of a sort was developed in Europe during the seventeenth century. At first the pieces were heavy and awkward, but by the middle of the eighteenth century both French and English designers had refined sofas and chairs into light, graceful pieces of furniture. However, it was not until our day that deep-seated lounging ease was built into chairs and sofas. Now the sofa is the most-used piece of furniture in a room and two or three upholstered satellite chairs are a necessity.

Upholstered furniture not only gives comfort but a pleasant feeling of solidity and color. Because of its weight and importance, the sofa (or sofas) should be located first in a room plan, not only to preserve the balance of the plan but because the sofa is the center of the main conversation group. Too many upholstered pieces are as unpleasant as too few. Fabric-covered pieces should be nicely balanced with open-arm chairs and with side chairs with upholstered seats. Of course, tables, chests, desks and other wood pieces give balance also.

Avoid tricky, unusual designs in upholstered furniture. When in doubt buy a Lawson sofa. Variations in covering will make this style compatible with any theme from modern to French Provincial.

Construction

TOO OFTEN upholstered pieces are bought like a dress, with emphasis on surface appearance —fabric, color, line and design—whereas workmanship and the hidden materials are the key to quality. Durability beneath the appealing exterior in the hidden frame depends on the way the wood in the frame has been dried and fitted together and on the webbing or other foundation and how it is attached to the frame. Other important construction features are the way in which the springs are tied, the kind, quality and amount of filling, and the quality of the edge construction.

There are three types of upholstered work— custom, production runs, and semicustom. Custom-built pieces are all handwork, often started and completed by one man. Production-run pieces use standard parts and are passed along a production line with different operators for each step. Semicustom pieces have standard parts and are made on a production line, but you may supply the cover, select the legs, the type of arm, decide whether or not a skirt is to be used and whether it should be tailored, pleated or ruffled. In the case of a sofa, the piece can be made any length you want from 52 inches to a king-size 108 inches. Standard lengths for sofas are 72, 84 and 96 inches. Such special service may take six to eight weeks and unless a standard size is selected, there may be a small additional charge.

These three grades of upholstered furniture

Upholstered furniture is comfortable and it also softens harsh lines. The blue upholstered chair seems to bring together graciously the old pharmacy case, the coromandel screen and the piano. The chair swivels. Four are grouped about a low table.

can be classed as inexpensive, medium, and fine or prestige quality. There may be a thousand to fifteen hundred dollars difference in price between a cheap sofa and an expensive, custom-made one. The difference in cost will be spread among the handwork, the kind of filling, and the cover. The effect of the fabric on the price can be seen when you consider that the same sofa may be covered with ten yards of cut velvet at fifty dollars a yard, costing a total of five hundred dollars, or with ten yards of linen costing five dollars a yard, a total of fifty dollars. Completely upholstered pieces are usually less expensive than those with an exposed wood top and bottom rail.

Chairs and sofas begin with a strong frame which is a combination of hardwoods properly put together with wood glue. Woods must be tough, durable, and cut and dried so that they will not twist, warp, split, swell or shrink. They must be able to withstand shock and to hold tacks and nails. Hard maple, birch, poplar and ash are preferred. Gumwood, too, is used in inexpensive furniture because it is easy to work with, but it does not hold tacks well. Hickory and pecan also are commonly used. Like gum, both of these woods take an excellent finish on exposed parts.

The frame is important and should outlast the rest of the chair, but the heart of the chair is the inner workmanship, the webbing base, the springs, the stuffing and interior covering. Building up the interior is done a layer at a time and is largely a hand operation. Increasingly, however, patented products are being developed to speed up and simplify the operation so that there is a growing divergence in methods between manufacturers. Traditionally, the base consisted of three- to four-inch interlocked fabric webbing applied back to front and side to side. Today, tempered steel webbing is often used; it has resiliency, doesn't stretch out and is more quickly installed than fabric webbing.

Most large upholstered pieces have coiled springs in the seat and back and small ones in the arms. In better-quality chairs these springs are firmly tied down with thick spring twine— eight knots to each coil. A good grade of burlap or muslin is stretched over the springs and tacked to the frames. Stuffing is placed over the burlap or muslin and a layer of white cotton felt is placed over that; then an outer muslin cover is put on. This insures a smooth outer surface.

Filling includes curled horsehair, sponge rubber, rubberized fibers of various kinds, Dacron, urethane foam, cotton felt, feathers, down—and, in less expensive pieces, moss, kapok and every possible combination of these materials. Loose cushion content may vary widely. Most production-line cushions are made of fine-tempered springs wrapped in envelopes of one or a combination of the filler materials listed above. Many states require a label stating the content. Don't fail to read it as a gauge of quality as well as a guide to care. It is a mistake, for instance, to clean foam rubber with a solvent; the rubber will dissolve.

Finally the dress cover goes on, the fine colorful fabric which will give glamour, excitement, drama. The selection may be made from a swatch at the store or you may supply the fabric. Delivery may take two or three months. If you buy a piece from the floor, be sure that you like the shape of the chair or sofa and are not attracted primarily to the color or texture of the covering.

If you supply the fabric, be sure that it is suitable. Upholstery fabrics fall into two classifications: pile and flat fabrics. Pile fabrics are mohair, velvets, cut and uncut, friezés, and velours. Flat fabrics are divided into two groups: the jacquard or woven patterns (damasks, tapestries, bouclés, brocades, and brocatelles) and the unpatterned group (plain weaves, twills, satins, basketweaves, etc.). These last, of course, may have printed designs.

All upholstery fabrics should be firmly woven to withstand strain and sifting dust. For hard wear select a pile fabric. One hundred per cent nylon is considered the most durable and easily cleaned. If you have cats or dogs, avoid looped piles or long floats in which claws can get caught. For family rooms, consider vinyl plastics.

Upholstery may match or contrast with the walls and carpets. Large pieces will be minimized if they are the wall or carpet color. It is quite correct to use the same color and fabric for draperies and all upholstered pieces or a different fabric for each. Many simple and effective color combinations are possible. You might use dark and light tones of one color for upholstery, such as beige, and add one smashing accent note such as orange, grass green or peacock blue. Again, the sofa and the two or three large chairs may be one color, such as blue, and another color, perhaps green, could be used as an accent on all pull-up chairs. The room will have more poise if you avoid using too many fabrics and too many colors.

Fine tailoring is the mark of good upholstery. Note in these pieces the crisp lines, the double welting on the sofa, the button-tufted pillow corners and the handsome fabrics. The wall is sand-blasted oak, the lamp adapted from a chandelier.

Graceful and feminine in line, this small Hepple-white sofa seems happily adjusted to the modern paintings hung above it.

Large and luminous, this graceful green-gold silk damask sofa is so closely color-toned to the wall-paper panel behind it that it does not look its full ninety-six inches in length. The cane-backed French chairs have shirred shield shaped pads.

Care and Maintenance of Upholstery

SINCE ONLY ONE side of the fabric is exposed, special techniques are necessary for cleaning upholstered furniture. Soaking with water or chemicals should be avoided.

- Brush upholstered furniture frequently, cleaning all crevices.
- Never use a vacuum cleaner on down-filled chairs; the suction may pull out the down.
- Remove spots as they occur, using a special upholstery spot remover. Test it on a concealed place before using it.
- For general cleaning, make a dry foam with a synthetic detergent and water. Apply with a soft brush or sponge. Wipe at once with a clean towel or dry sponge. Dry in a breeze or in front of a fan.

The ideal solution is to have all upholstery fabrics processed to repel stains or spots. Ze Pel, Sylmer and Scotchgard are used for this purpose.

Leather and plastic surfaces are easy to care for; both have a long life expectancy. Simply dust them occasionally and wipe up spills with a damp cloth. Never use detergents or cleaning fluids, furniture wax or polish on leather chairs. When washing is necessary, use a lather of saddle soap or mild baby soap, wipe dry and buff with a dry cloth or chamois. Plastic upholstery may be treated as leather although plastics are not as sensitive to strong cleaners. Those with knitted or reinforced backing are less subject to tearing.

Seat cushions will keep their shape better if they are turned frequently. Down pillows and others without spring construction should be plumped daily.

TERMS YOU SHOULD KNOW

CHAIRS

SIDE CHAIRS: Straight or dining chairs, with or without arms, originally placed against the side of the room when not in use; therefore the rear is usually not decorated and often the back legs are plain in contrast to carved front legs.

SLIP SEAT: A removable seat of a side chair. It is made by padding a solid base and covering with fabric. Four screws underneath the seat release it so that it can easily be re-covered.

SADDLE SEAT: An upholstered or solid wooden seat on a side chair which has a scooped-out shape for additional comfort.

UPHOLSTERED SEAT: A chair seat built up with webbing, shallow springs, burlap, a layer of cotton or foam, and fabric covering.

STRETCHERS: Side stretchers and cross stretchers are rods linking the legs of a chair together. They strengthen it and help distribute the strain. When the design does not permit the use of stretchers, corner blocks in the seat rail are doubly important.

APRON: The exposed wood frame sometimes seen around the seat rail of a chair. It may be scalloped or ornamented with carving.

SOFAS

SOFA: A seating piece with upholstered arms and back, a minimum of fifty-two inches long, usually of spring construction. Originally the cushion on a saddle for a camel.

COUCH: A long upholstered piece of furniture to sit on or lie on, also called a studio couch.

LOUNGE: A couch or sofa, especially a backless one with a headrest at one end.

SOFA BED: A sofa that opens by various methods into a single, double bed, or twin beds.

DAVENPORT: A large couch or sofa named for a nineteenth-century manufacturer.

SETTEE: A seat or bench for two or three with an upholstered seat and a wood or upholstered back.

DESIGN DETAILS: May refer to the basic styling of the piece or to dressmaker details and custom touches. Variations in the basic styling may refer to tufting, a channel back, unusual wings, arms or legs, and extra cushions. Dressmaker details include the skirt, pleats, scallops, shaping, swags and fringe. Design details also applies to trapunto work on the cushion and back, trimmings applied flat or in the seams, and to the covering or encasing of exposed legs with the cover fabric.

BOTH SOFAS AND CHAIRS

LOOSE CUSHION BACK: A deep lounge chair or sofa which has a loose, or removable, cushion back. The cushions may be loose or partially attached to the back.

DUAL-PURPOSE: A term which refers to sofa beds or any piece of furniture that has more than one use.

REVERSIBLE CUSHIONS. Loose seat or back cushions which have the same upholstery material on both sides and can be turned to distribute wear.

SELF-COVERED SEAT DECK: A term used when matching upholstery fabric is used on the deck (the surface of the seat on which the cushions are placed). All better furniture has this feature. Muslin is used on less expensive furniture.

SPRING EDGE: A term which refers to seat springs when they are extended to the front of the seat deck, enabling it to move up and down under pressure. This gives added comfort, but slipcovers for such chairs should make allowance for this action. **Tailored edge** is the term used when springs do not edge the seat platform.

GUARANTEE: A manufacturer's or store's promise that a piece of furniture will keep its quality for a given period of time. There is no law requiring that furniture have a guarantee, and very few are given on upholstered pieces. It is said that upholstered furniture loses 20 per cent of its retail value the first year and 15 per cent the second year—a total of 35 per cent after two years. The principal complaints on upholstery fabrics are shrinkage, color bleeding and water staining.

Flame-patterned tapestry covers this Knole-type sofa with ratchet ends, the button-ended bolsters, the two T-shaped seat cushions and four loose pillows. Simulated cork tiles cover the wall. Black table bases repeat the dark values in the pictures. Note how the sheen and pattern of the sofa cover, keyed to the mural above, minimizes the eighty-one inch length of the sofa.

LAMPS AND LIGHTING

ELECTRIC LIGHTING is one of the miracles of the twentieth century, but it is probably used less imaginatively than our other household equipment because we take it for granted.

The lighting plan offers an opportunity for creativity, from the architectural lighting to the selection and placing of the portable lamps. Pure utility—to further the ability to see after dark—is only a part of the aim of lighting. Mood, beauty, painting with light are all goals for home lighting just as they are for lighting in the theater, and the ability to produce these effects should be possible to some degree in all rooms. In modest rooms the effect can be achieved manually. Elaborate installations employ special devices, central controls and dimmers.

Sources of light should be varied for interest and should supply the quantity and quality of light appropriate for different tasks and occasions. For instance, if you are planning living-room lighting, think of the room as it will be when you need maximum illumination. Think of your last party. Were some of the guests seated in such poor light that they seemed cut off from the rest of the group? Do you ever have to move to a chair near the "good" light to read a letter? Does Mrs. X, who always brings her knitting when she visits, have to be steered to the only spot with adequate light for her work? Do wires trail treacherously across the floor to the bridge-table lamp? Is the piano well-lighted? Do you have to use a flashlight to see the dials on the television set or to find a book on the shelf?

Evidently a lot of light needs to be shed on illumination. There are four important aspects to consider:

Balanced lighting is the first thing to think about in a lighting plan. This means the elimination of dark corners and dim areas that make a room seem dreary and cramped. It means adequate light for specific jobs; it means using colors, fabrics, and accessories that contribute to the lighting plan. Balanced lighting makes all parts of the room usable. In rooms where books are important, a tall table lamp close to the shelves can send an upward flow of light across the bindings, or a special light trough at the top of the shelves can be put in. It is attention to such detail that gives a room balanced lighting. It takes a minimum of five lamps to light the average living room, and at least three to light a bedroom.

Softness as opposed to glare is important because it involves eye comfort as well as the aesthetic sense. In rooms with dark walls it is especially important to avoid extremely bright areas. The contrast with the dark walls will tire the eyes because of the constant muscular action involved in adjusting to light and dark areas. In rooms with dark walls, use reflector bowls if shades are translucent or coated lamp bulbs that have been especially treated to diffuse the light. Otherwise these shades will give a glaring light. Opaque shades are also useful in creating comfortable lighting as they reduce the sharp contrast between lighted lamp and dark walls. The use of a sufficient number of portable lamps will enable you to have variety of light and will make it easier to work out a pleasant adjustment between the type of shade and intensity of light.

Flexibility is indispensable. It simply means

Tôle chandeliers in black and gold are a good selection for almost any informal dining room. The handsome wall case with its imposing cornice and gay miscellany, crossing as it does both time and national boundaries, is worth studying.

the ability to provide low, medium, and high levels of lighting to meet the needs of different moods and occasions. The ideal method is to have two dimming systems: one system controls the background lighting, the chandelier and wall fixtures, the other the portable lamps. Dimmers are marvelous for bringing the lighting of a room to the desired level in the most convenient way. But if you do not have such a system you can still achieve several degrees of lighting with lamps that have clusters of lamp bulbs, each bulb controlled separately, or with three-way bulbs. For TV viewing, a brightly lighted room is not desirable, but there must be sufficient general lighting to counteract glare from the picture screen. For reading, sewing or desk work, you need both good general lighting and direct lighting from a properly shielded bulb of at least one hundred watts.

Reflected light from walls, rug, upholstery fabrics, accessories must be considered, too. You may find yourself with a startlingly brilliant or discouragingly dull effect if you don't take reflected light into consideration. White walls give a maximum of 90 per cent reflection. Black reflects only 2 per cent. Descending the scale from most to least reflection are cream, yellow, medium green, medium blue, dark red, blue-black. So, in rooms with light-colored walls, you can count on reflected light; in rooms with darker walls, you will need to plan particularly well-balanced lighting and increase the total available wattage.

These four factors—balance, softness, flexibility and reflection—can be achieved through the imaginative use of available light sources: architectural lighting, portable lamps and accent lighting.

Light Sources

Architectural lighting can best supply general lighting, or what engineers call "ambient luminescence." In a bedroom it is the general light that helps you find the earring that has rolled under a chest, that aids in make-up. In a dining room it is used in setting the table and clearing up afterward. In kitchen, bath and other service rooms it is the basic over-all light. In the living room it is the high-keyed lighting that sets the stage for a big, gay party.

Possible sources of general light include:
    Central fixtures
    Luminous ceilings and panels
    Cornice lighting
    Reflected light from any source

Architectural lighting in its many forms, incandescent and fluorescent, gives a general background illumination and may also be used for special effects—such as cornice lighting over windows and panels of wall light—and even for illuminating whole ceilings and walls.

In a new house, as a rule, an allowance is made for lighting fixtures. It is seldom enough. A fine dining-room chandelier and luminous ceilings in the kitchen and bathroom are extras worth considering. Stock units for luminous ceilings, modestly priced, are now available. They may be fitted together in blocks or strips to cover almost any area. But all such general lighting, effective as it is, tends to become impersonal and monotonous when used in living areas.

Portable lamps, pin-up lamps, and single or clustered pendants used off-center as a substitute for portable lamps are the principal sources of focal glow or the lighting provided for specific tasks and limited areas: the pool of light by your favorite chair, at the desk, beside a bed; the high-keyed specific light for reading, sewing, or study. Lamps are movable, adaptable, and do a good lighting job when they have large translucent shades. Lamps are beauty spots, too; they bring hospitality, warmth and charm to a room.

Accent lighting is used for beauty, gaiety, for highlighting unique features. It may be the concealed lights in a cupboard, the small recessed spotlights focused on a crystal chandelier, a painting, the music rack and piano keys or the silver on a buffet table. In a handsome dining room invisible spotlights may be adjusted to the exact size of the table top. Inexpensive but dramatic effects can be achieved with concealed portable spotlights tucked behind plants, at the base of a pedestal holding a piece of sculpture, or focused on a mobile. With careful adjustment, the shadow from the object can be placed on a wall exactly where you want it.

Other incidental but useful lighting includes a lighted house number; a luminous keyhole; pool and garden lighting; lighting in closets; baseboard lighting in the nursery, bathroom and at the top and bottom steps of a staircase.

133

Empire in feeling, this columnar lamp with its narrow shade and wreath-and-arrow finial is a classic also available in white, blue and green. The accessories informally arranged on the campaign chests are the casual sort that anyone might have.

1. Portuguese antiqued tin candlestick lamp.   2. A cylinder-shaped lamp 43 inches tall, of simple good design.   3. Three candle bouillotte lamps developed for a French game table, perfect for a desk.   4. A baluster base, painted any color or in wood finishes, a classic shape.   5. Quaint reproduction goose decoy lamps.   6. Children's folk art whirligig toy turned into a lamp for a country room.   7. Urn shapes are always elegant and satisfying.   8. Tôle or painted tin lamps of French origin are

frequently reproduced.   9. Pewter candlestick-base lamps are right for Early American rooms.   10. A student lamp with candle holders which can be raised or lowered. 11. Victorian opalene glass globe lamp with chimney.   12. Classic candlestick lamp with old gold finish mounted on a marble base.   13. Painted tôle, once an oil burning lamp with screw for wick and arrow finial.   14. Generously proportioned pottery lamp, a centuries-old shape.

How to Select Lamps

BUYING A PORTABLE lamp requires several kinds of knowledge if the lamp is to serve successfully its double function of accessory and light source.

Buy, if possible, for a particular location and have a tape measure in your bag and a note of the height of the piece of furniture the lamp is to stand on. If lampshade and table are properly coordinated, the glare from exposed light bulbs will not hit the eye whether you are sitting or standing. For sofas and lounge chairs the bottom of the shade should be approximately forty inches from the floor. A desk lamp placed in front of you should have a minimum of fifteen inches between desk top and shade. If the desk and lamp are primarily decorative this rule may be ignored. Wall lamps mounted above a bed are most successful when the bottom of the shade is thirty inches above the top of the mattress.

Major portable lamps in a room should be approximately the same height measuring from the floor to the center of the shade. If the five or six lamps in a living room are all different heights, the effect is one of confusion. Small accent lamps, however, are a law unto themselves.

Bases with simple classic shapes will have the longest life: cylinders, columns, urns, vases, balusters, converted oil lamps, candle bases and classic Oriental porcelains. Among the most pleasing Oriental forms are ginger jars, round and square beakers, temple and club-shaped vases. Materials for bases include tôle, glass, pottery, silver, brass, bronze, stone, wood and alabaster.

One advantage in these classically inspired shapes is that they are available in wood or cast stone and can be finished to specification and as easily changed later. For period rooms, finishes include tortoise shell, antique gold, silver or pewter, marble or porphyry; for contemporary rooms, bright, fresh lacquer. For traditional rooms, old objects can easily be wired. Antique shops are a treasure house of possibilities. In provincial or Early American rooms, such novelties as tea canisters, wine jugs, tall wood finials, carved wooden figures, large coffee grinders and even duck decoys may be wired and used for lamp bases. However, too much whimsey can be as cloying as too many sweets.

Shades are just as important from a lighting point of view as they are from a decorative one. The over-all rule that should never be forgotten is that shades should be simple in design. Some decorators insist on using the same shade material—linen, paper or stretched silk—on all the lamps in a room. There should not be more than one or two novelties, at most, and these should never be in complicated shapes—too deep or too shallow—or decorated with swags, beads, ruching or swirls.

The over-all problem of shade selection involves consideration of the size, pitch, proportion, density, color and texture. Whether the shade will be white or colored, translucent or opaque, depends on the room—its size, colors and the amount of reflected light you can count on. But all shades should have white linings to get as much reflection as possible from the shade itself. In a room where walls and fabrics are quite light you may need to tone down the quality of the light with white opaque shades and you may want to use a dark shade for contrast somewhere in the room. In general there is nothing more satisfactory than a white shade. Solid-colored shades should be thought of as accents.

The width of the shade is determined by the size and shape of the lamp. A shade sixteen inches in diameter gives a wide flood of light for reading. Shades that have wide openings at the top—and most of them do today— allow good upward light which contributes to the general lighting of the room.

Lamp Fixtures and Electrical Parts

EXAMINE THE working parts of lamps. Many lamps today have harps, fixtures which merely hold the shade in place with a finial and permit the use of one bulb. With harps, deep shades

Left. Nicely proportioned black and gold baluster-type lamps in a Regency setting. Right. The painted yellow tôle lamp fashioned into a fluted column looks quite at home on the skirted table.

are used to shield the eyes from the bulb both below and above the shade. When a lamp has a white glass or plastic bowl surrounding the bulb the brightness of the bulb is diminished and the quality of the light softened. Lamps with single bulbs may have a three-way switch and socket to accommodate a multiple-watt bulb for providing different intensities.

There are also lamps with two horizontal bulbs or with clusters of bulbs on swivel heads, sometimes arranged in a downward position around a central shaft, sometimes in candle-like fixtures. In lamps with clusters of three bulbs, a minimum of three sixty-watt bulbs will provide a quality of light comparable to that from a single one hundred and fifty-watt bulb.

When you buy bulbs, look for the new types which have been developed to give better light and better protection for the eyes. Better bulbs have a white inner coating that produces a controlled distribution of light and eliminates the bright spot discernible even in a frosted ordinary bulb. These bulbs are available in several sizes and interesting new shapes, with straight sides or flattened tops instead of the old pear shape. They come with controls for three degrees of light. Inner-coated bulbs are especially useful for lamps with no diffusing bowl.

Care of lamps should not be neglected. Shades will look better longer if they are brushed inside and out weekly, and bulbs should be wiped with a damp cloth. Dust is an enemy of light, whether on shade or light bulb. Darkened bulbs should be retired to halls and closets where a bright light is not required. When a bulb becomes dark it absorbs the light and may reduce lighting efficiency as much as 50 to 75 per cent.

TERMS YOU SHOULD KNOW

ACCENT LIGHTING: Staccato lighting for beauty's sake, and not utilitarian.

BUILLOTTE LAMP: A lamp, which comes in a variety of sizes and shapes, that takes its name from a popular eighteenth-century card game. Both base and shade are usually tôle, although some bases are silver or bronze. Originally one to three candles were used and the shade was shallow and opaque.

CORNICE: An ornamental horizontal projection used at the ceiling line. It may be of wood, metal or other material and may conceal fluorescent tubes. It may be used around the whole room or be placed over windows to shed light down onto the draperies.

COVES: Over-sized cornices, usually placed high on walls, concealing fluorescent tubes; coves throw light up and give indirect light reflected from the ceiling.

DIRECT LIGHTING: Light that goes directly from the source to the object it illuminates. It gives bright light, may be glaring, and brings out contrasts.

FINIAL: On a portable lamp, a plain or decorative ornament used at the top. It may screw into the harp or into a center socket in the shade frame.

FIXTURE: A permanently mounted electrical installation to hold either incandescent bulbs or fluorescent tubes.

FOOT CANDLE. A quantitative unit for measuring light.

FRAME-MOUNTED PICTURE LIGHTS: Small shielded clip-on lamps for lighting important pictures. In a museum or picture gallery these are acceptable, but they are seldom used in homes.

HARP: A looped wire that fits around the bulb and holds the lamp shade.

INDIRECT LIGHTING: Light that goes from the source to ceiling, walls, or other surface, from which it is reflected, giving soft general illumination.

PANEL LIGHTS: Lights "set" into the ceiling in recessed reflector boxes shielded by frosted glass panels or metal grids.

SCONCES, WALL LIGHTS, APPLIQUES, WALL BRACKETS, GIRANDOLES: Terms for lighting fixtures attached to the wall. Originally such fixtures were used to hold candles; now they are frequently wired. Sconces, as a rule, have a back plate. When the back plate is made of mirror glass the fixture is called a girandole.

SEMI-INDIRECT LIGHTING: A combination of direct and indirect lighting.

SOCKET: the recessed threaded depression into which a bulb is screwed.

TORCHERE, CANDLE STAND, FLOOR LAMP, GUERIDON: Terms that apply to floor-based candle- or lamp-holders.

138

Small flame-size bulbs are used in this fourteen candle chandelier. It is large in scale but has so little bulk it takes nothing from the size of the room. Walls above the dado and cafe curtains match. Sheer white muslin is made to fit the arched window.

ACCENT ON ACCESSORIES

AN ACCESSORY IS almost anything that can't be classified as major furnishing. Accessories may be serious, gay, witty, inexpensive or priceless; they may be new or old, hand crafted or machine-made. They may be beautiful, clever, amusing or "too, too divine." They are, in short, the verve, the prance, the "plume in the hat" sort of possession.

Without accessories a room is flat, dull and impersonal, like a hotel room. With the right accessories, even a hotel room can take on character and be gay, personal and charming.

Too often gift knickknacks are used as accessories. Such things don't say anything, instead they create confusion. They are usually too small and bear little relation to the color or theme of the room. Accessories, unfortunately, are too often used for sentimental reasons, not because they are appropriate. Well-chosen accessories can be the most personal feature of a room and can speak volumes.

Decorators report that on most jobs everything goes nicely until it's time to buy pictures and accessories. There the client draws the line. Years ago I handled an installation costing approximately $50,000. All the bills were approved without comment until the last one—a jungle painting priced at a modest $150. The uproar it caused was so unbelievable and unexpected that the animal peering through the leaves in the picture was christened "Mr. X"— the name of the agitator.

Another decorator gets approval on all details of a project except accessories. After the installation is complete he drives up with a station wagon·full of "goodies." These he moves in and arranges, and lets the client live with a properly accessorized room for a few days. Almost without exception the key pieces are purchased.

What Are Accessories?

BECAUSE THE SELECTION OF accessories is one of the most creative elements in decorating, it is difficult to classify them, or to guide anyone in the mystery of their selection because it is about nine-tenths inspiration. However, there are what might be called two categories: the useful and the purely decorative. Among useful accessories are fireplace tools, desk appointments, small boxes and chests, accent tables that hold an ashtray or bowl, flower vases, screens that shield something from view, clocks, candy jars and mirrors. Purely decorative accessories are the mantel garniture (except a clock), flowers, plants, pictures and sculpture, accent lighting, old books displayed for their fine bindings, collections of almost anything, from old wooden potato mashers to ancient Greek coins or lead soldiers.

In shopping for accessories it is helpful to further subdivide them into (a) formal, elegant or sophisticated and (b) informal, provincial, country or off-beat. For instance, even if they are amusing, old kitchen spoons, strainers or pancake griddles have no place in a room with

Horses are the theme of this collection used on chintz, plates and mugs. There is a weather vane horse on the double bonnet secretary and programs from the horse show on the easel. On the right, a Chippendale design.

Unrelated miscellany gives this room its charm. The pottery jug color matched

to the cabinet, the lion, the tiger and the pewter create a rhythmic feeling.

damask-covered walls and eighteenth-century mahogany furniture. On the other hand, an ornate gilt-framed Chinese Chippendale mirror has to be hung with a knowing hand in a room with board and batten walls, braided rugs and old pine furniture. No rule for using accessories in decorating or fashion is hard and fast. The knowing eye, the hand with flair, the innovator can juxtapose seemingly incongruous objects and materials with exciting results.

Materials used in accessories are endless, and learning a little about each one affords a fascinating education. The list includes bronze, brass, steel, pewter, silver, gold, iron and copper, pottery, porcelain, glass and crystal, tile and terra cotta, wood, basketry, leather, enamels and mosaics; stone, alabaster, marble, ivory and onyx; plastics, rubber and needlework.

One of the most startling objects I have ever seen used as an accessory was a six-foot plaster cast of a Greek statue casually standing knee-deep in ferns in a small Chicago apartment. "He" had been acquired at a Chicago Art Institute auction and had become one of the family.

A photographer with a penchant for traveling collects doors. They are a recurring note throughout his house and are so unusual that they can be classed as accessories. The first pair one sees are twelve feet high and separate the parking area from the garden. The entrance door is a nail-studded four-inch-thick slab of oak from a Mexican hacienda. In the bathroom, frosted-glass engraved doors from a French restaurant serve as a screen or room divider. In the baby's bedroom, low carved Spanish doors form a headboard. Over a sofa, painted Austrian doors taken from a mammoth cupboard give the effect of pictures hung on the wall, and a swinging mahogany café door with a stained-glass pane divides the dining room and kitchen.

Color is an invaluable help in giving direction to an accessory collection. Perhaps blue, amethyst, green or red is your favorite color. You will, no doubt, develop room themes in which your color is prominent, so whenever you see something you like in that color, it's a safe purchase.

The period approach works the same way. Today it is not necessary to adhere strictly to one period or even to one country. But it is important to consider texture and mood. Regardless of how handsome it may be, an elaborate crystal chandelier or ornate Sèvres vase would make little contribution to an Early American room. However, French tole lamps, English lustre pitchers or Italian pottery would be quite appropriate used in a maple-and-pine room because they are simple and provincial.

Accessories may be collected in terms of nationalities. In a recent United States World Trade Fair in New York artifacts from sixty countries were represented. Outstanding objects included African carvings and other primitive objects d'art; Mexican and South American accessories, both ancient and modern; Japanese, Chinese, Indian and Turkish curios; French, English, Spanish and Dutch bibelots; Scandinavian handicrafts. In fact, there isn't a place on the globe that will not offer fascinating man-made or natural objects: shells, rocks, wood, crafts and arts worth displaying.

How to Arrange Accessories

Arranging accessories is an art in itself. If they are just strewn around they will create an air of confusion. To be effective, accessories must have order and composition. The arrangements may be true "still lifes," but often it is necessary to think of comfort and convenience too.

Accessories may be hung on walls or from the ceiling; they may be placed on tables or chests or shelves; or on the floor. The mood or spirit and use of accessories may vary between rooms. For instance, table-top accessories in the living room will be quite different from those on bedside tables or on a counter in the kitchen. Some may have no fixed place, if they are to be shifted in use. However, balanced arrangements on mantels, tables or chests must be kept in precise order, or they will give a room a decadent, slatternly look.

In arranging accessories, consider line and shape, size, texture, theme and color. If there is sympathy between objects, an idea that links them together, they will almost arrange themselves. To develop skill, practice making compositions. By arranging and rearranging your small objects you'll learn the art.

Collections can be important in your decorating scheme if you give enough thought and study to the most effective way to display them. Used singly, many ordinary things have no charm, but used in masses they become interesting. In an old country schoolhouse converted into a residence, a collection of ten or fifteen castiron pancake griddles is displayed on one wall. A variety of old cooking tools hangs on a rack over a refectory table, and a collection of old carpet beaters forms a pattern on a blue-painted wall.

There are a few general rules. Keep your collections together. Don't scatter things around the room. Not only will the meaning and impact of the collection be lost, but the room will begin to look spotty. Shadow boxes lined with velvet, taffeta or small-patterned paper will set off little things effectively. Glass paperweights, coins and old spoons may be displayed in a recessed coffee-table top and protected with glass. Pictures, trivets—all objects that can be hung —may be grouped on a wall. Shelves, of course, are excellent for many objects.

Where Do You Find Accessories?

IT IS IMPOSSIBLE to tell anyone where to find just the right accessories for a room. Like buried treasure, accessories have to be discovered, not just bought. It may take years to find the perfect accents for your home. If you go downtown and buy the first object you see, chances are it will be meaningless.

Accessories may be family memorabilia, things with interesting associations found on trips or objects you have searched out in antique shops, thrift shops, secondhand stores, house-wreckers' yards. Visit white elephant

Shell prints hung on the wall and shells in the red corner cupboard are the mark of a collector or a summer at the shore.

A flower fancier created this small green world in an apartment. Note the Louis XV desk, the lace-topped cafe curtains.

145

sales. Let your friends know what you are collecting. Someone else's discard may be your treasure. Do not overlook museums in your locality. Many have shops where all sorts of fascinating objects can be purchased. In the shop at the American Museum of Natural History in New York you can find dolls from all over the world, ebony and ivory objects, small carved animals from Hong Kong and Jordan, and many other exciting things. An old house that is being torn down in the next block may yield lovely moldings, interesting old fixtures, doorknobs and decorative carvings. Learn as you collect, by studying your special subject in books and magazines published for

collectors. It may take years to acquire a sizable collection, but in the process you'll become an expert in some field. You will begin as a novice; with time you will develop the cautious taste of the connoisseur.

Collecting accessories sometimes requires a storage closet where treasures can be put until the day when they will become just the thing you need. The E's have three beautiful carved marble counters installed in their new house in Florida. They were so unusual that I asked about them. They were purchased for five dollars each in Chicago twenty years ago when a candy shop was dismantled, and only now have they found a permanent place.

How to Become a Collector

COLLECTORS WHO really have a mania for acquisitions and who pursue a fixed pattern are lucky souls.

Family hobbies, interests, enthusiasms or a profession sometimes supply a direction or offer a theme for accessories. A well-known Connecticut writer has, for instance, a quill weathervane on his house and a fine old corner cupboard full of antique inkwells—pewter, silver, china and brass. His den is lined with old engravings of authors: Shakespeare, Dickens, Rabelais.

Horses, dogs, your alma mater, flowers, trees, sports, music, travel, art, boats, books, fishing and hunting can all offer inspiration. Nearly everyone starts a collection at some time. Those who keep at it sometimes end up with valuable collections of museum quality. The peculiar enjoyment of owning and adding to a collection piece by piece over a period of years has to be experienced to be fully appreciated.

It's easy to become a collector. Just keep your eyes open and before long an object will choose *you*. It may be a pewter porringer, a bit of lace, a scarred wooden chopping bowl, a green-glass bottle, a letter postmarked before you were born, a gold filigree button, a Sandwich glass butter dish, a Staffordshire cat, a piece of coral. The attraction of a particular

object for a collector is inexplicable. But when you feel it, take the first step—acquire it and rejoice. You have started on an adventure.

Children are born collectors. If you grow impatient with the bits and pieces they first bring home, remember that many a fine collection was started in childhood. With a little tactful guidance your daughter may start collecting things that are new and commonplace now but that will have real charm in twenty years when she marries. One sixteen-year-old of my acquaintance has a valuable collection of majolica fruit and vegetable dishes that she has been adding to since she was five. A twelve-year-old attends antique shows with the hope of finding a child's or doll's chair at her price, and of a caliber to join the group hung on the wall of her bedroom. Another youngster searches out alabaster, wood and ceramic eggs; and an eight-year-old has become so engrossed in his collection of knives of all nations that he is an authority in the field. A well-known decorator has been collecting owls, in paintings and artifacts, for thirty years. Another specializes in Napoleona. Since his college days, a man in Chicago has acquired over one hundred and fifty tinsel pictures. He has only forty-five of the best now—the others have been sold at a nice profit.

146

CLOCKS AND MIRRORS

CLOCKS AND MIRRORS are usually classed as accessories; they are and they aren't. To call them accessories is about the same as calling your Uncle Joe or a good friend an acquaint- ance. Clocks and mirrors do play a decorative role but they also have a function, and as accessories there are ways of using them which increase their contribution.

Friendly Clocks

CLOCKS ARE inanimate, but they have a life of their own, and a room is never quite empty when there is a clock face on a table or on the wall. It will draw the eye as surely as a portrait, and will even give a room an aura of friend-liness. Experts in direct-mail gift selling have discovered that at least one face on a page of gifts helps sales. The face may be that of a person, a doll, an animal such as a Teddy Bear or, believe it or not—a clock. The companion-able quality of clocks makes their use in all rooms almost mandatory; but whether they have a happy tick-tock or a silent electric unit, they have the added features of beauty and utility. Use them on tables, desks, bookshelves and walls.

Large clock faces, whether the clocks are running or still, or grouped with pictures on a "scatter wall," have particular charm. As a mat-ter of fact, clocks are important collectors' items, and several old clocks may be grouped on a wall primarily for their shape and interest, rather than as timepieces. A young bride ac-quired nine old clocks, none of them valuable; they cost her from fifty cents to five dollars. She painted them all turquoise blue and hung them on the wall of her turquoise-ceilinged, white-walled foyer with great success. A serious collector, of course, would not be guilty of such desecration as painting a clock. Really fine old clocks should never have their original per-sonality obliterated.

Historically Speaking

THERE IS A fascinating history behind both the steady tick-tock of old clocks and the modern silent electric-powered or battery movements. Some of the most ingenious minds of all time have worked at the problem of keeping tabs on time. The earliest known invention was the sundial, which has existed since prehistoric days. To cope with keeping appointments when there was no sunshine, various types of flow-meters were invented, using either water or sand. The hourglass survives today for timing three-minute eggs and telephone calls.

Mechanical clocks came into use in Europe in the thirteenth and fourteenth centuries when unknown inventors produced the first ingenious mechanisms, some of which are still in running condition. The invention of the pendulum, in 1657, was a major contribution to accurate timekeeping. Most of the early American clocks had wooden movements because wood was plentiful and easy to work with, and metal was scarce. The clock industry in America began in the states of Massachusetts, Connecticut, Rhode Island and Pennsylvania. Early in the nineteenth century there was a period of bartering in which clocks were used as money —a number of clock movements could even purchase a house. A depression in 1837 ended that practice. When the clock industry recovered from the depression, movements of wood were abandoned.

Among old clocks that have become cherished heirlooms, the tall clock nicknamed "grandfather," is the best known. Early inventors added such interesting gadgets as astrological dials showing the phases of the moon and the relations of the planets to one another. Other clocks have had tidal dials geared for a specific seaport, or a sailing ship mounted on the end of a pendulum. These clocks had a loud, musical tick that is one of their endearing qualities.

The banjo clock, a famous early American wall clock, was patented in 1802 by Simon Willard, of Grafton, Massachusetts, one of the principal clockmakers of his day. The design of this clock has never lost its popularity, and can now be bought with electric works. Cases may be undecorated, but often they are gilded and hand painted with flowers or scenes; and sometimes a window in the base exposes the pendulum. A graceful relative of the banjo clock was the lyre clock, developed in Boston.

The pillar and scroll, one of the most beautiful of the early shelf clocks, was designed by Eli Terry, of Plymouth, Connecticut, about 1818. Scenic or floral designs were painted on the glass door panel below the dial, and brass finials, usually urn-shaped, were used on the pillars and the scroll top. These clocks originally had wood movements, ran for thirty hours on one winding, and cost about fifteen dollars. There were many imitators of this style. Its designer, Terry, served his apprenticeship with Seth Thomas.

Simon Willard's lighthouse clock was a departure from the usual shelf clock. These clocks were about sixteen inches tall with a bell-like glass enclosure on a tower-shaped base. Since few of them were made they are very rare today.

Wag-on-wall clocks with wood movements were made after 1790 by Gideon Roberts of Bristol, Connecticut. These are tall clocks without cases, and originally sold for about twenty dollars. For an additional twenty dollars a case could be purchased. Wall clocks were introduced because houses were more fully furnished by the late eighteenth century and floor space was becoming a consideration.

The French cartel was a wall clock of flamboyant, asymmetrical design. These eighteenth-century French clocks were of gilded bronze, and cases were designed by the great Paris designers of the period. English versions were of carved wood. Cartels have great beauty and distinction when properly used against rich wall hangings.

Steeple clocks appeared in the middle of the nineteenth century, when inexpensive springs replaced weights and gave the casemakers greater freedom; space for the drop of the weights was no longer needed. These clocks had twin Gothic steeples and were followed by a variety of small shelf clocks, including imitations of French clocks.

Whimsical clocks have been made over the centuries. A rare eighteenth-century French clock is in the form of a sculptured Indian maiden. The time of day appears in her eyes. A novel modern electric clock records hours and minutes on revolving bands, and an airy final whirling around serves as a second hand, all enclosed in a glass dome. An early timepiece was a gold water-powered contraption which the King of Persia is said to have given to Charlemagne in 807. This clock had twelve doors that opened in succession to allow little balls to roll out and fall onto a drum, thus striking the hour. At twelve o'clock twelve miniature horsemen appeared and shut the doors. A seventeenth-century clockmaker made what appeared to be a turtle swimming in a plate with a dial around the edge. A concealed magnet drew the turtle to the correct time on the dial, no matter where it was placed on the plate. These curious timepieces are examples of the ingenuity and imagination that time-telling seems to inspire.

Clock collecting is a fascinating hobby. Beginners might start with the less expensive items such as nineteenth-century kitchen clocks. There is much to be learned from them.

Clocks are collected for the unique elements in their working parts as well as for their cases, which are often works of art. There is real charm in this wall group.

Mural clock
French
eighteenth century

Pocket-watch clock
eleven inches high
electric

Lyre clock
Massachusetts
about 1830

Shelf clock
lighthouse shape
about 1815

Pillar-and-scroll clock
Connecticut, about 1818

DRAWINGS BY ERIC MULVANY

Whimsical electric clock
Bands revolve to tell time

ag-on-wall clock
ghted movements
modern

Electric pine-spice-box clock

Banjo clock
Massachusetts
about 1800

Table clock
Massachusetts
about 1790

Tall clock
astrological dial
Massachusetts
1772

Eighteenth-century French
Time's in her rolling eyes

Steeple clock, Connecticut, about 1845

A study of clock movements will enable a collector to spot an unusual movement in an apparently ordinary clock and perhaps make a rare find. The imitation French clocks that flooded the market in the last quarter of the nineteenth century are not difficult to come upon. They are interesting as a reflection of the taste of the times. A fine collection of old clocks can be seen in the Ford Museum, Dearborn, Michigan.

Mirror Marvels

LIKE CLOCKS, mirrors also have unpredictable characteristics—qualities which cannot always be determined before they are hung. These qualities relate to the elusive world of shadows and reflections.

Do you want sunshine to glow on a dark wall that the sun never reaches? Place a mirror there and watch it snare the light. Do you have a narrow hall or a small bedroom that seems to close you in? Stretch its boundaries with a mirrored wall. Would you like to enjoy your favorite view even if you have to sit with your back to it? Reflect it in a mirror. Would you like to expand a dining room? Then place a half-round table against a mirrored wall and it will appear to be round. Is a heavily patterned wallpaper a problem? Then hang a mirror on it. Do the upside-down reflections in ponds fascinate you and do you always look with pleasure at the reflections in the windows of the Seagram and the Lever House buildings in New York? Then use mirrors lavishly.

Mirrors have been used since the Greek youth Narcissus first admired his reflection in the depths of a forest pool. The earliest portable mirrors were polished bits of black obsidian and highly polished metal disks. In the Middle Ages, the "looking glass" was discovered. Since that time, the use of mirror glass has been prized for interior decoration, and the finest designers have lavished their art on frames. Venetian mirrors with elaborate glass-encrusted frames are justly famous. In England, Grinling Gibbon, Thomas Chippendale and Robert Adam made important contributions. In France, Le Brun is credited with the first outstanding architectural use of mirror glass in his design for the Galerie des Glâces at Versailles.

Mirrors have a place in every room in the house from foyer to kitchen, basement to attic, and even on the porch and in the garden. Traditionally, they are used over a fireplace or a sofa, between a pair of windows at the end of a room, over a chest or console in the foyer, above the buffet in the dining room. As service pieces, they find their way quite naturally into bedroom and bath.

Among the newer uses are mirrored glass doors which, when used in multiples, give the impression of a mirrored wall. They are, of course, wonderful for closet walls in bedrooms, but may be used elsewhere. One of the most handsome installations I have seen is in the New York apartment of Michael Greer, the well-known interior designer. At one end of his elegantly furnished guest-room-library is a mirrored wall which folds back like a screen to reveal a Murphy folding bed!

Quality Standards

THE MIRROR GLASS you select may vary with your need or plan. There are mirrors in which perfect reflection is wanted, as for make-up; purely decorative mirrors, where the frame may be the most important factor; and, finally, there are architectural mirrors for surfacing large wall areas with mirror glass.

For top-quality reflection, select twin-ground polished quarter-inch plate glass. Framed mirrors may have a beveled edge, unframed mirrors a seamed or regular polished edge. The less expensive mirrors are made from sheet or window glass. This is not ground or polished like plate glass and there are slight irregularities in the thickness that cause distortions in the reflection. Sheet glass is never beveled or seamed, although it may have polished edges. It is satisfactory for large architectural installations. Even without polished edges, the effect is excellent and there is considerable saving.

Window glass is also used for mirrors. The quality is determined by thickness.

Magnificent over-scaling is the chief element in this room: the huge lanterns, the heavily carved Spanish mirror, the big modern planter, the twelve-foot tree and even the ample size of the bowl of tomatoes and peppers outlaw use of small objects.

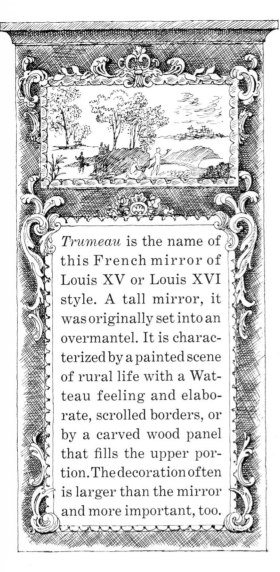

Trumeau is the name of this French mirror of Louis XV or Louis XVI style. A tall mirror, it was originally set into an overmantel. It is characterized by a painted scene of rural life with a Watteau feeling and elaborate, scrolled borders, or by a carved wood panel that fills the upper portion. The decoration often is larger than the mirror and more important, too.

Standing mirrors, used on chest or table, were popular as dressing mirrors in the eighteenth century. They came in many styles, with a straight, curved, or serpentine base. Glass was oval, shield-shape, square.

The *pier glass*, or cheval glass, has reflected many of the changing ways of life — and architecture — over the centuries. It was originally a tall, narrow mirror that was made to fill the pier, or wall space, between windows, and in the ceremonious rooms of the eighteenth century, pier glasses, with an elaborately carved panel atop each, gave great brilliance and spaciousness, gleaming at regular intervals amid the tall windows. Later, the term was used for bracket-hung mirrors that swung on portable floor stands and became popular as dressing-room mirrors. Many a nineteenth-century home had them, as well as true ceiling-high pier glasses. With today's revival of old furniture fashions, pier glasses reappear, as this one of the twentieth century.

Jigsaw mirrors were in favor in eighteenth- and nineteenth-century England and America. The earlier frames were ornamented by hand, top and bottom, with open-work scrolls; later frames, as well as other furnishings, were cut by jigsaw, one of the first tools operated by power. Though some jigsaw mirrors were crude, others were decorated with gilded and carved eagle and plume motifs.

The *rococo* mirror of the eighteenth century came in all sizes and a variety of fanciful shapes, like this old French mirror.

DRAWINGS BY ERIC MULVANY

mirrors

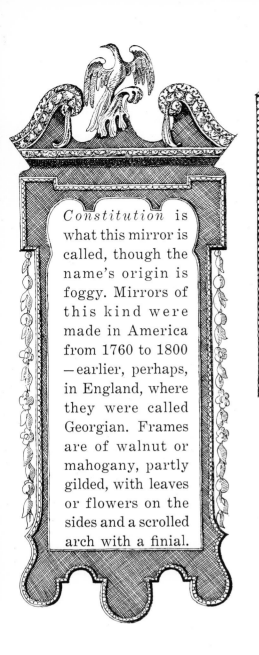

Constitution is what this mirror is called, though the name's origin is foggy. Mirrors of this kind were made in America from 1760 to 1800 —earlier, perhaps, in England, where they were called Georgian. Frames are of walnut or mahogany, partly gilded, with leaves or flowers on the sides and a scrolled arch with a finial.

Venetian mirrors used glass to ornament glass: colored glass or glass "carved" in leaf-and-flower design was often superimposed on borders, like the mirror sketched, a nineteenth-century one. Some resembled glass mosaic, with lead strippings between the fragments. There was no limit to their imaginative and intricate use of glass. Gilt wood was used in earlier mirrors.

Queen Anne frame, like this, retained its popularity long after her death in 1714. It is made of walnut, refined, uncluttered. The bonnet top, sometimes crested, is quite characteristic. Its history is amusing: The eighteenth-century mirror was considered a luxury, and it was taxed according to its size; so frugal Englishmen reduced their taxes by using two lesser pieces of mirror instead of a single large one, with the smaller of the two placed above the larger.

Country French mirror, Louis XV style, was rustic but elegant; often carved out of one piece of wood that was painted or heavily gilded.

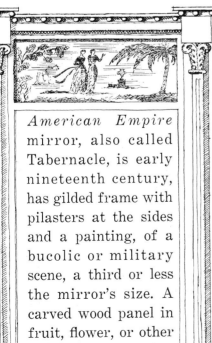

American Empire mirror, also called Tabernacle, is early nineteenth century, has gilded frame with pilasters at the sides and a painting, of a bucolic or military scene, a third or less the mirror's size. A carved wood panel in fruit, flower, or other Empire decoration may be used instead.

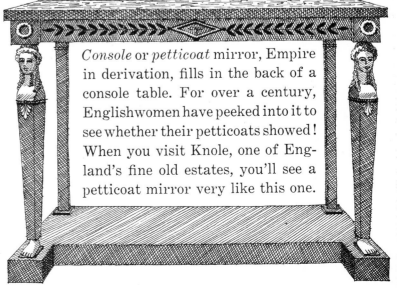

Console or *petticoat* mirror, Empire in derivation, fills in the back of a console table. For over a century, Englishwomen have peeked into it to see whether their petticoats showed! When you visit Knole, one of England's fine old estates, you'll see a petticoat mirror very like this one.

Care and Hanging of Mirrors

IF POSSIBLE, place mirrors where the sun will not strike them and where they will not hang over a register or a radiator, as heat causes deterioration of the backing. Any handyman can hang a portable or framed mirror using the same methods as those used for pictures.

Unusual effects can be had if reflections are carefully considered before the mirror is placed.

Mirrors weigh about four pounds to the square foot. For mirrors weighing less than thirty-five pounds, use twin-strand wire over two firmly embedded wall hooks, four inches apart; for a heavier mirror, place hooks farther apart to distribute the weight. Unframed wall mirrors which have been mounted and backed are generally attached to the wall with toggle bolts and plastic or metal clips which show at the mirror's edge. Two clips are usually used on all four sides. This method is also used for installing mirrors on doors.

Architectural mirrors hung without backing should be placed only on dry walls. Dampness damages the silvering on the back. As a safeguard, the wall directly behind the mirror, especially in new construction, should be covered with waterproof paper or polyethylene film, or the plaster should be sized to seal out moisture. Whenever possible, the mirror should be mounted out from the wall on a lath framework to allow for air circulation.

Repair of damaged mirror coating requires stripping off all of the reflective surface and resilvering the glass. Usually it is less expensive to have new mirror glass put in the frame. Incidentally, if you have a fine antique frame with the old glass in it, do not change the glass. It will reduce the value of the mirror and subtly affect its beauty. Old mirror glass was less mechanically perfect than it is today. The irregularities in the old glass and the graying effect of time are part of its charm.

Mirrors on the wall and mirrors on the sliding closet doors make this room glitter. The mirrors also appear to double the room size. The assorted frames on the mirrors over the bed are the needed gay touch.

BOOKS AND PICTURES

Books are like friends, and, really, no home is complete without them. Granted their primary use is for reading, they have a charm and often a beauty of their own and can do much to give a room a warm, pleasant, lived-in look.

Books singly and in pairs may be used with other accessories on desks and table tops. In a room with antiques, use handsome leather-bound old volumes. In a modern room, a collection of art books may be placed one at a time on a coffee table. By changing them from time to time, you can enjoy their beauty as you absorb their contents.

Far more fundamental is the housing of a library. In a family that uses books like oxygen or food, as a part of every-day living, keeping books under control can be a major problem. Accommodations for books may have to be supplied in living room and halls, bedrooms and family room, guestroom-studies and children's rooms. It may even be necessary to install a five-foot shelf in the kitchen.

Shelves may be of three kinds: built-in, assembled or furniture case pieces. If you own your house, built-in bookshelves may be worth the struggle of designing and building. Probably a country carpentry shop can knock together the least expensive bookshelf wall; well-made custom-built bookcases may be the most expensive.

A bookshelf wall should be designed carefully and may include door-storage areas, stereo, hi-fi, even television. First lay out a plan for the placement of the shelves and cupboard spaces on paper, using one inch or two inches to the foot. When the plan is satisfactory, with a soft crayon, a yardstick and a square, draw the plan full scale directly onto the wall where it is to be installed. A good shop will draft the plan full-scale on paper and tape it to the wall for your study.

Built-in shelves are, as a rule, finished to blend with the walls. In a wood-paneled room, use a natural finish. Or paint shelves to match woodwork or wallpaper. Often the shelves themselves are varnished, oiled or left unfinished although their edges may be painted. In hot humid climates paint sometimes softens and mars the edges of books.

Assembled shelves offer a simple do-it-yourself approach. There is a wide variety, ranging from shelves on metal brackets to combinations of shelves and cupboards. These are hung by several patented methods. There is a choice of shelf woods and finishes ranging through paint, Formica, teak and walnut. Even though installation is simple, care and accuracy in assembling and hanging are important. Use a plumb line to control verticality and a carpenter's level which you can rent at a hardware store to insure straight horizontal lines. Bookcases are architectural, and unless right angles are meticulous the results can be more maddening than a crooked picture.

Bracket shelves on wall straps are versatile and may be used for a small bank of shelves in a child's room or a wall-sized arrangement in the family room. Since the wall itself is the supporting medium and since book-loaded shelves have considerable weight, the supports must be placed to coincide with the two-by-fours in the wall. These can be located by tapping the wall, by testing with a magnetic device which registers the nails in the two-by-fours or by calcula-

picture on following page **Books are a decoration in themselves, but are hospitable to accessories. Here pictures, clocks, a treasure box and family memorabilia enliven the shelves. The calander clock is a family piece, the dolls head and galloping horse were childhood toys.**

tion from a corner. The supports are usually set twenty-four inches on center. If the shelves are not nailed or screwed to the two-by-fours, the weight of the shelves and books may pull the plaster off the wall.

If you don't trust the strength of a wall, if you rent or want the flexibility of easily moved shelves and cupboards, use a plug-in system or pressure-pole shelves. In both of these systems, floor-to-ceiling poles are the supporting medium. In the plug-in method, black anodized aluminum poles are braced on the floor and are plugged into a socket in the ceiling. In the pressure-pole system, spring ends in the poles hold them firmly between floor and ceiling. A wide assortment of shelves and modular cupboard units are available for all pole systems. Because of their exposed structural character, they are most effective in modern rooms.

Free-standing bookshelves or bookcases are, of course, the quickest and easiest solution. Next to inexpensive carpenter-built shelves, stacks of unpainted shelves and cupboards may be the least expensive, and if their assembly is plotted like a puzzle game, interesting walls with a built-in look can be developed. Finished bookcases, pier cabinets and chests or drawers in modular units with hutch tops are available in maple, cherry, walnut and mahogany, and in any style from modern to provincial. The least expensive may cost less than one fourth the price of quality units.

It is impossible to recommend a library's content—that is an individual matter and will vary with your business or profession and with your avocation and hobbies. Lawyer, banker, realtor, doctor, writer, businessman, housewife, teacher—each will want books in his own particular field.

A frequently asked question is, "Is it correct to use boxes, figurines and other accessories on bookshelves?" The answer is, by all means use space that is not filled with books for attractive still-life arrangements. Perhaps frivolous accessories interspersed in a serious medical or legal library might not be appropriate, but related accessories would undoubtedly add interest to either a home or office library. A doctor might have a collection of pestles and mortars, old herb canisters and bottles or chemist's flasks. A lawyer might display framed diplomas and small busts or engravings of illustrious members of the legal profession.

Books with handsome bindings may stand on the shelf like a picture; and pictures, too, may stand on shelves, as well as be hung from the shelf edge and cover several shelves; this is in harmony with the total wall composition. This technique is a helpful device while the library is growing.

Pictures

THE LORE, the fascination, the history, the magic of pictures is a world—a study in its own right—and a detailed discussion has no place here. However, unless pictures are stored and shown only in portfolio, the room designer must frame and hang them appropriately, and often, if there are to be pictures, the professional decorator guides their selection. Some knowledge of pictures is necessary.

Pictures may be divided into four large categories: originals, graphic art prints, reproductions and decorative prints. The term "original" is applied to any picture which is the direct work of the artist. Original paintings and drawings are one of a kind. Techniques used are oil, water color, tempera and gouache; collage, pencil, crayon, ink, wash, pastels, charcoal and variations of these.

ORIGINALS are the aristocrats of the art world, command the highest prices and are collected by museums and connoisseurs. This does not mean that they are out of reach of the average person. There has been a tremendous explosion in the number of artists in all parts of the country. Many are doing stimulating work and prices are sometimes within the average purse.

GRAPHIC ART PRINTS may be woodcuts, etchings, engravings, serigraphs and lithographs. These are made by the artist. Their value will vary with the quality, the technique used, the reputation of the artist and the number of prints made. In some

Small pictures scattered around a room can be distractions, but used in a mass they make an important contribution. Notice that the bottom and side of the group form a straight line. There is some variation at the top, but the effect is orderly.

cases, no more than fifty prints are made, and the plates are destroyed. This enhances the value of the print.

All graphic prints are made in much the same way. The artist makes a key block by etching on metal or glass with acid, by engraving on steel, carving on wood, or by using grease on stone (lithograph). Prints are made from this plate.

REPRODUCTIONS or facsimile prints of originals and graphic prints are made by several processes. These prints are surprisingly accurate in both color and texture and often are even made the same size as the original. There are three processes used for color reproductions: four-color, offset and collotype. The last of these is considered the most accurate.

DECORATIVE PRINTS form a less important category, and although they too are reproductions they are seldom referred to as such. Subjects include flowers, fruits, birds, butterflies, clipper ships and hunting scenes, as well as simple architectural or landscape subjects such as Currier and Ives and Audubon bird prints. Some of these prints have good color and design and a pleasant quaintness that makes them particularly charming in simple rooms.

Educate Yourself

THE ONLY WAY to get acquainted with pictures is to look, study, read and think about them. Start your education with several trips to a museum. There you can browse and acquire a feeling for pictures, begin to sense their history, learn to recognize the names of artists, their styles and techniques. Begin reading the art reviews in daily papers and weekly magazines. Search out local galleries. Start an art library with paperbound art books. Begin a portfolio of clippings of pictures. When the folder begins to bulge, classify it: old masters, primitives, impressionists, post-impressionists, and modern or experimental art. Put them into separate folders. In the modern art folder include examples of cubism, surrealism, collages, geometric abstractions and all the new techniques; you might even have a folder on "pop" and "junk" art.

The next step is to narrow down the field. When you visit a gallery, a museum, or look through a book or your collection, select the pictures you would like to own. The personal element in picture selection is always important. Two pictures may be equally good from a technical point of view, but one excites you and the other doesn't. Trust your own reactions—in fact, encourage them. Next, allow and expect changes in your taste. As you learn to *see* pictures, some you once admired may seem trite and uninteresting because your taste has developed and changed.

Follow local art exhibits in galleries and museums. Your first purchase may be made at an outdoor art show. There is no proof that the price will be less than you would pay elsewhere, but the choice may be larger. Simply by studying the picture, you will develop your taste.

The question, of course, comes up: Should the pictures be selected to suit the room? The answer is yes and no. If the room suits you, then the pictures you select for it will also be appropriate.

You can spend ninety-nine cents for a reproduction at the supermarket or a million dollars for an old master at an auction. It is this range of price that frightens many people. Actually, you can name your price. A good original oil painting may not cost more than an electric range or refrigerator, and if you love it you will enjoy it for a longer period of time. A water color may be had for the price of a dress, and a pencil sketch may cost no more than a hat or a pair of shoes.

Discussing pictures this way is not meant to equate them with merchandise bought and sold in a store; its purpose is to take the fear out of buying art, to say: "If you wish, you too can own a fine picture, and, like a trip to Europe, once you have indulged, the second time is inevitable and easier."

A desk corner offers an opportunity for developing an intimate feeling. Here the silhouettes mingled with framed family photographs, the Victorian brackets and the unstudied objects on the desk have warmth and great character.

Frame Carefully

IN BOTH FINE and decorative arts, framing plays an important role. I was not too impressed with what framing could do to a picture until I saw one of my own amateur daubs come to life when set off by a handsome frame. Width, color, texture, depth and feeling of the frame must all be coordinated with the picture. Mats and glass are not used with oils. Sometimes, however, a narrow liner or inner frame is used as a transition to the frame itself. Such a frame extension may be wood or fabric.

The size of both molding and mat will vary with the boldness of the picture, the size of the room and character of the furniture. Molding widths range from a quarter-inch to six or seven inches. Try the molding against the picture itself.

Average frame choices are as follows:

Size of Picture	Width of Frame
20″ x 30″ to 30″ x 40″	2½ to 3″
16″ x 20″ to 20″ x 30″	1½ to 2″

Frame extensions on oil paintings should be equal in width on all four sides. Mats of varying proportions and materials are used on etchings, prints and other media. They give strength, add size, and help contain the picture. As a rule, narrower frames or moldings are used with matted pictures than with unmatted ones. In matting pictures, it is usual to make a slightly narrower margin at the top than the bottom. A water color sixteen by twenty inches can take a mat that is two inches wide at the bottom. In most cases, the mat should just cover the four edges of the print; however, for etchings and other plate-marked prints and for those which have an engraved title or signature, the mat should be cut out to reveal such markings.

Incidentally, if you have a picture of the artist, a clipping or story about the picture, or the date when the picture was painted make a note and paste it on the back of the framed picture as a permanent record.

Where to Hang Pictures

LARGE DRAMATIC pictures are best displayed alone, and may become the focal point of a room when hung over a sofa or a fireplace. Small pictures are more effective in a large grouping on one wall rather than scattered around the room.

Scant use of pictures gives a room a bare-boned look. Many pictures create a warm friendly air.

For example, in a fifteen-foot-square studio apartment in Greenwich Village, the wall over the marble fireplace carries one large forty-inch painting with four paintings of assorted sizes grouped on both sides. On the opposite wall, over the sofa, there are also nine paintings, the center one about thirty-six by sixty inches. Far from being busy, the room is calm and restful because the pictures supply all the color and pattern. Walls, upholstery and rug are all in a light to dark pinkish-beige. In the same apartment, three red-framed white-matted nudes (a lithograph, an etching and a pencil sketch) hang in the bathroom. The small kitchenette boasts a bulletin board displaying six small Mexican primitives.

In a house in Maryland, ten paintings of varying size hang on a brick wall. Most of the paintings were done in Barbados and have high-keyed colors, but the brick wall and adjoining wooden wall are deep-toned and neutralize the boldness of the pictures.

Pictures may be hung at any agreeable height. In a foyer where they will be viewed from a standing position they should be hung as nearly as possible at the eye level of the average person. However, in other rooms, people will usually sit as they view the pictures. They may then be hung lower if a satisfactory relation can be worked out with the furniture. There is more danger of hanging pictures too high than too low. To counteract this tendency, especially in modern rooms, a picture or two may even be hung beside a table or chest rather than above it—for the pleasure of floor sitters.

Made by the owner, this picture is on a cypress wall. Dresses, pantalets, shoes and stockings are real garments cut in half. The necklaces and buttons are also real. The faces are embroidered. The whole is appliqued to black velvet and is under glass.

Scatter Walls

THERE ARE MANY guides for hanging picture groupings, but the best one is your own eye. If there are only two, three or four pictures in a group, a formally balanced arrangement is usually best. A pair of pictures may hang side by side, or one above the other. A third larger picture may be placed between them to make a trio—or two pictures of different sizes may be placed above or below the first pair. Larger groupings may be arranged with a free hand, but the final effect must have a feeling of composition or order.

Plan one. Hang pictures of widely assorted sizes and shapes, so that the outside line of the frames forms a straight line. The pictures hung within this space are fitted together like a jig saw puzzle. Sometimes the straight line is preserved only at the bottom and sides; an uneven line at the top is given definition by the cornice at the ceiling line.

Plan two. Hang pictures of assorted sizes using asymmetric balance. Their placement should develop a sense of boundaries and tension, i.e., an interplay between the pictures that seems to hold them together. When the pictures are of minor importance, it is interesting to intersperse other artifacts: a bit of carving, a clock, several pairs of antlers, a small mirror.

Often this question is asked: "Is it correct to hang framed family photographs?" Family photographs, if used imaginatively, can be intimate and delightful in practically any room. I think of a hall with photographs hung from floor to ceiling, making a veritable record of the family. The photographs include prize dogs, horses and records of travels, as well as the children at all ages.

In the den of another house, blue-black felt walls are completely covered with photographs of hunting and fishing expeditions. These are interspersed with red and blue prize ribbons won for target practice and bowling. Among the photographs are a fish or two and several antlers. A safe rule for the use of photographs is to avoid a timid approach; use them lavishly, or not at all.

Another recurring question concerns the types of pictures to use in Early American or country rooms. The choice is practically unlimited, although, to build up the feeling of the room, pictures or objects popular before 1900 are the most appropriate. Flower, fruit, butterfly, mushroom and bird prints are always pleasing. Audubon bird prints, Currier and Ives prints and Godey's famous fashion plates are possibilities. Don't overlook portraits—quaint old ones are good. Other possibilities are framed samplers and other needlework pictures, framed and matted pages from old scrapbooks, deeds of land, old maps, old shop signs, even collections of old bottle labels matted and framed.

The important thing with pictures is to feel free to do what you want and to feel, when you do it, that you understand the field and are leading from knowledge, not ignorance. I am reminded of a large scatter wall of pictures and objects in a house in Westchester. It was most impressive, and not until it was closely examined could you see that most of the pictures were clipped from magazines. The frames were old; many of them were bought at auction and cost less than a dollar. In fact, the total cost of pictures and frames on a ten-foot wall over a big maple chest was only twenty-nine dollars. Gradually, as the young couple who own the house can afford it, better pictures will be substituted.

Another young couple who live in a loft space in Greenwich Village have huge wall areas. On one wall are massed thirteen frames of all sizes and shapes, but only five have pictures in them—pictures painted by friends in the Village. The empty frames contribute "pattern" and will eventually be filled.

166

A combination entertainment-dining room. Ten oil paintings of various sizes give a mass of color over the black-green sofa. The wall opposite is lined with books with built-in hi-fi, and television on a turntable so that it can be viewed from the sofa.

ROOM
REVIEW

 4

FOYERS AND HALLS

SMALL COMPACT spaces like foyers and halls offer a particular challenge. Given the right idea, they can be practical and effective and set the mood of a house or apartment. Without that small extra touch, they can be very dull.

One long narrow entrance hall with no place for furniture was painted white and given a terra-cotta tile floor. The drama was introduced by the addition of bleached-oak ceiling beams, one handsome antique wooden figure mounted on a bracket near the door to the living room, and a wrought-iron ceiling lantern. The hall closet had a bleached-oak door studded with nailheads and equipped with handsome hardware. The door was mirror-lined, with a bracket basket large enough to hold a pocketbook mounted on it. The walls, shelves and coat hangers were covered with red cotton damask. This simple but practical Renaissance hall led into a book-lined room with natural linen upholstery and draperies, Oriental rugs, and old oak tables and side chairs.

The following questions may help to focus the problems involved in designing a foyer:

- Are the adjoining rooms formal or informal?
- What colors are used in adjoining rooms?
- Is there any space available for furniture?
- What type of lighting is called for?
- How can a mirror and a place for hanging wraps be included?
- What type of rug, carpet or surfacing would be practical on the floor?
- What can be done to make anyone seeing the foyer for the first time smile with delight?

Walls in foyers with a formal feeling may be mirror-lined or fabric-covered with simulated tent ceiling. There are fine murals and large-scale dramatic papers for halls. Classic damask-patterned papers are usually successful in black and white, red and white and even white on white. One pleasing foyer papered in a white-on-white damask paper has a white vinyl floor, white doors, white painted console with a mirror over it, and a brilliant crystal chandelier. The drama lies not in the all-white hall, but in the adjoining all-red living room, glimpsed through double doors.

Walls in foyers with informal feeling may be casual, gay or whimsical. There is an almost endless assortment of wall surfacings with quaint calicolike patterns. There are colonial scenics and stenciled borders. A white-washed brick or simulated brick or board wall makes a delightful statement. Perhaps you are ambitious enough to locate authentic old boards for the foyer of a house with a rustic look. In a fascinating country house in the Midwest, the walls in the foyer are papered with old newspapers dating back to the 1880s. A fine collection of old iron trivets and tools is displayed. In the country house of a "rock hound" in Sussex County, New Jersey, the walls in the large hall are papered with the blue-and-white tracery of geodetic maps of the county. Each map is studded with actual ore specimens, indicating exactly where they were found. In a small foyer in Michigan, the walls above a green dado are completely covered with old flower prints. In a modern house in California, there is a small greenhouse at the right of the entrance doors which creates a fabulous effect of light and greenery in a wood-paneled hall.

In a much-used foyer, in narrow halls and for stairwells used by children, consider washable paper or one of the vinyl-coated surfacings that will submit gracefully to scrubbing.

Floors in halls and foyers get hard wear and should always be ready for dress review. There is endless dispute about the perfect choice for flooring. Those who recommend carpets and rugs like them for their easy care and quietness. The hard-surface adherents also claim easy care. Vinyl floors, marble, tile and parquet floors are handsome for formal halls. Painted and spattered floors with braided or hooked rugs are right for Early American halls. Brick,

slate and flagstone also create a provincial feeling. Since the space in a foyer is usually small, it is sometimes worth while to be extravagant in solving the floor problem. The floor is a conspicuous area and accounts for easily a third of the over-all effect.

In selecting a rug or carpet for your foyer, think of the color of the dust in your neighborhood. The nearer the carpet color harmonizes with it, the better it will look. A dark-brown carpet in a white-dust area can be a real source of grievance. Even if the foyer has a smooth-surfaced floor, the stairway should be carpeted to reduce noise and give greater safety.

Furniture for Foyers

THE CLASSIC FURNITURE grouping for halls is a chest or console flanked by chairs, with a mirror above. This combination serves all needs, a chair for the caller, a surface for bags, gloves, mail, keys and a mirror for a last glance. But there are endless other possibilities, many of them "iffy." That is, if there is a powder room or a closet door equipped with a convenient mirror, a hall mirror may not be necessary. In large halls or foyers, additional furniture may be needed to create a furnished look. Possibilities include:

Highboy	Love seat
Armoire	Wing chair
Desk	Screen
Bench	Grandfather clock
Secretary	Hi-fidelity console
Chest	Fountain

Large halls are often made to do double duty. In a large hexagonal foyer painted white, a white painted piano and two white benches with red velvet cushions keep company. An apartment foyer has a narrow table with banquettes along one side used for dining. A wide center hall in a two-story colonial house in Connecticut is lined with books, has a large desk and serves as a study. An upstairs hall in another spacious house has been turned into a sewing center.

Back halls, bedroom halls and other passageways may not be wide enough for furniture; in such cases the walls must supply interest. They offer a wonderful place to hang family photographs or to display a hobby, such as a mounted and framed button or butterfly collec-

tion, or perhaps a showing of your own weekend adventures with a paintbrush.

Lighting in halls should be designed to give a hospitable glow. In a small and simply furnished hall, the fixture or fixtures may be jewel-like in importance; certainly, the lighting should accent the mood of the room. A pendant or ceiling fixture is first choice. It takes no floor space and spreads the light. In addition, there may be wall brackets flanking a mirror or a lamp on a console or chest of drawers. If the hall has an important piece of sculpturing, a picture display or other dramatic feature, a spotlight may be called for. In a long passageway, ceiling lights will be repeated every eight to twelve feet. In a modern house, a luminous plastic ceiling or large illuminated squares or circles may establish the right mood. The long bedroom hall in a flat-roofed house in North Carolina has wonderful daytime lighting supplied by round plastic domelike skylights.

Wall collections like those already mentioned are decorative; however, for convenience, there should be a large and visible ashtray for the inevitable cigarette. A wastebasket may be mounted on the inside of a closet door, and in a climate where it is needed often, there should be an umbrella stand handsome enough for display, such as a large jardiniere. In a country house, the umbrellas could share space with a collection of walking sticks. A charming and personal collection of canes, long and short, carved, plain and with gold and silver mounts, still stands by the door of Theodore Roosevelt's home on Long Island.

Foyers should be an introduction to the family and the house. The crisp green walls, handsome mirror and settee, the pier cabinets and vinyl floor with a black octagon center medallion give a gracious traditional welcome to the caller.

Many houses and apartments do not have separate foyers—the entrance door leads directly into the living room. If this is the case, try to create a feeling of separation. If space permits, a desk or upright piano placed at right angles to the wall may serve as a divider. A screen or a pierced wood fin wall is sometimes used for this purpose. In a long apartment living room with the entrance door at one end, a fin wall five feet wide was installed at the end of the room, about six feet from the entrance door, with a five-foot traffic space at each end. On the hall side, there is a console and mirror; on the living-room side, bookshelves.

In a house in Grand Rapids, Michigan, the entrance area was also used for dining. One wall was mirrored and a half-round table was used against the mirror-glass wall, giving the illusion of a round table. This dining area was separated from the passageway by five garden urns always filled with green laurel leaves.

In a house in Florida, a wallpaper mural was used on the wall by the entrance door. A five-foot wall was installed to separate the door from the living room, which created an alcove for the sofa and also perfect privacy.

172   **Brick, slate and fine wood give individuality to this gracious center hall. Moreover, there is a place to put a package or hat and gloves or a calling card. The living room can be glimpsed. The see-through circular staircase leads to the bedroom.**

PERSONAL LIVING ROOMS

WHETHER YOU WANT it to be or not, your living room is a revealing personal statement. The amount spent has little to do with the atmosphere, the character, the feeling of the room. At a glance, it will be clear whether there is awareness, sensitivity, taste, and discrimination. On the other hand, it will be equally clear whether there is an obsession with possessions, a desire for display, a concern with decorating formulas and convention. The room will reveal your interests, or lack of them, in books, pictures, plants, bric-a-brac. It will expose your concern with what other people think. It will whisper, shout, shyly point out or broadcast the whole story.

A delightful, meaningful living room can re-sult only from living a rich, full life and having a basic cultural drive. If you have the interest and energy to acquire a wide general background and have an innate curiosity about books, pictures, flowers, furniture, you need never worry about having a dull living room. Oddly enough, a well-furnished mind almost inevitably produces a living room with personality. The only decorating job I ever gave up was for a young New Jersey couple. After working with them for several weeks, I discovered that their only interests were TV and racing on the highways in their sports car, going nowhere at all. I could find nothing in their lives with which to launch an interesting room. My ideas on good living were not theirs.

Decorating Is Work

WHETHER YOU do it yourself or work with a decorator, designing a room is always fascinating, but it requires study, visualization and a real "stretching of the little gray cells," as Agatha Christie's Hercule Poirot would say. The usual decorating job divides into three parts: about one-third common sense, one-third science and one-third art. Neglect the common sense and the room will not be comfortable; overlook the science and it will not be practical; ignore the art and the room will not have warmth, beauty or charm.

Soul-searching could be substituted for the term "common sense"; it involves an honest appraisal of yourself and your family and may be the most difficult part of the job. It will call for a crystallization in your mind of the highest form of family life you feel that you can achieve. If the living room is the only communal center there will be different requirements than if you also have a family room, a recreation room, a den or library. Review such questions as these:

- How many are there in the family?
- What are their ages?
- What are their interests?
- How often do you entertain or have visitors?
- Are these affairs casual, informal or are they usually very formal?
- Do dogs, cats, birds or other household

174

Above. The friendly furniture and bric-a-brac has been assembled over a period of thirty years. Mantel and beams were salvaged from a Maine house. An ancestor was the captain of the sailing ship in the picture above the fireplace.

Below. French Regency furniture, cut velvet upholstery and a handsome wall cabinet with doors open to display books and accessories will give lifetime pleasure.

pets share the room with the family?

- Should books be included in the plan?
- Do you play games? Would a bridge table in a permanent place be pleasant?
- Where will the TV be put—in the living room or elsewhere? Are you a hi-fi family?
- Should the plan include a piano or other musical instrument?
- Will you frequently serve tea, coffee, cocktails in the living room?
- Have you any hobbies, activities, collections that could be woven into the decorating plan or that require special storage?
- Are there enough desks in other rooms, or should a desk be included in the plan?

After this firm and honest appraisal of family life, review budgetary limitations as well as the furnishing you already have. Next, picture an average evening with the family when they are all at home. Where will each one sit? What will each person be doing? What changes of activity will take place through the evening? Now, picture an evening with guests—large groups, small groups—and just how dinner guests, for instance, would gather and move about throughout an evening.

Will you make a clean sweep of your present furnishing and start afresh? Will you keep a few pieces and build around them? Or, to stretch your dollars, will you have to keep all basic pieces and do a face-lifting job with color, fabrics and accessories?

If your budget has some flexibility, work out a floor plan before settling this point. This is the best way of determining which pieces to keep and what must be added. This plan should be worked out to scale on graph paper and should be arranged and rearranged like a puzzle until a satisfactory solution has been achieved.

Recently I spent days of study on the floor plan for the living room of a small house. The requirements were seating for from eight to twelve people for dinner and bridge; the sofa had to be long enough and suitable for use by an occasional overnight guest; furnishings were to be a combination of old and new for sentimental as well as budgetary reasons. Such specific requirements are both helpful and difficult, but usually lead to a workable and comfortable room.

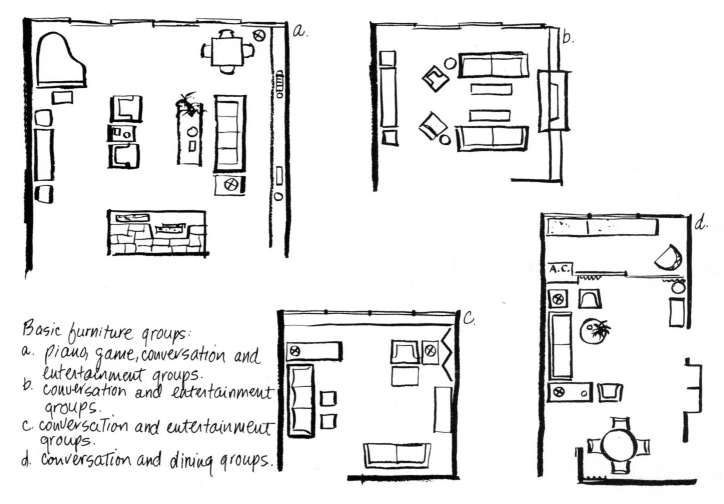

Basic furniture groups:
a. piano, game, conversation and entertainment groups.
b. conversation and entertainment groups.
c. conversation and entertainment groups.
d. conversation and dining groups.

176   Country French furniture sets the mood of this pleasant conversation group, with one end table serving a double function. The sturdy furniture and simple color scheme give a feeling of unity to which the wallpaper lends sophistication.

Gracious and Comfortable

Group Furniture

In DEVELOPING floor plans, learn to think in terms of groups of furniture, not single pieces. Single pieces are meaningless, like separate musical notes; and, unlike Noah's animals, groups should not be limited to twos. Three, four or five pieces in a group are better. Group arrangements may be built around sofas, desks, pianos, game tables, chests or consoles. Small groups of furniture may be expanded by adding three to six, even eight pieces. These groups may be looked upon as chords—combined with other chords, they complete a composition.

The basic furniture inventory for an average living room might include the following:

A sofa and two lamp tables
Two occasional chairs and a coffee table
One arm chair and table
A desk and chair
A breakfront or case piece, if there is no fireplace

Small living rooms may accommodate only two or three groups. Larger living rooms may have room for one large grouping and several smaller ones. Once these chords, or groups, are established, fitting them into a room is comparatively simple. Before deciding where they · go, however, mark all doors on the floor plan—traffic lanes must be kept clear. Indicate architectural centers of interest. If there is a fireplace or an important window, the major grouping should balance it or center on it to form what is called an axis or center pole. The lesser groups will drop in around it.

Once the plan for the furniture arrangement is completed, it's time to develop a picture, an idea, a color theme, to lead you through the maze of selecting wall coverings, fabrics, carpets and accessories. Without this over-all concept or picture of the completed room in your mind, the whole business of decorating is one of confusion and agony. Design begins inside, not outside. Know what you want to accomplish and you will have a red-carpeted guide to its completion.

The theme that gets you started may be almost anything. You may have an idea that you want something bold and dramatic. You may want color to play an important role. Perhaps you have a paisley shawl to use as a kick-off; Oriental rugs or a floral chintz may inspire you; or your desire for a calm, soothing, quiet atmosphere may be enough to carry you through the problems of selection. Perhaps your taste for antiques is keen—then you may want to feature a collection of white ironstone, pewter, woodenware, or crystal. You may decide to combine old and new furniture in as elegant a manner as your budget will permit.

Once the desk work and dreaming are over, it's time to go shopping with scientific fervor. This is when a decorator may be most appreciated. Professionals know sources and values and may save hours of time, study, shoeleather and shopping. If you are the type for grand gestures and are sure of yourself, go ahead and buy as you find it—one thing at a time. But if you like to play a sure game, make an over-all survey of fabrics and rugs; get color samples and furniture measurements; and only when all pieces and colors fit together, place your orders.

Don't rush the job; work slowly for best results. Know that it may take six months, a year, or more, to design, shop, get furniture delivered, carpentry work done, draperies made and installed, and just the right accessories and pictures.

The completed living room may be wholly different from those of your neighbors; in fact, it will be, if you have delved into yourself and your family and have developed your own personal interpretation of your life. There is no one "right" look, no one "right" color scheme or one "best" furniture style. There are as many looks as there are families. Make yours a personal living room.

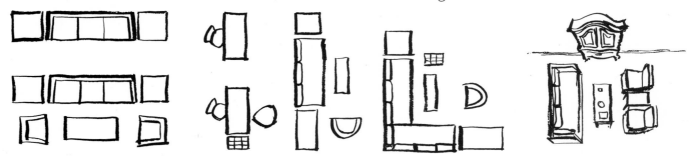

180 Study the lines of the end table and coffee table, the graceful curve of the cornice and the lady with the high-waisted Directoire dress and you will discover the room's French ancestry even though at first it may appear to be Early American.

PLEASANT DINING ROOMS

THERE ARE MANY pleasant ways of dining and serving meals; it's fun sometimes to eat in parts of the house other than the dining area, as well as in the garden. Winter Sunday suppers around the fireplace in the living room, beanhole beans for the gang, after an August outing, in the lower end of the yard, "fourses," that is, English tea at four on Saturdays in the family room, and watermelon carved and served in the kitchen on the Fourth of July— these can become family traditions. Notwithstanding the quality of such occasions, a separate dining room where meals can be served with a reasonable amount of pomp and circumstance is most desirable.

As one young woman said, "With four children and an ambitious husband on the way up, we can't afford to eat out often. Eating in the kitchen made us all careless of table etiquette. Now we have a dining room, and it has solved the problem. Dinners are served there every day and it has revolutionized our manners." In fact, the return of the dining room is giving women more pleasure than any change in house floor plans in years.

Dining rooms are easier to design than living rooms; the dining room is a more specialized room, and there is not the problem of providing for a diversity of activities. Because most of the furniture is made of wood, the excitement of color may be lacking unless walls, floors, and windows are treated imaginatively.

Conventional dining-room furniture is bought as a suite: a table; four, six, eight or a dozen chairs; a buffet; a china closet; and/or a serving table. A breakfront may replace a buffet, and in smaller rooms the china closet may be omitted entirely. However, if you have imagination and will, endless furniture variations and combinations are possible. In one handsome white-walled dining room, a big coromandel screen was placed along one wall where the buffet would normally be placed. It was flanked by serving tables; matching servers were placed on the wall directly opposite, on each side of the kitchen door. In another home, where a great deal of entertaining is done, built-in cupboards with wire mesh doors line two sides of the room, taking the place of wall furniture. One table, large enough to seat six and easily accommodating the family of four, is placed against one wall with a banquette (an upholstered bench) on one side and chairs opposite. In addition there are two square tables with velvet floor-length skirts. With these three tables, one of which is 34″ x 68″ and the other two 34″ x 34″, four possible table arrangements can be made: one huge table 68″ x 68″; one 34″ x 108″; an L-shaped plan; or two tables, each 34″ x 68″. This room is always ready for two tables of bridge plus a reserve table for refreshments. Moreover, the three tables create a delightful party atmosphere.

In less formal rooms try Welsh dressers, cupboards with hutch tops, corner cupboards, old washstands, brass French-bakery racks, tilt-top tables, grandfather clocks, a stack of Korean chests; even a highboy may offer drama, as well as storage space, and take the place of more conventional pieces.

Don't be afraid to mix woods or finishes; but unless you have a special flair, keep formal pieces in formal rooms and informal pieces in informal rooms. Oak, walnut, maple, pine,

French Provincial is the most versatile of furniture styles. Like a camelion, it reflects whatever it is used with. It can be elegant used with silk, but in this dining room paneled with old boards, it is pure country.

A dining room formula: hang a dove basket on the wall, white muslin curtains at the window; paint the chair

turquoise, use a black tablecloth, a head of lettuce center-piece and a home-made crystal chandelier over all.

cherry and painted pieces hobnob pleasantly in Early American or country dining rooms. Satinwood, mahogany, fruitwood and walnut tables and chairs will bow graciously to each other under the glitter of a crystal chandelier.

It is usually a good idea to assemble the maximum number of chairs a dining table will accommodate. If they are rarely used together, the extra chairs may serve nicely in other parts of the house—to flank a console in the hall, in the bedrooms or at a desk in the living room. All the chairs may be armless, or you may have host and hostess chairs with arms. Only in very large rooms is it possible to accommodate armchairs at all places at the table. If the chairs have slipseats, they can easily be reupholstered. The change in cover and color is pleasant, and in a young family where spills occur such changes are often necessary. Painted chairs relieve a "woody" look and are gay in such colors as coral, white, green and cerulean blue. Antiquing will add to the richness of the finish.

Walls and windows take the decorating lead in the dining room. Because this room is used for relatively short periods, high-keyed colors and bold patterns are effective. These may be combined with one or more wood-paneled walls, a chair rail or a dado.

Use Unexpected Colors

DON'T HESITATE to paint or paper the walls red, deep orange or terra cotta, gold, pine green or dark blue. These colors have the refreshing impact of the unexpected. But if light colors are preferred, go to extremes. Paint walls and woodwork white, use yards of white damask or organdy at the windows, lay a white vinyl floor accented with black lozenges, and, if it's a small room, paint the table and chairs white too! In winter, use red upholstery on the chairs, a red velvet floor-length table cover, and pictures in which red and orange dominate. In summer, change all the red accents to green, green, green, or mingle green and blue.

There is a wide assortment of wallpapers which will decorate for you. Scenic patterns seem to be made for dining rooms; damask patterns, gold or white snowflakes or fleur-de-lys are also handsome. For a formal dining room consider flocked papers. Wallpaper murals are also effective, even if used on only one wall.

The dining room may also double as a conservatory or library. A window full of plants, not tiny ones, but big and bold, can give an aliveness to a room that is priceless. Walls lined with bookshelves will do the same thing. Inevitably, you will discover that someone in the family will be the "Autocrat of the Breakfast Table." Reference books at hand will find their way to the table to clinch arguments.

If yours is a dining room with one wall missing—that is, opening into a kitchen or living room—the decorating of the two rooms should merge. Usually the space is small, and the table and chairs may supply the full quota of furniture. Wall treatment of adjoining rooms need not be identical. The room opening into the dining area may have plain-colored walls, the dining area a pattern which, although in harmony, nevertheless will set the space apart. Screens, room dividers, and even curtains on a ceiling track can make the separation more complete.

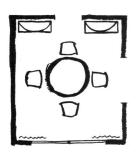

Small dining room with serving tables flanking door. Round table good choice.

Large dining room with breakfront china cupboard, and two serving tables, and two upholstered arm chairs.

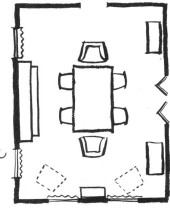

Once a country schoolhouse in Illinois, it is now a home and houses a fine collection of eighteenth- and nineteenth-century antiques. Notice the trestle table, the two spindle-back chairs, the painted chairs, the hand-woven rag carpet and the pots.

Light Theatrically

SINCE THE EVENING meal is the most important meal of the day for most families, the dining room is primarily a "nighttime" room, and calls for careful and complete wiring so that many degrees of lighting are possible, from calm general illumination to dramatic high-keyed and pinpoint lighting. Check off the following possibilities against your dining-room plan:

Chandelier	Ceiling spots
Pendant lights	Cupboard lighting
Wall brackets	Candlelight
Valance lighting	Picture lighting

A ceiling fixture, a handsome chandelier, is almost a must and can combine general and dramatic lighting if it is Luxtrol-controlled so that the lights can be dimmed. Tiny lamps that simulate candles are now available. If these are used, their light may be magnified by using ceiling spots which are set to light only the table. The bottom of a chandelier should be about thirty-seven inches above the table top.

Wall brackets make handsome decorations but should be placed so that no one sits facing them during the meal. However, when the table is off center for a buffet party, the brackets may offer ideal light.

Lighting concealed behind window valances may give both indirect lighting on the ceiling and dramatic down-lighting on the curtains. Draperies and curtains should be light in color to get maximum reflection. Cupboard interiors painted a light color and featuring fine china and glass collections may deserve special illumination. Fine pictures may also be lighted with a spot from the ceiling. In one dining room a large picture on a wall is lighted by a ceiling spot. This illumination, plus candles on the table, is adequate for special occasions when a dramatic atmosphere is desired.

188   Drama in the dining room: a 36-inch high goddess of the garden reigns over all and happily carries flowers or wears garlands of greens as the seasons change. The matching seat cushions and curtain lining are beautifully understated details.

FAMILY, DEN AND RECREATION ROOMS

THE SUBJECTS of activities, projects, and making things may seem far afield from decorating; but actually, they are as closely related as a hen and an egg. The house that is not planned for home activities and the creative use of leisure time is a desert and a jail. Children should be exposed to the arts of creation and the pleasure of tinkering and dabbling at home. If there is no place planned for such activities, it is likely that nothing will be done. The homemaker who is always griping about "messes" both man-made and child-made is a wet blanket putting out the glow of creative urge.

In a small house the hobby center may have to be in the living room. I know of several small apartments with week-end art studios lurking behind screens. In another small house, in Kentucky, the piano is in the master bedroom. One understanding soul tolerates her husband's metal file cabinets in the foyer because there is no other place to keep them. A bride, mature beyond her twenty years, has turned the living room of her first apartment into a den-study. She quickly realized that her husband wouldn't be happy without his books, desk and research equipment. "So," she said, "Peter gets his study now, but it's a break for me because I will have a brand-new living room when we move into a house in a couple of years."

Special hobby rooms have a parade of names and individual requirements which may vary with every family. The list includes:

Den	Photographic
Library	dark room
Studio	Little theater or
Music room	projection room
Game room	Carpentry shop

Family room	Greenhouse
Rumpus room	Home office
Recreation room	Swimming-pool
All-purpose room	cabana
Attic	Flower-arrange-
Basement	ment room

One family blithely refers to their much-used workroom as "The Glory Hole." These rooms may be shared by adults and children, though the household is lucky that can have separate areas for each. Adult work or study rooms may be in the most remote corner of the house, in the basement, attic or partitioned area of a large garage, or even in an adjoining shed or barn.

When the children are small, the playroom or family room should adjoin the kitchen. When children approach teen age, they and the family will both be happier if a separate area can be salvaged for teen projects and parties. It is no fun for teens to entertain friends with the family breathing down their necks.

Practically any available space can be requisitioned for any activity area. A woman in Indiana turned one bedroom into a dormitory for her three boys so that the third bedroom could be a play-work area. An architect turned the dining room of his house into a study-office. Then, by knocking out a wall of the kitchen and enclosing a porch, he created a handsome eating area overlooking the garden. Another family lined a wide upstairs hall with bookshelves, put a round table with four chairs in the corner, dropped a light over it, and called it the family room. Space is where you find it. Generally two hundred to four hundred square feet are needed.

Built into the wall of a den, this entertainment closet has easily operated bi-fold doors. There is a bar behind the black chair. The exposed brick wall, open-beamed ceiling and natural colors give warmth and unity.

A Remodeled Basement

Acrylite triangular skylights and a prefabricated fireplace converted an unused attic into this charming quiet retreat.

Crow's-nest for a budding space scientist and a horticulturist. Under-eave bunk beds are on one side, built-in chests opposite.

Next door to a marina, this·small shed roof cottage features sea-worthy vinyl upholstery in white, blue and olive green.

A prefabricated igloo firepot is the center of a conversation group which features a vinyl-covered, brass-studded trunk.

194

Garage into family room is the story behind this relaxed scene. One wall was surfaced with pecky Cypress, the others with a wallpaper featuring French theater posters. There are three activity areas, for conversation, dining and hobbies.

"Decoration" may be the wrong term to use in connection with such a special room, but without question the space will be more useful, more conducive to work or play, and easier to keep in order if it is a designed room. Creating such a room makes a wonderful do-it-yourself project.

The requirements are simple. Smooth-surface floors are suitable, possibilities include wood, painted concrete, asphalt tile, vinyl asbestos, cork or linoleum. They are easy to install and maintain. Since noise is frequently a factor consider soundproofing the ceiling.

Walls, for the most part, should be working walls, with shelves or closed cupboard space. At least one wall should be designed for display of artwork, collections.

Lighting requires special attention. Light speeds the hand, reduces accidents and saves eyesight. Some sort of general nonglaring light is called for plus specific light for the activities involved.

Furniture should be simple and may be new or makeshift, secondhand or salvaged from the attic. But, no matter what its original condition, it should not be left in a shabby derelict state. It should be reconditioned by refinishing, painting, regluing and bracing. Use plastic-surfaced upholstery.

An increasing amount of furniture is geared to special rooms, such as metal-legged molded fiberglass chairs and tables, garden and terrace furniture, classic ladderback chairs and folding director's chairs. Maple and pine furniture is ideal. Tavern tables, captain's chairs, wall cupboards with closed bases and open shelves above have a casual quality.

And don't forget color and some frivolity. All the furniture could be painted orange, violet, green, blue or yellow. Perhaps this is the place for a red wall.

Below. In a minute and a half, this sewing room can be converted into a guest room.

Left. This is the guest room in a country house, once a stable. The walls and floor are painted white. Hats from around the world and fantastic paintings supply color.

197

BEAUTIFUL BEDROOMS

COMFORT, CONVENIENCE, charm—these are the three guides to keep in mind in designing bedrooms. A bedroom may be used continuously for longer periods of time than any other room and should be designed for daytime as well as nighttime use. It is a room with a real job to do —it has to send you out into the world each morning refreshed and happy. The chances of success are better if you have slept well, are pleased with what you see when you wake up, and if everything you need is conveniently arranged.

A bedroom should cater to the idiosyncrasies of the occupant. This is the place to frame and hang personal pictures, to use the family keepsakes, to display trinkets acquired on trips, to create a sense of life's continuity. A bedroom can be turned into a private theater for hi-fi concerts, for TV or radio. It can be a quiet place to read, write, sew or plan the week's menus. It can be a place for confidences with your husband and the children. It may open onto a private terrace and be your own gymnasium and solarium. If it's well planned, the bedroom may be the only truly twenty-four-hour room in the house.

Master bedrooms are less overwhelmingly feminine than they used to be. Possibly the banishment of delicate pastels and froufrou dates back to women's getting the vote. In any case, a feeling of greater sophistication characterizes bedroom decoration today.

If you insist on pink bedspreads, dark-brown walls and cherry-red bolsters will keep the room from being insipid. In a white room, grass green or brilliant blue may give vitality. In a lavender bedroom, blue or deep violet will add spice to the scheme. Many master bedrooms today are large enough to include both a sleeping area and one or two other groupings: a TV corner, a reading group, a desk and bookshelves, or a table and a pair of chairs convenient for breakfast or tea. Such groupings are pleasant both for parents and teen-agers. For the parents, they make the room a comfortable retreat; and the youngsters have a chance to entertain in the living room without worrying about Mom and Dad.

There is a wide choice of bedroom furniture in all styles. It may be purchased as a matching suite of five to seven pieces, or selections may be made from a coordinated grouping of furniture offering from sixty to two hundred pieces. Perhaps the most interesting method of assembling bedroom furniture is to acquire one piece at a time, new, old or just because it's a love.

The Bed

THE BED IS the first and most important feature in the room; and the heart of the bed is the box spring and mattress. It's the piece on which to spend lavishly and get the best; it will come closer to affecting your health and your disposition than any other article of furniture in the house.

Inner-spring mattresses have a core of metal

Red, black and white supply endless fresh combinations. Here matching wallpaper and curtains in a toile de Jouy pattern are used with an airy four poster with bolsters.

Fresh as a Garden in Spring

coils either held upright and connected with metal clips, or encased in separate muslin pockets. Both types of construction are fine, and several degrees of firmness are available from "soft" to "very firm." Padding on top and bottom of inner-spring mattresses varies widely: cotton, cotton felt, curled hair, sisal, lamb's wool, latex and urethane foam are used alone or in combination.

Latex foam mattresses are made of the milky sap of rubber trees whipped into a froth and baked into forms. For children, foam-rubber mattresses on a firm plywood base make satisfactory, easy-to-care-for beds. For adults, latex mattresses should be placed on firmly padded box springs.

Urethane foam mattresses are made of a synthetic resin which is whipped to a froth, baked in forms, and then cut into the desired size. These mattresses are as light as a pillow to handle, and make the weekly mattress turning and airing a breeze. They, too, should be used on plywood or a firmly padded box spring.

The newest luxury in a box spring and mattress is a frame, connected with a motor, which works like a hospital bed, so that you may have a choice of positions by merely pressing a button. For the inveterate reader in bed, the TV viewer or invalid, these mechanized beds are worth the investment.

The bed frame itself may range from an inexpensive steel frame on casters—the basic element of a so-called Hollywood bed—to a handsome bed frame with a headboard or head- and footboard both. Upholstered or padded headboards are handsome; they have a custom look when covered to match the bedspreads or draperies. Material used should be processed for soil resistance.

Wooden bed frames are available in many styles. Panel headboards are usually the least expensive wood models. Fourposters are classic. Low fourposters are informal and seem to demand chintz and patchwork quilts. High fourposters have great elegance. Traditionally, there were always four posts. Today, sometimes only the headboard posts survive. Extra drama can be given even to a very simple headboard by painting it. Canopy-curtained beds and bonnet-topped bed frames are romantic, luxurious.

Novelty headboards are limited only by your own imagination and inventiveness, and almost anything may serve, such as segments of decorative iron fences, old brass headboards,

A sloping ceiling supplies a base for a bed canopy in a room for a young picture collector. The headboard has graceful lines.

Fabric-covered walls frame the window with a valance which continues around the room. The curtain hides air-conditioning.

202   Bold black-and-white plaid used in a room with gold walls and draperies would be pleasant. But it is the unexpected blue accent that gives this room its sparkle.

millinery display racks, or boards from an old red barn, held together with heavy black iron hinges.

Bedside tables are usually too high and too small. The top should be on a level with the mattress. The size may be gauged by the floor space available and the comforts you require. Tall lamps are needed for lower tables, unless the lamps are mounted on the wall. Wall-hung lamps that can be raised and lowered and are controlled by a switch or a cord are ideal. Depending on individual requirements, there should be space available on the table top or in an easily reached drawer for:

The electric blanket control
Bedside alarm clock with luminous dial
Telephone, color-keyed to the room
A transistor radio
A remote-control switch for TV
A thermos for ice water, hot bouillon or coffee
A book or magazine
A beauty and manicure box
Facial tissues

Other Furniture

Chests of drawers: Not so long ago, a low chest or dresser and a high chest, or chest on chest, or a chiffonier, were considered standard equipment for bedrooms and were a part of all bedroom suites. Now there are no rules. Selection may be made from an enormous range of chests and storage pieces. The size of the bedroom, the space available, whether or not there is built-in storage, and the presence or absence of a dressing room should influence the type of

chests selected. A low chest and high chest may still be the perfect solution for an average-sized bedroom with hanging storage only.

A double chest, or so-called Mr. and Mrs. chest, is often used instead of a standard chest. It requires a long wall space, and dimensions should be carefully checked before purchasing one. Twin chests that can be used together or separately offer greater versatility.

Modular units of varying heights designed to fit side by side are ideal for small rooms. They fit under the high windows so often used now and are available in both modern and traditional styling. A fine old highboy or a reproduction also supplies storage with great style. Such pieces may be used in small or large rooms, in halls or, for that matter, in living rooms or dining rooms.

When basic storage (drawer or shelf, in addition to hanging storage) is supplied by a closet wall, chests may not even be necessary in the bedroom and unusual furniture pieces can take their place. In one handsome room, a French armoire was placed opposite the beds. It was lined with blue-and-violet chintz and now houses the TV, a collection of handbags and hats. In another room with white walls and blue toile draperies and bedspread, a big Welsh

dresser was used opposite the bed, accessorized with books and interesting bibelots. Bookshelves and a desk may fill a need, or a complete built-in wall with closed and open storage may be the most useful treatment of space. A dressing table in a bedroom is a possibility.

Seating units may be few or many, depending on the size of the room. A pair of straight chairs and one small upholstered chair should be on your "wanted" list. A chaise longue, a love seat, a sofa, a wing chair and a bench are other desirable pieces. Two mirrors, one for make-up, and a full-length one on the back of a closet door are useful. Search for a handsomely framed mirror to hang over the chest.

A wall-to-wall carpet is a delicious luxury in a bedroom. It feels wonderful underfoot and is no harder to take care of than other floor coverings. Since the bedroom does not have heavy traffic, inexpensive carpeting may be used. With care, such a bedroom rug will last almost forever. In country rooms or Early American rooms, woven rag rugs, oval braided rugs and hooked rugs offer the perfect background. In warm climates, smooth-surface flooring with a throw rug by the bed is a good solution. Terrazzo, ceramic tile, slate, flagstone, cork, linoleum, vinyl and even marble are possibilities.

Furniture Arrangement for Single Rooms

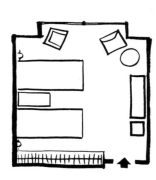 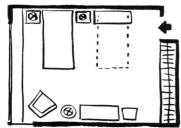 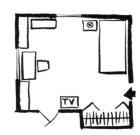

Furniture Arrangement for Double Rooms

 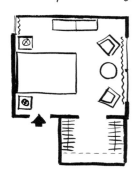 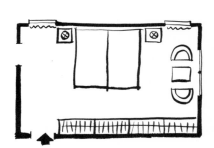

204

CHILDREN'S ROOMS

AFTER THE GLOW and excitement of preparing the first nursery, children's rooms are often overlooked as decorating projects. Certainly they require a different philosophy, a different point of view from that used in furnishing other rooms; but the right facilities may be even more important.

Children are intuitive. Expect them to wreck things and they will. Put them in a beat-up room where everything is dull and dingy and they will bang it up some more. Let them hear you say, "There's no use in fixing up the house until the children are older," and they will set out to prove your decision right.

The current lack of respect children show to property can very often be traced to a lack of beauty and order in the home. The New York City school comptroller reports that a new school could be built every three years for the price paid to repair wreckage caused by vandalism in school buildings. Nevertheless, children are more responsive to beauty than their elders. They recognize form and color, and often paint delightfully themselves.

The Nursery

IN PLANNING THE baby's room, both baby and parents should be considered, especially if it is a first baby. If everything in the room is washable, a nursery can be a sweet and pretty dream room, all butterflies, bows, and roses, in pink, blue, yellow or apple green. The baby won't mind what color it is if he is kept cozy, changed, and fed at regular intervals, but the pretty room will be enjoyed by parents and admiring guests.

A bassinet, a chest, a counter surface such as the top of a chest for dressing and changing the baby are the necessities. Display shelves for the inevitable collection of stuffed toys, and a comfortable chair—perhaps a rocking chair for feeding the baby—are next on the list. Windows should be equipped with flexible controls for light and air; a screen is also useful for controlling daytime and nighttime light. A screen prevents drafts as well, and reduces what must seem like a vast acre of space to an infant. How would you like to be tucked in at night in a bed in the corner of Grand Central Station?

If possible, one bathroom should be equipped with the baby's needs, a basin for bathing him, a tray for his supplies. There should be another baby department in the kitchen, entirely separate from the family supplies, for baby's pots and pans, measuring cups, spoons and sterilizing equipment.

As the baby begins to take notice of his surroundings, to sit up, stand up and toddle around, do everything you can to insure his safety. Remove fragile, breakable, pointed or sharp-edged things from his reach. Two-to-four can be a sticky, grubby period in which coercion may be the only effective way to discipline him. But a four-year-old has developed a sense of reason and "no" can change to heart-to-heart talks and disciplines which are a preparation for community life.

205

A Room for a Little Girl

What has all this to do with decorating? It demonstrates the importance of understanding the problems, needs and interests of the child, or children, who will use a room.

A canopied double-decker may not be the usual thing, but it can be done quite simply by screwing a wooden frame to the ceiling, using it as a base of the operation.

Children Are Creative

IF CHILDREN'S ROOMS are planned and the youngsters are given some leadership and direction in caring for them, it's amazing to see how responsive, how important, what proud little peacocks they become. Moreover, pleasant surroundings in childhood inculcate an instinctive response to good design that will give lifetime pleasure. One proud four-year-old who had just acquired his first professionally decorated room invited everyone who called at the house to come and see it.

A child's room is his castle, his shelter, his laboratory for discovering the art of living. It should not be a serene retreat; it should be a wonderful, colorful, stimulating, creative, ego-enriching place, developed not from a five- to six-foot point of view but from his own forty- to fifty-inch height. The room should have great flexibility and adaptability to changing interests and enthusiasms. Basic changes in scale and philosophy may be needed every few years —approximately at the ages of four, eight twelve and sixteen years.

The under-eights, both boys and girls, need a minimum of furniture, a firm bed, a low chest that can be painted and repainted, with easy-to-operate drawers, a low table twenty to twenty-four inches high, three or four small chairs so that little guests can join the play. There should be low shelves for books and toys, and possibly a row of assorted boxes or large baskets for classifying, sorting and storing treasures.

The floor should be designed as a base of operations. Smooth, washable flooring is perfect for building blocks, Erector sets, scooters and the like. One wall should be designed for display of pictures and other artwork. Ideally, this wall would be paneled in cork, pegboard and blackboard for various purposes. The child's own pictures should be displayed there as well as pictures clipped from magazines or museum picture postcards. As the child's interests expand, the poster wall may favor such subjects as boats, airplanes or automobiles, or perhaps wildflower, insect and ore charts. If the child is musically inclined, a collection of composers would be appropriate. Such a wall can also be used as a holiday wall and changed with each month of the year. Remember that the area reachable from the floor up is more important than the area from chests or table tops to the ceiling.

During the child's first eight years, this poster or "growth" wall may be very largely a parent's responsibility. Then the child will automatically take over. A normal child will have

Plenty of storage space is essential in a boy's room if any order is to be maintained. The big blackboard is for fun and lessons.

A curtain on a ceiling track gives privacy to a small baby and creates a cozy corner in a big room another child could share.

Chests which can be assembled like blocks are ideal for children's rooms.

absorbed from the exhibits almost without knowing it a breadth of knowledge and understanding about the cultural and scientific world that will inevitably pay high dividends.

Closets can be made into two-level affairs, with a low bar and reachable hooks and shelves for the child's use and a higher rod, possibly curtained, for storage. Mirrors, too, should not be placed above chests but hung, like panels, beside them.

Boys' Rooms

THERE ARE AT least two important turning points in every child's life: when the infant learns to look after himself—somewhere between six and eight years—and when the child becomes an adult, somewhere between 14 and 18. Recognize these two vital times, cater to them and help the child through them without fuss, and you are an "in" parent.

Bobby goes to school, acquires a pal, meets other boys. His world widens, and before your eyes he is a man in embryo. He wants no part of the prettiness and ruffles of a baby's room. He becomes involved in sports, hobbies, matchbox and rock collections, birds' nests, and snakeskins. He wants nothing touched in his room; it is his domain, his club, his cave. All

210

you can do is supply what he wants—a retreat, a place to entertain his friends, to stimulate his imagination.

Walls may be lined with shelves and pegboard; floors smooth-surfaced, colors masculine—pine green and beige; brown, orange and cream; red, white, and blue; or school pennant colors. The window treatment should be simple: Venetian blinds or shades or café curtains of denim hung on a pole with brass rings.

Furniture should be basic and placed so that it leaves a center space free for action. The play table should be replaced by a big study desk with a good lamp, preferably hung from the ceiling or wall or screwed to the desk so that it won't be knocked over. A radio is almost a

A calico wallpaper, ruffled curtains and an old-fashioned hit-and-miss rag carpet set the mood of this nostalgic child's room. Inexpensive maple furniture was used.

necessity, and life is very nearly perfect if there is a cast-off TV set available. The proudest possession of one future engineer who is now ten is an old sewing machine which he found and put into working condition.

The bed should be firm, equipped with sheets and blankets with boxed corners. Some youngsters vote for sleeping bags which are stored in a closet during the day, leaving the upholstered box spring and mattress neat and tailored. A sleeping unit for overnight guests is essential. It may be the second or even the third deck of a bunk bed, a trundle bed, an ottoman that opens into a bed, a folding bed or an extra sleeping bag.

Washable, sturdy, dark tailored spreads are mandatory; select corduroy, denim, cotton tweed and similar firm, boy-proof fabrics. All upholstery should be reinforced plastic fabrics.

If two boys share a room, furniture and belongings should be separated physically, and by color if this is feasible. As nearly as possible, it should be a twin room: two cots, two chests, two desks, two chairs, two shelf areas, two poster boards, two closets or at least a divided one. The blue for Bobby, the green for Teddy, to eliminate quarrels over possessions. A sense of ownership is important to a child; it helps make him feel wanted—a part of the family.

Then, suddenly, there is an interest in girls. A boy learns to drive the car, enjoys dancing, starts worrying about his hair; his voice does funny things. At spring-cleaning time he may say that he would like to clean some of the junk out of his room. It's time at last to put away childish things, get rid of the scuff marks and convert his room from a retreat for the gang into a place to store sports equipment and to sleep.

Girls' Rooms

SHE'S SIX YEARS old. She is interested in her dolls, her painting set, her books. She wants a pretty room, a bed with a canopy, even a dressing table and a slipper chair. It can still be a washable room, with cotton rugs, chintz or gingham bedspreads, curtains and slipcovers; walls pink, blue, yellow or lavender; and perhaps painted furniture.

By the time she's twelve or fourteen, the roses, ruffles and pastels may seem babyish. Then it is time to develop either a studio room for a budding artist or career girl or a classic bedroom with a large dressing table, if parties and beaux are beginning to be an important part of life.

The right choice of furniture at this time can form the nucleus of the furnishings for a future home of her own.

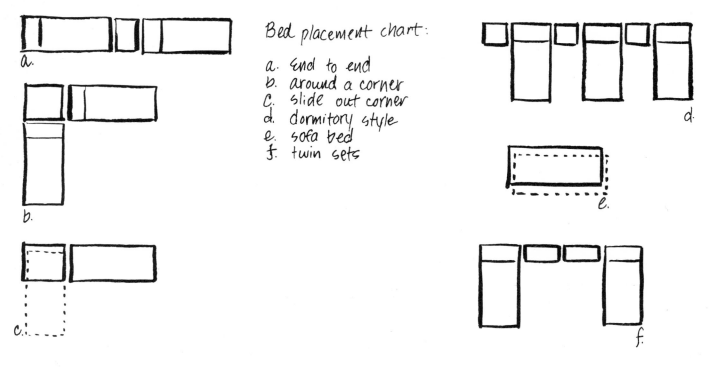

Bed placement chart:

a. End to end
b. around a corner
c. slide out corner
d. dormitory style
e. sofa bed
f. twin sets

What young princess wouldn't like this room with its wire bed and crown-topped draperies? White brick wallpaper was used in back of the bed; the other walls are pink.

LUXURIOUS BATHROOMS

PROBABLY THE LARGEST bathroom in the country is in a house in Texas. It is a marble-lined room approximately sixteen by twenty-five feet, with a window wall opening onto a landscaped and high-fenced terrace. Two crystal chandeliers, gold-plated fixtures, a palm tree, a chaise longue and a small painted breakfast table and chairs create an aura of luxury.

A bathroom of quite a different nature, in rapport with the Early American flavor of the rest of the house, has wallpaper on walls and ceiling in a pattern that simulates old newspapers, and a tongue-and-groove board wainscoting. The wooden water-closet seat, ruffled curtains and hit-or-miss rag carpet, the wired lantern hung from the ceiling, towels with fringe or lace edging, a collection of old framed prints and a wall-hung magazine rack are as right as they can be. The final amusing detail is the door, which is vertical boarding with black cast-iron strap hinges and a half-moon cut-out.

Another unique bathroom is in a house in up-state New York on a site blasted out of a rocky hillside. The water for the sunken bathtub spills in over a natural outcropping of rock, which was left undisturbed by the blasting. In the wall above the sunken tub are sliding glass doors that open onto a rocky paved terrace forty feet above a deep pool. The floor-to-ceiling towel rack is a tree trunk with short branches which hold the towels. The powder room in this house has a Japanese motif and is approached by three stone steps. The lavatory counter is made of a plastic laminated Japanese silk brocade with an imperial chrysanthemum design. The walls are plastic laminated bamboo; a Japanese lantern supplies light.

The most beautiful bathroom I have ever seen was in Paris, and might have been copied from one in Versailles. It had a free-standing green marble tub, a white fur rug, and a white upholstered chaise longue. The walls had Louis XV paneling, alternating painted wood and mirror glass. On the green-painted panels were hung gold-framed flower paintings from a rare old botanical book. Tall French windows were hung with full, sheer lace-trimmed batiste and opened onto a small iron balcony overlooking a parklike garden.

These exceptional and handsome bathrooms typify the new excitement that now surrounds this erstwhile neglected room.

Equipment and Materials

THE EQUIPMENT AND the decorating plan must suit the use of the room. A general classification of bathrooms, each of which requires slightly different treatment, includes:

Family bathroom
Master bathroom
Man's bathroom
Woman's bathroom
Children's bathroom
Guest bathroom
Powder room
Mud room

214   Twin basins, a room-wide mirror with a luminous panel over it, ceramic tile walls, a slat windowshade combined with a floor of Arizona stone provide character here.

WATERPROOFING is a necessity for all bathrooms, regardless of size. Steam and a certain amount of water sloshing must be expected. Fortunately, today there is a wide choice of waterproof materials for walls and floors.

Permanently waterproof walls may be of marble, ceramic tile, Formica, Textolite, Micarta, Carrara glass, enameled or plastic tiles, or similar materials. These may be used to line the bathtub enclosure and extend to a height of thirty-six or forty inches around the rest of the room. Above this line, paint, plastic-coated fabric or washable wallpaper may be used. In a small room, a non-directional patterned fabric or paper, continued across the ceiling, makes an interesting effect.

Blue and white strips of Formica on walls meet matching strips in the vinyl of this exceptional French Provincial bathroom.

In the American tradition, beige and white Formica tile, black iron hardware, rug, towels and a buggy seat provide the charm.

Victorian and rose-strewn, the carpet is washable vinyl tile. A Formica-topped dressing table hides the laundry behind doors.

Oriental in theme, the shoji screens, mats, tea caddy and Chinese table form the mood. Note the terrace for contemplation.

216

FLOORS may be vinyl or ceramic tile, asphalt or rubber tile, linoleum or even brick flagstone or marble.

CEILING TILES will help absorb sound, and in new construction, bathroom walls can be wrapped in fiber-glass blankets, urethane or other sound-deadening material. Clothes closets located between bathroom and bedroom or hall walls will also act as sound mufflers.

WATER CLOSETS: A great aid to a quiet bathroom is a slightly more expensive one-piece quiet-flush water closet. This type is highly efficient and almost noiseless in operation. There is also a growing interest in the wall-hung type; these give a neat appearance and facilitate cleaning the floor because a mop can be used underneath.

BATHTUBS come in many sizes and shapes. Your selection may be influenced by the size and shape of the room and who uses it. For older people and children, square tubs have advantages because of the corner seating arrangement. There is also a choice of low or high bathtubs. A tub sixteen inches deep allows for plenty of splashing. The best choice is probably an enameled cast-iron tub with an acid-resistant surface that will not scratch or chip. Enameled steel tubs are lighter in weight and are also acid-resistant, but may scratch and be noisy. Ceramic tubs are handsome but are so heavy that they may require floor reinforcement.
Shower heads should be included with bathtubs. For children, it is convenient to have both a high and a low shower head, as well as a fixed water-temperature control gauge. A separate stall shower in any bathroom is a pleasure.

LAVATORIES, or washbowls, are beautifully styled and have been the real leader in turning bathrooms into bath-dressing rooms. In children's bathrooms standard bowls are adequate, but a twenty-by-twenty-four-inch bowl, large enough to bathe the baby, costs less than ten dollars more than the standard seventeen-by-nineteen-inch model. In the master bath use a countersunk bowl in a marble, tile or Formica counter, with a wall-size mirror above. For luxury bathrooms, there has been a revival of painted china bowls decorated with roses, or gold fleur-de-lis.

FAUCETS are no longer taken for granted. There is a world of difference both in cost and performance between the cheapest, good-quality and luxurious ones. Avoid the cheapest. Insist on drip-proof models. These may have solid handles that turn on by pushing or pulling instead of the old spoke-and-wheel type, and they will not have washers that have to be replaced. For sheer luxury, there are gold-plated faucets in many forms, including swans and sea horses. They operate no better than standard-quality models. Perhaps faucets which mix hot and cold water are most important and should lead the agenda in remodeling projects. When selecting plumbing fixtures and tiles for long-term use, avoid violet, black, maroon or other extreme colors. Dark colors show watermarks and fingermarks and are difficult to keep clean in hard-water areas. Gray, beige, white, pastel yellow and green allow a wide latitude in the selection of colors for walls, towels, carpets and shower curtains.

Twin-mirrored storage cabinets with built-in lights are set into the plaster-paneled wall over the double-basin counter. Shower is a glass-doored compartment. Wallpaper repeats the color of the fixtures.

A rippled glass panel and built-in ceiling lights insure good lighting. Handsome gold-plated hardware accents the luxurious look of the grape-colored, Formica-surfaced, built-in cabinet. Note the spacious effect provided by the large mirror.

Pink pegboard offers an invitation to hang things on the wall over this round-the-corner dressing table with charcoal Formica top and choice of small mirrors. On the floor is a shaggy white cotton carpet. The flowers lend a touch of red.

This is a compartment bathroom and laundry with an oriental flavor. Clothes hampers are built in beneath the wash bowl and laundry equipment is behind doors on the opposite wall. This area can be reached from hall or adjoining master bath.

ACCESSORIES MAY BE lavish. In bathrooms with modern styling, use sliding glass mirrors, wall to wall, concealing the shelved interior of the medicine cabinet. In traditional houses use mirrors in classic frames. If the bathroom is small and the only space for a mirror is the door of the stock medicine cabinet, the mirror of that utilitarian object put into a handsome frame will give it an entirely new look.

Crystal, tôle, and gardenlike wire baskets all make charming lighting fixtures. Coach lamps, candle brackets and round Victorian lamps may flank mirrors. Light coming from both sides of a mirror eliminates the dark shadows cast by one overhead lamp and permits more skillful make-up.

Pictures, sculpture, plants are all attractive in bathrooms. Shells, driftwood, apothecary jars and bottles can be used, depending on the mood and style of the room.

Other conveniences worth finding a place for are an electric clock, a reserve supply of paper towels, a wastebasket, laundry hamper, scale for weight-watchers, a reserve supply of soap and tooth paste, a hook to hang a robe on, if possible a table or counter on which to place things, and perhaps even a transistor radio and telephone. Adequate towel racks are a necessity. A ventilating fan, a sun-tan lamp and an auxiliary electric heater in the ceiling or wall are desirable. If your home has an intercom system, don't forget to include the bathroom.

Plain or Fancy

THE FAMILY BATHROOM is the most difficult to plan. Efficiency, foolproof surfacing, a place for everything and a neutral-toned background are advisable. Bright-colored towels can carry the color load; even a different color for each member of the family would be practical and bright. A paper-cup dispenser may also be worth considering.

CHILDREN'S BATHROOMS may change somewhat with the age of the child, just as their rooms change. For an infant, the bathroom will contain his bath facilities, scales, diaper can and clothing supplies. Later these will be stored, to make way for multitudinous floating toys. This bath should be stoutly waterproof. Only when the baby period has passed and the teens are approaching need the girl's bath take on a note of femininity and boy's bath acquire wall-mounted magnifying shaving mirrors, perhaps even exercise bars and other masculine requirements.

MASTER BATHROOMS, like all bathrooms adjoining bedrooms, may have a related or identical color scheme. The bedroom may be a blue and green, with plain blue walls; the bathroom may have the same color scheme with patterned walls. One very handsome red-walled bedroom with Empire furniture has an adjoining bathroom with red woodwork and red-and-white striped wallpaper. The ceiling fixture is an inverted Empire helmet. Soap dish, accessories and pictures are all Napoleonic.

Another bedroom, with white walls and black-and-white damask-patterned linen draperies, a brown nylon velvet bedspread and dark seventeenth-century oak furniture has an adjoining bathroom with white-washed pecky cypress walls. A room-size skylight with colored panes casts drifting yellow and orange shafts of light on the textured walls.

A POWDER ROOM is desirable in any house, but almost a necessity in a two-story house. It may be generous in size or fitted into minimum space in a closet or under a stairway. A powder room may be installed in an area no more than four by four feet or two by six feet. In the first, a minimum-size corner lavatory is recommended; in the second, a built-in lavatory can be placed across one end.

Since the powder room may be small and have no window, it is doubly important that the decorating be gay, colorful, even whimsical.

A MUD ROOM may take precedence over a powder room in a household of young children. If this is the case, a waterproof paper on the wall and practical appointments that are easy to keep neat and clean should prevail.

220

GLAMOROUS KITCHENS AND LAUNDRIES

THERE IS A new look and a new approach to kitchen design. Along with Telstar, astro-exploration and other marvels of this age, science has turned the handling of food—storing, preparing and serving—into a pleasure instead of a chore.

Two hundred and fifty years ago, when the country was young, the kitchen was the heart of the house and sometimes the only room. Around 1800 came the industrial revolution. The kitchen lost status, the cook moved in, and family living moved out of the kitchen into the back parlor. The kitchen turned into a dingy heavy-duty workroom centered around a big black coal stove.

Then, circa 1930, engineers eyed the kitchen, made job analyses, time-and-motion studies, and applied straight-line production techniques to the kitchen. Under their direction, kitchens became clinical white marvels of efficiency. But developments did not stop there—waste disposers, built-in ovens, freezers and vinyl floors were yet to come. These, plus more imaginative house plans, larger windows and better ventilation, made a whole new concept of kitchen planning possible.

Today, in the second half of the twentieth century, we have the glamorous kitchen with a decorator look. It is a new kind of room, both handsome and efficient. The kitchen is again a living area, a center for play, cooking and eating, the hub of the household. It may share a fireplace, sliding glass doors, handsome lighting fixtures, draperies and upholstery with a neighboring area. No isolation room is this.

Handsome though the room may look, to receive a high score the work area must be efficient. All kitchen plans begin with the placing of major appliances and storage. Then only should appearance take over. Such questions as these must be answered:

Where will the children come in from school and where will they play?

What route will be taken to move groceries from car to kitchen?

Which door will be used for serving meals on the back terrace?

How long is the trip to the front door?

What is the service route to breakfast and dining rooms?

Finally, where is the "back door"—the door most used by the children—and is it easy and safe to operate? A sliding glass door leading to a terrace is a delight and gives an air to the kitchen, but it is not a substitute for an old-fashioned door on hinges that can be opened with one hand, that the children can operate themselves and that is not so prone to collect finger smudges.

Since kitchens are used primarily during daytime hours, adequate daylight is desirable. However, the mania for a window over the sink is archaic. Dishwashers and prewashed and frozen vegetables have eliminated long hours at the sink, and it may be desirable to have the window in a more serviceable and possibly more entertaining location near the dining area. Luminous ceilings, skylights and sliding glass doors can supply high-level light, day or night.

Placement of Appliances

BEFORE GETTING down to specific planning, it is again necessary to study yourself and your family in order to have a kitchen that's right for you. There are kitchens for families with young children, for teen-agers and for families of two. There are kitchens for good housekeepers and slap-happy housekeepers. There are one-cook and two-cook kitchens, gourmet kitchens, old farmhouse kitchens, French kitchens and sophisticated city kitchens. Regardless of the style, all kitchens require three basic-appliance work centers linked with a continuous line of counters and cabinets. Work normally flows right to left: from the refrigerator-mixing center to the sink-dishwasher to the range-serving center. The sink is logically placed between refrigerator and range to save steps. The work area itself should be reasonably compact in order to save steps and to leave space for dining, games, serving, lounging, the laundry and other activities.

If you are remodeling, work out ways and means of closing up doors or whatever is necessary to have a dead-end work area—one that is not interrupted by traffic. Such changes are important, and the extra cost can easily be justified by greater efficiency. As a matter of fact, study the whole service area: the back porch, utility room, pantry, kitchen and dining room. It may be possible to take out a partition or two and have a truly magnificent space to work with.

When the architectural plan is complete, place appliances first. Working with time-and-motion studies, kitchen planners have developed four basic arrangements that offer the greatest efficiency.

The U-shape work center is most efficient, with the sink-dishwasher in the loop of the U, the range on one arm and the refrigerator on the other, and counter space linking the three appliances.

Next best is the L-shaped plan, preferably with the range on one side and the sink and refrigerator on the other. The fourth corner

Why shouldn't kitchens be beautiful? Study those at Williamsburg, Cooperstown and Old Sturbridge and you'll find they can be! Here, there's a pass through to the dining room. Old tools mingle with the latest sold.

A

may be a dining area.

The third type is a corridor or pullman kitchen. These kitchens are usually narrower than the others and the appliances line the two sides. If there are doors at both ends, bisecting the work area, a pullman kitchen is inconvenient except in two-person households without children.

One-wall kitchens, often used as an extra

This pullman-style kitchen with handsome wood cabinets and tile counter is aided immeasureably by built-in surface units and oven. Even though the kitchen is small, both a dishwasher and an under-counter washer-dryer have been included. Because doors are both at one end, there is no traffic to disturb the work area. This is very nearly a perfect small kitchen even though planning started with the awkwardly placed off-center window.

A

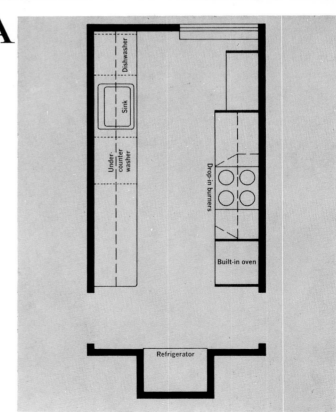

B

kitchen upstairs, in a recreation room, or in a small apartment, have range, sink and refrigerator on one wall linked with a counter and cabinets above.

Variations of these basic plans include the peninsula and island plans. Both of these variations may be added to U and L plans in large kitchens and may include an appliance or counter space only.

An efficient U-shaped kitchen developed in a minimum space, plus a peninsula snack counter. Equipment includes a range with an eye-level oven, a combination washer-dryer and a dishwasher. The space between counter and upper cabinets has been used to good advantage and top cabinet space attractively stores decorative accessories. The floor is carpeted. Cabinets are steel with chromium handles and have lights over the counters.

B

Kitchen Cabinets

A MINIMUM OF ten square feet is recommended for a family kitchen to supply enough space for work counters, storage and all the large and small appliances needed in today's kitchen. The following checklist of necessary or desirable appliances shows the extent of today's mechanization and the impressive amount of electric wiring and gas connections needed.

Automatic saucepan
Automatic skillet
Blender
Can opener
Clock radio
Coffeemaker
Dishwasher
Electronic oven
Exhaust fan
Food mixer
Freezer
Intercom system
Juicer
Portable mixer
Radio
Range
Refrigerator
Rotisserie and/or oven
Telephone
Television
Toaster
Waffle iron
Waste disposer

The major appliances are accommodated in the basic plan. Storage must be supplied for the small appliances either in the lower or upper cabinets or on the counter, and the convenience of their location is important in the final efficiency of the work area.

There is a choice of steel or wood cabinets. Steel cabinets have gone utterly giddy; white is still available, but the selection includes all the colors of the rainbow, as well as black and bronze. Neat steel cabinets are models of efficiency. They also come with wood-paneled or plastic-laminated doors.

Wood cabinets give a warm homey look that is particularly appropriate in kitchens that form part of a larger living area. Use curved provincial moldings for a Spanish or French kitchen and square paneling and black H & L or butterfly hinges for an early American look.

Formica and other plastic counter surfaces are a delight to care for. However, in a large kitchen, consider using several materials for counters. Alongside the range a ceramic tile insert won't be harmed by a hot pot, a wooden chopping block is convenient at the preparation counter, and gourmet cooks may demand a marble insert for rolling out pastry.

Dishes, glassware and basic supplies must be stored. Find an area where shallow storage walls without counters can be installed. Such shelf storage is almost indispensable for china reserves and supplies. The perfect solution is a walk-in pantry such as grandmother had.

Decoration

THE ADJACENT area for dining or play, or a combination of the two, may often supply the key to the mood of the kitchen. Since a kitchen is a work area, it must be efficient; since it is part of a living area, it must be gay; and since we are not as puritanical about work today, beautiful "un-kitcheny" lighting fixtures, pictures, accessories can cheer the eye and the heart as they do in the rest of the house.

Study photographs of modern kitchens; note the plants, the over-scale lighting fixtures, the accents of pure color. In provincial kitchens, note the use of tile, the natural-wood finish, the blue-and-white checks, the baskets and copperware. In Early American kitchens there may be old tinware, wooden molds and weathervanes. In the Victorian kitchen, curlicue rattan chairs, urns and apothecary jars are exactly right.

Don't be content with just anything on the floor. For provincial and colonial kitchens consider linoleums with a spatter or brick pattern and vinyls that simulate flagstone or tile. Real brick, ceramic tile and flagstone are handsome but much harder on the feet.

Vinyls and linoleum with marbleized and terrazzo effects are fine in kitchens.

A play space for the children close by but separated from the kitchen is one of the most wanted house features of young families. Here is the perfect plan plus a fascinating family dining area with a fireplace set in a shingled wall.

When a cookie board is not a cookie board, it may be posing as a door or drawer front in a cabinet. Here an efficient one-wall kitchen is separated from the dining area with bi-fold doors. Note elegant cupboard and table.

An in-a-wall laundry with stacked washer and dryer. On the left is a closet and the laundry chute; on the right a bar with a draw top and glass supply, and a dining area with a delightful wallpaper mural featuring an 18th-century laundress.

A laundry of this type can be fitted into almost any closet off the kitchen or off a hall near a bathroom in the bedroom wing. The decorated doors suggest a screen, the straight-line motif could be easily made with colored gummed tape.

228

The Extra Kitchen

TWO-CAR AND two-television families have become commonplace. Now we have the two-kitchen family.

In one two-story house in California, a door opens into an upstairs hallway and, behold! A complete apartment kitchen with under-counter refrigerator, two electric cooking units and storage above. Wonderful for early-morning coffee or tea, for children, or when someone in the family is ill.

In a New Jersey home with three teen-agers, an on-grade basement game room has sliding glass doors opening onto a back terrace and swimming pool. The children do all their entertaining there, and a kitchen in a closet in one corner has saved the sanity of the rest of the family. A Michigan family solved the same problem by building a cabana, complete with kitchen-bar at one end of the swimming pool. Even an extra sink on a terrace can be a convenience for washing hands, flower arrangement and barbecues.

In Philadelphia, an imaginative couple converted their two-car garage into a suite for the husband's mother. The most indispensable unit is an in-a-closet kitchen where she can prepare her own meals when she wants them, and dine with the others as an occasional guest. The whole family is delighted with the arrangement, which gives them all maximum freedom.

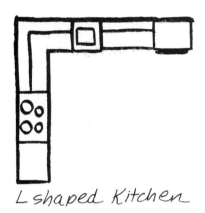

L shaped kitchen

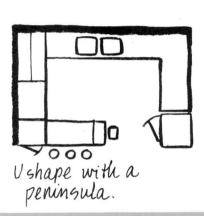

U shape with a peninsula.

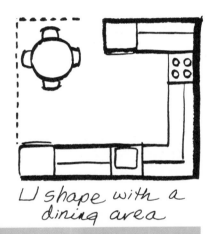

U shape with a dining area

Laundries and Utility Rooms

LAUNDRIES, though not without the possibility of glamour, are, in a sense, orphans looking for a permanent home. Traditionally, the laundry was in the corner of the basement. Basements have all but disappeared, the new washers and dryers have revolutionized wash day, and going up and down the cellar stairs has been labeled hard labor. So laundries have moved upstairs—but where?

Laundries may share space in the kitchen or family room or occupy a separate utility room in the kitchen area. In the South, especially, they are often placed in the garage; but increasingly laundries are found in the bedroom wing, in an alcove off a hall, in the bathroom or in a utility room back to back with a bathroom, so that only one plumbing line is needed. This location is sensible because most household laundry originates in the bedroom wing. An outside door can open from the laundry so that children can enter there without going through the rest of the house. A laundry in the bedroom wing is not satisfactory if the bedrooms are in two widely separated wings of the house.

Usually a minimum of space is allotted to the laundry. Sewing, mending, even the ironing, are done elsewhere, often in view of television in a bedroom or family room.

Good lighting is needed in a laundry, as well as a waterproof floor and walls. Some shelves or storage space for supplies are desirable. The color and character of the laundry should share that of adjoining rooms.

CLOSETS MAKE ALL THE DIFFERENCE

POSSESSIONS ARE AT once a joy and a problem. They are often the key to joyous occasions. The problem is how to store them so they can be kept in good condition and easily found when wanted.

During the last fifty, twenty, even ten years, possessions of the average family have increased so enormously that they have overflowed any reasonable assortment of closets supplied by architects and builders. Storage space in this affluent age may be needed for such items as sister's twenty sweaters, the boys' fishing togs, mother's thirty pairs of shoes, father's business, sports and formal clothing, and everyone's special garments for spring, summer, fall and winter.

Bicycles and the baby carriage have always been a problem; but now there are suitcases, photographic equipment, ski, tennis, skating and camping paraphernalia to be dealt with, along with terrace furniture, winter draperies, Christmas accessories and items constantly in demand, such as folding bridge table and chairs and the household accounts. And everyone's growing collection of books and records has to go somewhere. If the interior designer does not help solve the storage problem, clutter will overwhelm each room and frustrate the family.

Out-of-Sight, Close-at-Hand

TODAY EVERY household, whatever its size, whether in an owned or rented house or apartment, needs organized storage. In fact, there should be a supply closet for every room. Indispensable for most households are:

- Linen closets—one is needed for general household linens, if there are not separate closets in each bathroom and bedroom. A separate closet is needed for table linens and kitchen towels.
- Bedroom closets, which may include both hanging and drawer or shelf storage, for personal wardrobes.
- Coat closets—one near the front entrance for guests, and a family coat closet near the back door where the children come into the house.
- Cleaning closets—should be arranged on every level or for each wing of a house.
- A sewing closet—may be a part of linen closet or laundry.
- A luggage, sports, and hobby closet for bulky storage of things used occasionally.
- A seasonal storage closet—may be provided in an attic, basement, or garage.
- An accessory closet—a joy if space can be found for it.
- A household supply closet (once called a pantry) for canned goods, light bulbs, cleaning compounds, reserve supplies; a necessity if shopping is done only occasionally.
- A tool closet—the only method of keeping order for the do-it-yourselfer.

Shelves for storage may be twelve to thirty inches deep. It is amazing how much storage

230   **Living room storage solved with a painted armoire with mesh doors hung with shirred muslin. It accommodates Hi-Fi, TV, records and books. The yellow painted interior and gray-green trim make a nice contribution.**

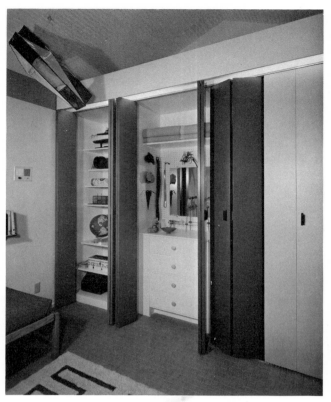

A closet wall in a boys' room with bi-fold steel doors provides game, drawer and hanging storage.

This ten-inch deep cupboard in a stairwell accommodates vast quantities of miscellany.

Twenty by twenty-four inches taken from a closet is used for an efficient housekeeper's desk.

Fourteen inches deep and forty-eight inches wide, this closet stores a service for twenty-four.

space can be taken from a room without perceptibly affecting its size, if this alteration is handled inventively. Decorative doors—sliding panels of mirror glass, louvered doors and shoji panels—have contributed to the acceptance of room-wide closet walls.

Look for storage space:
- In unused corners
- Flanking windows and doors
- Flanking a deep fireplace
- Under stairways
- Between rooms
- In halls, garage and basement
- In attics and utility rooms

Walk-in closets, if deep enough, may be divided into two closets with sliding doors. Open the hall door and there is a neat coat closet; slide open the door at the back and discover space for storing such things as the baby carriage, folding bridge table and chairs and other miscellany.

A small bedroom may seem twice as large and have more than twice as much storage, if, instead of chests, a closet wall is built along one side of the room with both hanging and drawer storage behind doors. Bedroom closets for all ages can be made to hold more if needs are carefully studied. In a long closet one small section might have a high pole for evening dresses, another section might have two poles for two-deck storage of blouses, skirts, jackets and shirts. A third section might have a standard pole about six feet six inches from the floor for dresses of ordinary length and for coats.

Neat and Pretty Too

THE INTERIOR construction and decoration of a closet will vary with its use, but the space should be organized for convenience, neatly kept and well-lighted. Closets can be attractive, too. Walls, shelves and doors may be papered. With painted walls, braid or molding in a contrasting color may be used for shelf edging. A contrasting color scheme may be worked out. A pink closet would be pleasant in a green room. A red-and-white-striped closet would be delightful adjoining a blue room. Closet floors may be painted to match the walls or surfaced with white vinyl, or carpeted to match the room (be sure the carpet has been mothproofed). Hangers may be painted to match the walls.

Service closets will be more flexible and hold twice the volume if they are lined with pegboard for hanging storage. One woman arranged her closet storage so efficiently and attractively that her guests are as fascinated with the sliding shelves for linen, the neat pegboard-lined cleaning closet, the handsome foyer guest closet and the wall-hung tool closet as they are with the rest of the apartment.

Storage That Goes With You

PORTABLE STORAGE—storage walls of movable furniture—can also make a major contribution toward solving storage problems, especially for renters. There is a wide range of possibilities, from unpainted shelf units to factory-type steel shelving. This shelving comes in a variety of finishes, is bought knocked-down, and can easily be moved when you move. Every year brings improvement and variety in the design of these mobile storage walls.

SMALL APARTMENTS

SMALL HOUSES and apartments, and even bed-sitting rooms have one over-all problem—lack of space. The first essential in decorating a small area is the right state of mind. If you feel sorry for yourself, whether you are eighteen or eighty, the situation will never right itself. Accept size limitations and turn the room arrangement into a game, and decorating the smallest space can become a fascinating project.

The goal in a one-room apartment may be a living-room look even though facilities must be provided for every activity: sleeping, dressing, cooking, dining, entertaining, the pursuit of hobbies, TV, hi-fi, books, art and storage space for seasonal clothes and other possessions. If an apartment has been properly designed for one-room living, an attractive, comfortable plan is reasonably easy to work out. There may be an alcove for dining or sleeping, a bath-dressing room and fairly adequate storage space. But if your room is simply a square or rectangular box, your wits will have to be sharp. Open your mind to the possibilities of space.

Do not plan to use standard dining-room furniture—buffets, china cupboards, draw-top tables; or standard bedroom furniture—double bed, dresser, high chest. If you have such furniture, store or sell it. Divide the space into activity areas and assemble the essentials. In many cases these activities will overlap. Nevertheless, to test your plan, think through the routine of a day, move and change and shift furniture until you have achieved convenience.

For sleeping, the choice is wide. If there is an alcove, a single or three-quarter box spring and mattress will fit nicely, and there may be space for a small chest and a night table. This area may be shielded from the living room with a screen, portieres or a room divider. The same fabric or color may be used on walls, bed and curtains, to unify the whole area.

If other activities are more important to you than sleeping, the alcove may be requisitioned for dining, an office, study, art or a music center. Sleeping is then moved into the main area. The choice will be either a sofa-bed that opens for sleeping, a boxspring and mattress piled with cushions, or a day bed. Still another choice is a Murphy bed that pulls out of a closet or armoire.

Storage is a major part of the problem. There must be a place to store clothes, books, magazines, china, pots, silver and bric-a-brac. Every possibility should be considered. A handsome high chest, armoire, secretary, desk or break-front offers great storage possibilities, and could be used as a focal point. Instead of using small tables to flank the sofa, use small chests. There may also be space for a small high painted chest in the bathroom. Plank and bracket shelves which you can take with you will store books and collections, and are decorative besides. If storage space just doesn't exist, flank a window with shelves or hanging space. Mount draw curtains out from the wall to conceal the shelves. Any handyman or do-it-yourselfer can cope with the boards and brackets needed for such simple construction.

Unpainted furniture departments are a good source for extra storage units. Chests and bookshelves can be piled up to create quite imposing storage walls. These have the advantage of being easy to knock down and take with you.

234   **The red-and-yellow color scheme launched by the rug marks the magic in this apartment living room which is never gloomy and offers both comfort and convenience. Note how even the pictures help the color scheme.**

Cooking and dining arrangements may take many forms. Storage can be created in a small kitchenette by surfacing all available wall and door surfaces with pegboard for hanging pots, pans and tools. A screen with a pegboard back makes an excellent divider for an in-a-wall kitchenette. Quite remarkable culinary feats can be accomplished on a chest or behind a small bar using only small appliances: a broiler, coffeemaker and electric frying pan.

One clever young author on a small budget managed for three years to do all her cooking in three electric percolators. Everyone loved her soup and salad meals followed by dessert and coffee. She served them on antique dishes, with silver that she had collected a piece at a time in England, and they were accompanied by candlelight and good talk. She did not lack guests.

Good food alone is not enough—it must be served attractively. If space is crowded, it isn't always possible to have a table reserved exclusively for meals. Rather than both a small coffee table and a small dining table, consider a larger double-purpose coffee table. If you do not object to mechanical furniture, there are nicely styled tables that can be raised and lowered. Desks also make good double-purpose pieces for study and dining.

A deeply cushioned sofa is nice to have, but avoid bulky upholstered chairs that are hard to move around. Select, instead, light open armchairs, peel tub chairs and side chairs.

Wall treatments are often dictated by landlords; but be as imaginative as possible. Mirrors are ideal for expanding space and have the same influence on a room that a lake has on a landscape. Large paintings can give drama and interest even to small rooms. Collections of pictures are good, too. One elderly woman has a scatter wall of pictures over her table-desk that traces her family's travels through three generations. It has become a great conversation piece since it includes two paintings on silk her grandmother picked up in China in the 19th century, as well as a small painting made by her godchild.

Colors may be light or dark, depending entirely on what effect you want to achieve. White and light colors make spaces look larger. However, a black wall may practically disappear. Incidentally, landlords dislike dark colors and wallpaper and may make an extra charge for them.

Fun on a Shoestring

Dining and conversation areas in a one-room apartment with a sleeping L. The simple white, black and green color scheme gives an airy look.

A bachelor's room, keyed to the striped fabric used on the sofa bed and in the Roman shades. The primitive painting, bold rooster and accessories do the rest.

A couch for a bed, a desk-study corner, a French garden table and painted chairs
for dining plus personal trivia make this one-room apartment a home.

TABLE TOP ART 5

COLLECTING DINNERWARE

TABLE SETTING, in the larger sense, is an art within an art, a gentle and endearing avocation that requires great sensitivity. It calls for an understanding of the fundamentals of design and color, a gourmet appreciation of food, and a broad knowledge of dinnerware, silver, glass, linens, fruits, vegetables and flowers.

Rules of etiquette do not present the major problem—these can be learned from reading books. What a table-setting artist needs are imagination and well-stocked shelves of components. With such a supply, the table designer is as free as an artist with his paints, a cook with a full and varied larder, or a woman of fashion with a knowingly collected wardrobe. A cupboard overflowing with matchmates, things that go together, is the secret of the table setter's art.

Collecting a proper supply takes years of devotion as well as some long-term thoughts about the family living pattern, a working knowledge and personal philosophy, and an honest appraisal of the cultural direction your family has taken. What profit is there in having an exquisite set of fine china, long-stemmed goblets, silver candelabra, and lace tablecloths if you live in a remodeled dairy barn and favor pine and maple furniture and country antiques? Why have a large assortment of soup bowls if your family does not like soup? How can you have a happy feeling about a cupboard of assorted casseroles, covered and uncovered, if your family has not progressed beyond meat and potatoes for dinner?

The aim in assembling a collection of table accessories is not to prompt the family or guests to say, "What a beautiful table!" but rather, "That dinner was a dream." This means perfect coordination between the likes of your family and your guests, the menu and the table service. If this aim is kept in mind, the perfect accessories for your table can be acquired one by one, rank extravagances will be avoided, and your cupboards will become a treasure trove.

Even if you yearn for individuality, start with the basic sets that correspond to a basic dress or a basic suit. Sets of flatware, dinnerware and glassware, will make possible the service of almost any menu. The perfect accents—the eight red lacquer bowls, the pewter plates, the majolica salad service—may take years to find, but you will treasure them all the more.

Start with China

DINNERWARE IS THE flat unimaginative term covering the wonderful world of pottery and plastics, the plates, cups, saucers and bread-and-butter dishes used in meal service. A minimum of two services is basic—one for every day, a sturdy, colorful service; and one for festive or formal dinners and occasions.

If you plan to carve a name for yourself, don't

241

be too conservative in your selection, don't get something just because it's safe. If a pattern can be described as safe, the chances are that it's faceless china—it either has no pattern or at most a few timid, uninteresting little floral scrolls scattered over it, lost in a sea of white.

Whether your set is to be plain or elaborate, select a positive design that makes a clear statement, that looks as though it was made for an individual rather than to conform with mass taste.

Some years ago a designer spent months developing a glaze that would make a self-color spatter pattern when fired, which would be different on every piece of china. The pattern was what might be called an act of God because it could not be controlled. The effects were delightful and as varied as snowflakes or the clouds in a mackerel sky. However, after examining the plates and comparing them, unimaginative customers brought them back to stores with the complaint: "Look, these plates aren't the same—they don't match!" They raised such a fuss that the manufacturer has gone back to a listless identical glaze with no pattern.

Pottery, Earthenware and China

BEFORE BECOMING involved with actual selection of dinnerware, it is desirable to know something about its history and development. Everything you find in the "china" department is not china. This classification covers pottery, earthenware, stoneware, porcelain and china, as well as melamine plastic.

Pottery bowls and jugs were made by primitive man. Bits and pieces can be traced back thousands of years. In his steady evolution, primitive man passed through three cultural stages: food gathering, food producing and craftsmanship. It was in this third stage that the making of pottery developed.

Imagine the excitement when, by chance, it was discovered that clay used to line baskets hardened and kept its form. The drying out was probably first done by the sun, later in an open fire and eventually in an oven. At some early period man also learned that covering the clay surface with sand before baking produced a hard surface, or glaze, which made the vessel waterproof. Dishes, bowls, platters, jars and cups from Syria, Palestine and Mesopotamia rank among the finest relics of ancient days. Some have outlasted wood and metal. Pottery is still one of our most interesting and useful materials. Each country over the years has developed characteristic pottery shapes and patterns that are still in use today. Among well-known native potteries are Mexican, French, Italian, Spanish and Japanese ware. They are decorative and make for gay, handsome tables. The patterns are colorful and bold and call for coarse linens, wood, pewter and copper accessories.

Twentieth Century Wares

POTTERY IS HEAVY, an informal friendly type of tableware, but it is not as durable as china and earthenware. Pottery dishes break and chip more easily, the glaze eventually scratches and crazes (cracks in minute lines) and the body beneath the glaze is porous. However, these wares are inexpensive and favored for the friendly, informal character they give to a table.

Earthenware is highly refined pottery in which finer clays are used. It is fired at a higher temperature than pottery, but at a lower temperature than china and for a shorter time. The result is a softer ware, porous under its glazed surface, not as durable as china but not as breakable as pottery. Earthenware should not be washed in boiling hot water or put in the oven to warm; this may cause it to craze. When crazed, chipped or cracked, the porous body will absorb liquids and darken.

This ware was developed in the early eighteenth century by French and English potters searching for the secret of making china, and it continues to account for the largest volume of dinnerware made and sold.

Earthenware is made in a wide range of price and quality. Inexpensive domestic wares may be less than a third the cost of a fine English starter set. In fact Queen's Ware, Wedgwood's

242   **A pretty tea service, a fine mahogany chest and charming padded French provincial chairs are unpretentious and appealing. The folding painted muffin stand is a ubiquitous English piece sometimes called a curate.**

earthenware, still made in traditional eighteenth-century patterns, is often prized above china for its gracious quality.

Ironstone, stoneware or stone china are different names for the same ware. This is not china—that is, porcelain—but it is an interesting and durable ware. It became very popular when it was first developed and continues to hold a distinctive place because of its tough quality and beautiful forms. Hard, close-grained clays are used in the manufacture of ironstone ware. It is fired at higher temperatures than earthenware and is actually fused, but the body is dense, without the translucence of china. Almost every cupboard in the country in the nineteenth century could produce some stoneware, often with copper lustre decorations. Today its popularity is being revived.

China, or chinaware, is porcelain. The Western world calls it china after the country of its origin. For a long time, its manufacture was a carefully guarded Oriental secret. Even though pieces may have reached Europe in the Middle Ages, it wasn't until the seventeenth and eighteenth centuries that the West developed a real "china mania."

The secret of fine china, or porcelain, is in the mixture of clays and stone and the very high temperatures at which they are fired. China will take hard wear and even when chipped or cracked will not absorb moisture. When flicked with the fingernail, it rings like a bell and it has a translucence that pottery and earthenware do not have. It is the strongest ceramic dinnerware made.

Fine English china has a minimum of 25 per cent bone ash added to the mix; some wares have up to 50 per cent of calcined bone. This produces an even harder, though crisper, ware. Among the well-known makers of English china are Wedgwood, Spode, Coalport and Minton. French Sèvres, Limoges, and Theodore Haviland table services are equally famous. In Germany, such names as Meissen, Dresden and Rosenthal stand for fine china; in Italy, Ginori. Arabia of Finland makes all grades of dinnerware from simple pottery to the most delicate china, and is famous for fine design. In the United States, Lenox, Franciscan and Syracuse make fine china. In 1962 Lenox added a very white bone china to its list of achievements. The list could go on and on.

Coarser china—high-fired, heavy and not translucent—a close relative of stoneware, has been developed for restaurant and hotel use. It is also available as range-to-table ware for the home. It is not to be confused with fine china.

"Plastic is for picnics" may have been the theme song ten years ago but not today. There is still a type of plastic ware (polystyrene and urea-formaldehyde) that is chiefly suitable for such use, but these days melamine plastic dinnerware is smartly styled, handsome on the table, stalwart in the dishwasher or when dropped, and can hold its own for any occasion that is not strictly formal. Colors range from pastels to black, and patterns are similar to those used on pottery and earthenware. Melamine plastic dinnerware has a marked resistance to chipping, breaking and cracking. There is, however, some marring and staining, more evident on dark, solid colors. Plastic dishes should not be heated or used as ashtrays. When buying plastic dinnerware, look for uniform texture, smooth edges.

Shopping for Dinnerware

FOR EVERYDAY meals, select a ware that is easy to handle, store and use. Earthenware, stoneware or coarse china and melamine are all good. Round shapes stack better than square or free-form, and handle more easily in washing. Avoid embossed patterns that will collect dust or food and have to be cleaned with a brush. For quick table setting, do not select directional patterns, such as a tree that has a bottom and a top which must always be placed exactly on the table. A snowflake, for instance, has no top and bottom and requires no positioning. Cups should be simple, rounded shapes with big loop handles which are easy to grasp. The cup should fit firmly into the saucer. If you use a dishwasher, do not select a gold- or platinum-trimmed pattern; detergents and hot water will wear off even the finest quality.

Less frequently used fine china may be selected with more abandon and less stringent adherence to practical matters. Fine china may be bought by the place setting rather than as a set. An individual place setting usually includes dinner or luncheon plate, tea or salad plate, bread-and-butter plate, cup and saucer. Better wares are usually sold in place settings from

Heart-warming provincial gaiety is the mood created by this table with its red-and-white checked table cloth, rose-splashed pottery plates and unusual wine dispenser. The fabric-covered shelves and cupboard lining are worth noting.

245

open stock. After you determine how many place settings you need, other pieces may be considered: cereal dishes, soups, platters of various sizes, vegetable dishes, gravy boat, creamer and sugar. Even though yours is an open-stock pattern, you may want to buy extra cups and saucers right away in anticipation of breakage or guests.

Less expensive wares may be assembled at a price in sets of various sizes:

A seventy-two-piece set is a service for twelve and consists of twelve five-piece place settings, plus twelve soup plates.

A forty-eight-piece set is a service for eight and consists of eight five-piece place settings, plus eight soup plates.

A twenty-piece set is a minimum service for four and consists of four five-piece place settings and no extras.

The following chart gives average sizes of the various pieces in a set of dinnerware.

Service plate	11″ to 12″
Dinner plate	10″ to 11″
Breakfast or luncheon plate	8½″ to 11″
Tea, salad, dessert plate	7″
Bread-and-butter plate	5½″
Cereal bowl	6″ to 7″
Flat soup plate	7″
Covered soup tureen	6″ to 7″
Platters, oval	12″ to 16″
Chop plate, round	12″ to 15″

Other serving pieces available include:

Vegetable dishes, open or covered
Sauceboat for gravy, stand attached
    or separate
Teapot and coffeepot
Sugar and creamer
Covered butter dish
Cake stand
Salt and pepper shakers

Don't Stop with a Set

A COMPLETE SERVICE in one pattern can be slightly overwhelming and is certainly unimaginative. However it is easy to add accent pieces when you find things that will contribute to the beauty of your basic service. When you make your find—on a trip, in your favorite store, at a secondhand shop or at a church bazaar—you can say with confidence, "Ah, this belongs in my china cupboard," if you will keep in mind the color and character of your basic service.

What are these collectors' items, these delights that somehow make meals taste better? Consider round deep soup bowls with lugs for serving New England clam chowder, black bean soup or borscht; flat-bottomed soup plates for main-dish soups and stews such as baked fish chowder or *boeuf bourguignonne;* covered bowls for use on the terrace; brown pottery bowls to fill with onion soup, top with cheese and pop into the oven; mugs with handles for soup-and-sandwich meals; and glass bowls for cold summer soups. Some or all of these, plus the classic soup plates of your set, can help you serve any soup or stew with style.

Extra place or service plates, though far from necessary, can do wonders to launch a meal. Pewter, wood, stainless steel or silver place plates are impressive and a lifetime investment. If the china to follow is of simple design, lavishly patterned place plates make a felicitous opening. Red or blue glass plates give élan to a table gleaming in the candlelight and cast a glow on cheeks; make a simple mushroom soup look like ambrosia.

Dessert plates from around the world are a good investment: glass, lacquer, china, pottery, enamel, mother-of-pearl, pewter and silver are possibilities. Look for deep-dish English desserts for puddings with sauces; flat decorative eight-inch plates for pie, and to use as place plates with glass bowls; and don't forget there are *pot-de-crème* sets and fluted ramekins for individual *soufflé au chocolat* or *crème brulée.*

Special menus may prompt special dishes. When Russel Wright serves one of his famous curry dinners, he uses charcoal-black dinner plates, but the curry and condiments are spread out in as varied a collection of containers—bowls, boxes, vases, baskets—as you could hope to see. They make a real contribution to the distinctive flavor of the meal.

A friend from Down East specializes in old-fashioned Saturday night New England suppers with baked beans, brown bread, cole slaw and apple pie with cheese. To give these events an authentic flavor, she always uses her blue-and-white Fitzhugh-pattern Spode; jelly and pickles are heaped into dishes of Sandwich glass; there is always a spoon holder on the table, little butter dishes, a caster set and, often, a celery holder displaying its bouquet of celery.

246   **Palm leaves, pineapples, melons and other exotic fruits clustered around a wood carving give a Polynesian flavor to this scene set for an informal supper party. The plates are on the table and the soup is in the bain-marie ready to serve.**

Care of Dinnerware

DINNERWARE, LIKE everything else, wears out with use; however, careful handling will extend its life. Breakage presents the first challenge, abrasion and cutting the glaze on china the second.

Glaze on pottery is a hard substance but not as hard or tough as steel. The sharp edge of a knife under pressure will mar the surface of a plate. Moreover, just as one glass may scratch another, so one plate or cup rubbed across another may mar it. This is particularly true when they are wet. Fine china should be stored with a felt pad between each plate, and plates should not be scraped against one another.

Underglaze decorations are protected against damage by a glass film. But on-glaze colors and metal decorations—gold, platinum and silver—are not so durable. They are damaged by repeated washing at high temperatures, by corrosive soaps, and by prolonged exposure to acids, fruit juices or vinegar. Rinse and wash them as soon as possible with mild soap in a plastic or enamel—never aluminum—pan lined with a towel or rubber mat at the bottom. Do not use a dishwasher for fine ware or gold-, silver- or platinum-decorated pieces.

Also remove your diamond ring when washing china, as a diamond will scratch almost anything, and a casual scratch across a plate will leave a scar.

TERMS YOU SHOULD KNOW

COUPE SHAPE: A plate which has no rim or indented center portion.

DELFT: Earthenware first made in Delft, Holland, with a colored tin glaze.

GLAZE: A coating of glass lending brilliance to the surface.

JASPER WARE: Black stoneware left unglazed, either with classic decorations in relief or without; made by Wedgwood, late eighteenth century.

LOWESTOFT: Soft-paste porcelain usually decorated by Chinese-derived patterns on underglaze blue enamel. Originally produced by factory in Lowestoft, England.

LUSTRE: A surface film made by firing metallic pigments on pottery or porcelain.

MAJOLICA: Highly decorative pottery with tin glaze made distinctive with vivid colors, made in Italy and Spain. Its opposite number in France is called faïence; in Holland, delft; in England, earthenware.

OPEN STOCK: A term used by retail stores and manufacturers to designate patterns which will be kept in the line for a stated number of years or for an unlimited time.

PYROCERAM: A cross between glass and ceramics. Adapted to dinnerware in 1962, it combines great mechanical strength with the appearance of china.

QUEEN'S WARE: A fine cream ware or earthenware made by Josiah Wedgwood.

RELIEF DECORATION: A raised pattern. This may be made by modeling, incising, piercing or by applying molded low-relief borders.

RIM SHAPE: This is the traditional form for plates. A depressed center section is bordered with a two-inch flange or rim.

SEMI-PORCELAIN and SEMI-VITREOUS: Terms sometimes used for earthenware.

SGRAFFITO: Decoration, usually scratched through slip to a different colored body.

SLIP: A clay thinned and flowed over another clay to color it or decorate it.

UNDERGLAZE: Colors applied before the glaze is put on and fired.

RAINBOW OF GLASSWARE

GLASSWARE SHOULD BE treasured, collected, used and displayed. Intrigue, mystery and romance are associated with its early development. About 98 per cent of the glassware sold today is plain crystal glass, notwithstanding the wide variety available. Crystal glass is correct for every occasion but this does not rule out the charm, excitement and pleasure to be had from light-struck colored glassware on a table.

One of the most beautiful tables I have ever seen was set for a large dinner at Chatsworth, England. The table linen was white, the china and silver elaborately patterned, but it is the glassware I still see: a tall cobalt-blue goblet for water, a simple ruby-red wineglass, and beside it a heavily cut, long-stemmed green wineglass, also individual blue glass salt dishes and four cobalt-blue-and-white footed compotes for bonbons. The multiple-color effect in twinkling candlelight had the impact of a stained glass window as it patterned the tablecloth with shifting color.

Equally dramatic in a more subtle way was a table set in a dark-blue-walled room in California. The round table, set without a cloth, was white marble, the centerpiece was a mass of white waxy camellias, the napkins monogramed white leatherlike damask, the dinnerware white also. The final note was the long-stemmed Venetian latticinio glass goblets. This table gets an "A" for restraint as well as for memorability.

A third table I have never forgotten was set for an informal luncheon at the White House during the Roosevelt administration. No china appeared throughout the meal. Both place plate and bouillon cup were crystal glass; the main course, a salad, was served on glass, as was the ice-cream dessert and after-luncheon coffee. The mixed bouquet containing blue delphiniums, which accented Mrs. Roosevelt's blue eyes, was also arranged in a glass bowl.

Let us consider, at this point, various aspects of glass: its manufacture; its use for table and beverage service; decorative glassware, including antique glass; and its care.

Why It's the Way It Is

THE MAKING OF glass predates both china and silver. Like pottery, it was an accidental discovery. Glass is sand and soda ash fused into a liquid with great heat, then hardened. Glass beads have been found which are thought to date back to 2500 B.C., and in any museum featuring old artifacts you can see opalescent small glass bottles from Mesopotamia which date back to the seventh century B.C. But it was not until many centuries later that the technique for blowing glass was discovered. Glassmaking became an important factor in the economy of the Roman Empire, and from there it spread throughout Europe.

Variations in the body of glassware are made by addition of elements to the basic mix.

LIME GLASS is used for most tableware. The basic mix is varied by the addition of lime ash, which toughens it.

LEAD GLASS is used for fine glassware, especially cut glass. The basic mix is varied by the addition of lead oxide, which produces a denser, heavier, softer glass with refractive brilliance. Flicked with a fingernail, a lead-glass goblet rings like a bell.

COLORED GLASS is the result of adding metallic oxides to the mix. The first colored glass was accidental; it was due to impurities in the sand and soda used. Now the making of colored glass is an exact science.
Yellow is obtained by the addition of iron or carbon; red by the addition of gold or copper; green by the addition of copper or chromium, blue by adding cobalt and copper. Glass is made both by hand and by machine. Go through any commercial factory that makes goblets and other glassware and you will be impressed with the hand processes and painstaking care which still persist. Great skills are involved, which are often handed down from one generation to the next.

UNDECORATED GLASS, simply clear bubbles of air, is often the most beautiful, but it's evidently difficult to leave a plain surface untouched. Many methods of decorating the hard surface of glass have been developed. Pressed patterns have already been mentioned. Glassware is also decorated with cut, engraved, etched and sandblasted patterns.
In addition to the methods outlined, colored enamel decorations are increasingly popular in informal glassware, and gold and platinum bands are used in fine tableware. The most satisfactory gold decorations are fired on. They are applied by hand, silk screen, decalcomania or spray gun.

Glass tableware is shaped by one of three methods:

OFFHAND BLOWING is the method passed down for 2,000 years. A gob of molten glass is picked up on the end of a blowpipe. The craftsman forces a bubble of air into the glass gob just as a youngster blows bubble gum. By twirling, rolling and twisting, the artist can develop any shape he wishes. Offhand blowing is a disappearing craft. Today it is used chiefly for art glass.

BLOWN MOLDING is a quicker, more exact way of shaping glass. Instead of free blowing, the gob of glass is blown out against the walls of a mold that determines the shape and size of the pieces. Originally this was done by a craftsman, but in 1903 Michael J. Owens of the Libbey plant in Toledo perfected the first automatic bottle-blowing plant. This machine technique has now been adapted to the making of inexpensive table and cooking glassware.

PRESSED GLASS was an American development about 1825, and it put glass into every household. The most famous factory was at Sandwich, Massachusetts. Instead of being blown, molten glass was dropped into a mold, and a tightly fitting plunger forced it into every part. The resulting glass lacked brilliance. This was soon corrected by developing all-over lacy and crosshatched patterns on the mold, which were transferred to the glass. The pattern on cut glass has a crisp edge and the inside of the piece is smooth. Pressed-glass patterns have a soft edge and may be uneven to the touch inside. Original Sandwich glass is a collector's item.

Set in the English manner without mats this pleasant informal luncheon table features fine blue-and-white ware, Waterford crystal tumblers and wine glasses, pistol-handled knives and three-tined forks with table spoons used for soups. The fruit and flowers on the sideboard are arranged in an épergne.

A Beverage and Table Glass Wardrobe

As WITH CHINA, it is pleasant to have at least two sets of glassware for the table, a formal set and an informal set. The formal beverage set will, of course, be stemware, and the informal set may be either tumblers or footed tumblers. Glass plates may be interchangeable. For instance, green glass plates might be quite handsome used with either a formal set of gold-banded Lenox china or with informal ivy-wreathed Napoleon Queen's Ware by Wedgwood. Blue glass plates would be handsome with blue-and-white Spode Old Salem or with all-white ironstone china.

Develop a feeling for the shape and texture of glass, study the shapes of glassware in museums and in old paintings. Take pleasure in the great variety of textures, colors and shapes available.

The charts show the pieces needed for a basic glass table service. However, the use of glass when wine is served is much more elaborate. You'll need many shapes and sizes.

251

Cocktail glass: For mixed cocktails and apéritifs, minimum capacity 3 ounces.
Champagne: May have flaring saucer shape, widest of all stemware, with hollow stem, or may be tulip shaped. 6 ounces.
Goblet: For water—about 10 ounces.
Red wine: An all-purpose dinner wineglass, smaller than the goblet, but may be the same shape. It is often called a claret glass.
Dessert wine: Also called port wine glass. Is used with dessert and fruit at end of meal. Cocktail glass may be used instead. 2 to 3 ounces.
Cordial: No standard shape, minimum 1 ounce.
Brandy inhaler: Also called "balloon" or "snifter"; holds 18 ounces, but small quantity (2 ounces) fine brandy should be served in it.
Frappé liquor: Larger than cordial (3 ounces) to accommodate shaved ice. (Champagne glasses may be substituted.)

TUMBLERS AND FOOTED TUMBLERS

Old-Fashioned: Fat, squat glass; should be served with muddlers. 8 ounces, also come in 12-ounce size.
Highball: To hold two or three pieces of ice with drink, minimum 12 ounces.
Whiskey and soda: For short drinks use less ice. 12 ounces.
Pilsener: A tall, footed tumbler; holds a full can of beer or ale. May also be used for parfaits, milk shakes, iced tea, coffee or eggnog.
Water tumbler: 10 ounces
Tea tumbler: 12 ounces
Juice tumbler: 5 ounces

Rules are only made to be broken. Today more than two wines are seldom served during a meal, and whether the wine is red or white makes no difference if it is pleasant with the food being served. Today's hostess makes her own simplified variations. Traditionally, however, this was the plan followed for formal meals:

Oyster course:	Rhine wine (white)
Soup:	sherry
Fish:	white wine
Entree:	champagne
Roast:	red wine
Salad:	red wine
Cheese:	red wine
Dessert:	champagne

Other glassware for dinner-table use includes six-inch and eight-inch plates for salad or dessert, glass bowls or nappies for dessert, cold soup or finger bowls and low-stemmed sherbet glasses, which may also be used for a first course of seafood. Glass mugs and punch cups also fit into the entertainment picture.

For table service, other glassware pieces to consider are:

Salts and peppers	Hurricane chimneys
Salad and fruit bowls	Ashtrays
Punch bowls	Creamers and sugars
Cake stands	Water pitchers
Candlesticks	Cocktail shakers and
Candy dishes	decanters
Epergnes	Vinegar and oil cruets

Care of Glassware

GLASSWARE HANDLED carefully will have a long life. Certain precautions are worth observing. Quick changes of temperature will crack glass. Do not pour boiling water over glasses, especially stemware. Do not put ice in a glass that is still hot from washing. A silver spoon standing in a glass will take some of the heat, but not always enough to save the glass from breaking if hot water is poured on or into it. Always rinse glasses after use. Milk curds will harden in the bottom of a glass and make it difficult to clean.

Fine gold-decorated china, gold-rimmed goblets and "Chantilly" flatware establish
a French feeling which is accented by the unusual tôle basket and square urn.
The straw flowers and artificial lemons are fastened to a chicken-wire foundation.

Vinegar cruets and flower vases which have become brown and cloudy can be cleaned with detergent or ammonia water. If the neck of a bottle is too small to insert a brush, drop in a tablespoonful of uncooked rice and shake it hard. The friction of the rice will help loosen the soil. Cloudy pressed or cut glass can also be brightened by soaking in warm detergent or ammonia solution before scrubbing.

If two glasses stick together, put cold water into the inside one and stand both in warm water. They should then separate easily. Stand glasses with head up on shelves to avoid chipping the drinking edge. If the foot or rim of a glass is chipped, gently file the rough edge. Wash decorative glass in hot sudsy detergent water and drain dry; if you don't wipe, the glass will have more glisten.

Tray settings for a TV dinner repeat the blue-and-green room color scheme and give even a simple meal a gourmet flavor.

Blue-and-gold patterned fine china and a white shelf-to-table majolica centerpiece look their best against a blue cloth.

TERMS YOU SHOULD KNOW

WATERFORD: A famous eighteenth-century Irish glass with a characteristic geometric crosshatch cut and a sturdy shape on a low baluster stem.

TIFFANY GLASS: An opalescent glassware developed in this country at the turn of the twentieth century.

CRYSTAL: The term applied by the French to flint glass. It comes from the Greek **charice.**

BOROSILICATE GLASS: A cooking glass with boric oxide added to the mix, which makes it resistant to thermal shock.

MILK GLASS: An opaque white glass. The opacity is achieved by the addition of fluorides and other substances. Opaque glass can be made in any color.

CASED OR OVERLAY GLASS: Glass made by coating crystal or milk glass with colored glass. By cutting out the top layer and leaving the bottom layer, a pattern develops, white on color or color on white.

CUT GLASS: An early development for adding patterns to the surface. It is done by an abrasive machine or by hand. Waterford glass is the most famous, although late Victorian cut glass is most plentiful.

ETCHED GLASS: The pattern is etched with acid and is usually shallow and lacy.

255

ENGRAVED GLASS: The patterns are developed on a wheel or by diamond point by artists. Today used principally for art glass.

BOHEMIAN GLASS: A fine cut glass with diamond engravings; usually refers to red or blue glass decorated with clear tracery.

VENETIAN GLASS: This glass has been famous since the eleventh century. It is delicate, clear, blown glassware, renowned for its thinness, fanciful shapes and colors. Its variety of form and fancy has never been excelled.

FLINT GLASS: An old term for lead crystal.

PONTIL MARK: A scar left on blown glass where it is broken off the "punty," a long iron rod used to remove the glass from the blowpipe.

LALIQUE GLASS: A French glassware designed and made by a sculptor. It is a heavy, decorative ware.

ORREFORS: A well-known Swedish glassware of high quality.

STEUBEN GLASS: Fine American crystal, famous for quality and beauty. Exquisitely engraved pieces of Steuben glass are sometimes used as diplomatic gifts.

LATTICINIO GLASS: A Venetian glass with thin lines of milk glass alternating with crystal; usually there is a slight swirl to the flow of the lines.

SANDWICH: The Boston and Sandwich Glass Company located at Sandwich, Cape Cod, 1825-1888, is best known for its fine pressed glass. This factory also made cut, engraved and molded tableware.

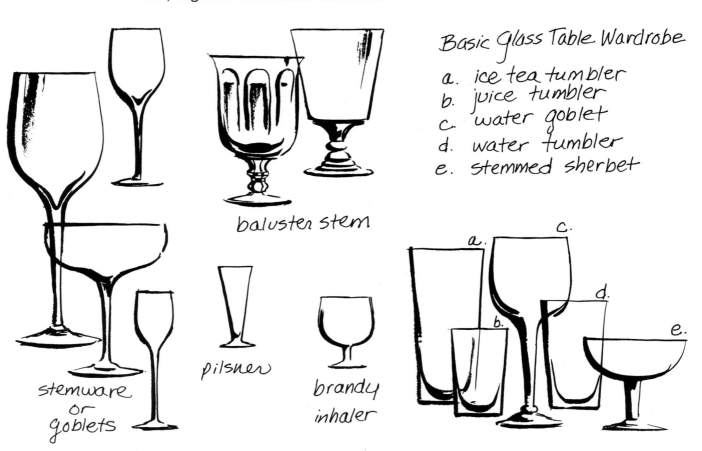

baluster stem

Basic Glass Table Wardrobe
a. ice tea tumbler
b. juice tumbler
c. water goblet
d. water tumbler
e. stemmed sherbet

stemware or goblets

pilsner

brandy inhaler

TABLE GLINT AND GLITTER: SILVER AND STAINLESS STEEL

METALLIC NOTES, notably silver, give glamor, beauty, sheen to a table setting. Silver, wood, bronze, pewter and pottery bowls and plates date back to ancient times, but table setting did not become an art until silver spoons and forks for eating were developed in the seventeenth century.

Reproductions of some of the old patterns are still being made: the plain rounded end of old English patterns, the rattail on the back of the bowl of a Queen Anne spoon, the pistol handles and three-tined forks characteristic of the George III period. The shell motif and fiddle shape are particular favorites and are still reproduced in sterling, silverplate and stainless steel.

A limited amount of thin old silver flatware can still be found. Soft coin silver was used for flatware in the early days; it was melted and cast into silver bullion whenever there was a financial emergency in the family. The pieces of flatware that escaped the melting pot are apt to be paper thin from use, with worn bowls and twisted shapes.

Flatware: Basics and Bonanzas

FLATWARE, LIKE CHINA, should be bought in sets so that practically any menu can be served. However, it is nice to expand a set beyond the basic pieces, by becoming a collector of unmatched extras. Matching silver on a table gives an orderly look, but unmatched pieces not used in the place setting or added as an extra note such as fish knives and forks add a pleasant fillip.

Flatware may be divided into two basic categories—that used for individual place settings and that used for serving. A minimum place setting includes place knife, place fork, teaspoon and salad fork. The next piece to add is an oval (not round) place spoon, which can be used for soup or dessert. In a six-piece place setting a butter spreader is also included.

Extra teaspoons are useful to have. Older silver services may offer forks and knives of two sizes—larger ones for dinner, smaller ones for luncheon. Start with the more versatile luncheon size, which can be used for salad and dessert if the dinner size is eventually added.

Extra pieces that are nice to collect:

Serving and carving spoons and forks
Fruit knives and forks
Demi-tasse spoons
Fish knives and forks
Seafood or oyster forks
Iced-tea spoons
Individual steak knives

Serving and accessory pieces may match your pattern or not. They come in a wide variety including:

2-piece steak set	Gravy ladle
2-piece roast set	Sugar tongs
Pierced tablespoon	Sugar shell
Plain tablespoon	Cheese serving knife

picture on following page — **Who would ever think that fine china, a wooden horse, iron candelabrum, straw mats, sterling silver and violets could get together happily on the same table?**

Serving fork	Lemon fork
Salad set	Pickle fork
Pie server	Jelly server

Sterling silver, plated silver, stainless steel flatware—whichever you choose—is a sound investment in dollars, service and pleasure. Your flatware will give longer and sturdier service than almost anything else you buy for your home. It should be the best you can afford, and, to give lasting satisfaction, it should have a classic design.

Sterling Silver is a permanent investment, a lifetime pleasure. Legally it must contain 92.5 per cent of pure silver. Copper is added to harden the silver and increase its wearing quality.

New silver patterns are brought out every year to satisfy the demand for something new and different; however, some of the most distinguished patterns have been in use since the turn of the century, and some for much longer. Classic patterns continue to sell because of the excellence of their design. Among them are simple modern and colonial patterns, graciously curved eighteenth-century designs, ornate and handsome baroque designs.

Young brides should not select a sterling silver pattern on a whim. Inevitably, after a few years, taste matures and improves and what one once thought so beautiful may no longer satisfy. A classic pattern is always a wise choice. When buying sterling silver, check the strength of the shanks of spoons and forks, the balance in the hand of all pieces, and the design, both front and back.

Plated silver flatware is a silver-coated hard white metal, usually nickel alloy. The coating is applied by the process of electroplating. Quality silver plate has a heavier coating of silver with reinforcement at points of wear, where it rests on the table and on scraping edges. Compare pieces and prices—the difference lies in the development of the design, the finish and the weight of the silver coating.

The best you can afford is the best investment. With careful use, a quality plated service will last several decades. Since plated silver is often a second service it is usually bought in four- or eight-piece sets. The plated silver service may not include salad forks and bread and butter knives. Silver-plate designs compare favorably with sterling patterns; there is a wide choice.

Stainless steel is the Cinderella of the flatware family. It started in the kitchen, but because of its fine styling, finishing and good performance, it now graces the dining table. It is strong, easy to care for, rustproof and resistant to stains. It is styled in a wide variety of patterns, but the finest are simple Early American and suave contemporary designs. Many of the major silver companies now make a stainless line, and there are imports from Scandinavia, Germany, Italy and Japan. Prices vary widely, depending on the quality of the design, the finish and whether or not the knives have hollow handles. Look for smooth edges, freedom from pit marks, well-shaped tines.

Steak knives with ground steel blades are growing in popularity for table use as well as barbecues, and may be used with a silver place setting.

Hollowware

SILVER OR OTHER metal serving pieces are handsome and unbreakable. At the top of the list of desirable metal serving pieces are a water pitcher and meat platter. Nice to have, too, are candlesticks or candelabra, a sauceboat, a covered vegetable dish and a twelve- or fourteen-inch tray. Salts and peppers and a pair of compotes are also useful. Other possibilities include teapot, tea kettle, creamer and sugar, coffeepot, wine cooler, chafing dish, pepper

Red-sprigged plates rest on pewter place plates instead of mats. Fiddle-handled flatware, baluster-stemmed goblets, and the ring on the fringed napkin seem right against the old brick wall with its primitive pictures.

Mustard-colored pottery and red lacquer create a Far East flavor. The shell motif is repeated in the plate, the flatware and the covered salt dish.

Ivy-ringed earthenware blends with the leaf-and-melon patterned green majolica, the green tumbler and the easy-to-care-for woven straw mat.

Blue-and-white ironstone china is pleasant with the blue pottery hexagonal bowl and the butter dish. The napkins repeat the angular motif.

Milk glass goblets, pink lacquer and white coupe plates with "Colonial Tipt" stainless steel flatware add up to a fresh modern setting.

mill, trays in assorted sizes, cocktail shaker, bar accessories.

Hollowware pitchers, trays and platters of sterling silver are available but very expensive. Stainless steel pieces have modern styling; sterling silver and plated silverware offer a wide range in traditional styling.

Almost all hollowware lends itself to more than one use. Be guided by your need, not by the name of the piece—a sauceboat, for instance, can be used for candy, nuts, olives or flowers as well as sauce.

Pewter hollowware has a special charm when combined with pottery, stoneware and earthenware in informal services. Pewter has been used for the table for centuries. In the Middle Ages only the well-to-do owned it, which accounts for the handsome shapes of many of the old pieces.

Pewter is an alloy, the principal component of which is tin. Old pewter is not recommended for use with food. Modern pewter is harder and perfectly safe, although it is softer than stainless steel and should never stand on a hot stove or be put in an oven to warm.

Pewter place plates, candlesticks, tankards, salts and peppers and porringers are distinguished acquisitions.

Care of Tableware

PROMPT WASHING, rinsing in hot water and quick, complete drying all help to retain the fine lustre of metal wares. Use a mild soap or detergent when washing by hand. In an automatic dishwasher, follow the directions supplied by the manufacturer of the dishwasher. If left to dry in the air after washing, metals will water-spot.

All metals are susceptible to scratches. With reasonable care, deep cuts and nicks can be avoided. Don't weep over small cuts and scratches; eventually, polishing will blend them and your silver will have the soft lustre—the patina—of old silver. When polishing silver, use lengthwise, never circular, strokes.

The electrolytic method of cleaning silver, although often used, is not recommended for fine silver. In this method, the silver is put in an aluminum pan or in an enamel pan with aluminum foil fitted into the bottom. It is then covered with a strong detergent solution and allowed to stand until clean. This method removes all shading in the pattern as well as tarnish and produces a white look instead of a deep silver sheen.

Heavily patterned silver will not show scratches and nicks as much as plain silver does; but use is a beauty badge of silver, and daily use—rotating the pieces in your set so that all receive equal wear—is the best treatment you can give it. It has been said that silver dies when it is not used.

After contact with eggs, salad dressing or excessive salt, tarnish marks may show. Light cleaning with a reliable silver polish will remove tarnish at once. To reduce tarnish to a minimum, store silver flatware in a tarnish-proof box and keep hollowware in tarnish-proof flannel bags. Polyethylene bags are also effective in retarding tarnish. If hollowware is not in constant use, put some gum camphor into the bag to keep moisture out. Do not close bag with elastic, as rubber permanently mars silver.

All stainless steel is not of exactly the same composition. Some of the less expensive grades and some imports occasionally darken and show discoloration; this can be easily removed with any scratchless polish.

Discourage the family from prying covers off, digging or scraping with table flatware. This is the way spoons are worn down, knives twisted, fork tines pushed out of alignment.

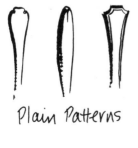

Plain Patterns

Ornate Patterns

Traditional

modern

TABLE COVERS

TABLE COVERS MAY be simple, unusual, practical or exotic. For special occasions, the choice of cloth offers a great opportunity for drama. Flair is fine and may be unlimited if neatness and orderliness are maintained.

Today there are no rules to observe, such as damask tablecloths for formal occasions, mats for informal ones. You may make your own decisions.

For every day, most of us are utterly practical about table covers, but being practical does not rule out beauty. Have a supply of plastic mats —straw, bamboo and paper—anything that is gay and colorful, and drip-dry or spongeable. Better a grass mat than a soiled tablecloth; better a plastic mat than a rumpled plastic tablecloth; better a drip-dry mat than no cover at all.

With unpatterned dishes, use dark or light solid-color mats and cloths, and patterned ones too, for variety. With patterned dishes, use solid-colored mats and cloths or, for variety, a stripe or plaid that looks well with your pattern.

Party tables put fresh demands on a table-cover supply. You should have at least one set of fine linen mats and perhaps an embroidered or lace cloth for formal events; but it is also fun to surprise your friends occasionally with an unusual "dressmaker" cloth.

A dress designer I know, who is also a great hostess, is apt to use almost anything for a table cover: a sari she picked up in India, a Chinese temple robe, a vivid Mexican rebozo or an unhemmed length of gold lamé that she will later turn into an evening dress. A decorator who is also a great party-giver specializes in "bedspread" cloths. They are ninety inches long without seams, washable, durable and dramatic. Her favorite is a white quilted mattress cover, cut round and edged with deep fringe. Another is a patchwork quilt, a third is a tufted bedspread with a round medallion design which just fits the top of the table.

Your supply of table linens will, naturally, vary according to the size of your family, the amount of entertaining you do and the amount of service you have. A minimum list of table linens includes:

1 large colorful tablecloth for buffet meals
12 large matching or coordinated napkins for the buffet cloth
2 sets of dinner place mats and napkins
3 sets of luncheon place mats and napkins
3 sets of breakfast place mats and napkins
12 to 20 cocktail napkins

Centerpiece Concoctions

FOR FAMILY meals and informal dinners a centerpiece may be omitted. However, there is no reason for it with so many quick and easy ones available. Every household should have a centerpiece cupboard stocked with accessories that can go from shelf to table without benefit of flowers or other adornment. Below are two lists of centerpieces, one of containers requiring fruit, flowers or plants, the other of shelf-to-table objects.

picture on following page
This is the traditional Christmas look: rich red damask background, handsome white cloth, shining silver and glass and a bountiful harvest arrangement of fruits with a choice of punch or champagne.

Centerpieces To Use with Fruit, Flowers or Vegetables
Baskets
  wicker
  wire
  silver
Epergnes
Bowls
  silver
  glass
  pewter
  metal
Vases
  ceramic
  glass
  silver
Jars
Planters

Centerpieces That Can Go from Shelf to Table
Covered soup tureen
  or casserole
Candelabra or
  collection of
  candlesticks
One or more figurines
Arrangement of shell
  or driftwood
Ship's model
Covered lacquer bowl
Collection of glass
  paperweights
Covered copper pot
  or tea canister
Cluster of candy jars
Old scales, caster
  set or coffee
  grinder
Decoys
Collections of
  pottery

It is, no doubt, possible to assemble a charming plastic bouquet for occasional use, but don't let it become a habit. A Paris decorator makes a practice of tucking two or three exotic flowers, real or artificial, into leafy plants just to amaze guests. But the very permanence of plastic flowers makes them monsters. One of the charms of flowers is their fragility, their brief existence. They are like a kiss, a pleasant thought, a delightful occasion or as the Japanese would say, "a guest who knows when it's time to leave."

Dried flowers are colorful and pretty, but they, too, should have only a brief period of exposure before they are removed and wrapped in polyethylene to wait, until the next time they fit into the table theme. Dried bouquets date back to colonial days and can be seen in many restoration houses. Interest in this period has led to the revival of the art of dried flower arrangements.

Use vegetable and fruit centerpieces too, and don't hesitate to mix in a few flowers. Study old Dutch paintings for inspiration and imaginative details. For a spring table, a beautiful bundle of asparagus tied with ribbon and topped with a few flowers could well be a conversation piece. Eggplant and yellow-green grapes in a basket with a few leaves make a picture. Glossy green peppers in a white bowl set off a green-and-white table. Tomatoes heaped in a white compote may be more handsome than roses on a red-and-white table. On a long table, a row of three compotes, each topped with a big yellow grapefruit resting on precisely placed ivy leaves, have an air. A cluster of old glass bottles in assorted colors, with perhaps a daisy or rose tucked into one or two, is fresh and colorful.

Unusual objects of all kinds offer the charm of the unexpected. Antique celestial globes, a choice collection of old flatirons, old cast-iron banks, or antique children's toys, make delightful compositions.

In the winter, gourds in a basket may be used and reused, and even a bowl of nuts or eggs may strike a pleasant note. A friend in California is fascinated with sprouting seeds and vegetables and often uses big fat Bermuda onions with long curling sprouts for a centerpiece. Potted plants and water-grown leaves are good standbys. Ivy, philodendron and pachysandra all grow in water, and can be enjoyed as centerpieces; meanwhile they will root, and can then be transferred to the garden. To make small potted plants seem more important, arrange them on a tray or in a basket.

The selection of the container and the flowers must be coordinated in mood and color with the dinnerware and the linen. The easiest and often most effective tables to arrange feature one color. It is difficult to improve on an all-yellow, all-pink, all-blue or all-amethyst table. Do not, however, rule out the beauty and excitement of "clash" colors and the stimulation in the use of pink and red, yellow and orange.

Questions and Answers on Table Setting

Q. Should napkins match the color of the cloth or mats?

A. They may; but have a set that contrasts, too. For instance, with green mats,

An after-skiing buffet featuring baked lentils, hot mulled cider and salad on a table laid with a coverlet, a drum full of flowers and accessories.

blue or white napkins would be interesting; with pink mats, red or deep-blue napkins would add spice; with red mats, black or white napkins would be dramatic.

Q. When are bread-and-butter plates used?

A. Bread-and-butter plates are technically correct for all but formal occasions. However, bread-and-butter plates increasingly are being omitted from informal meals. We all eat less bread and it's one less plate to wash.

Q. Where should napkins be placed and how should they be folded?

A. For formal meals with maid service, the napkin is placed on the service plate; when you sit down, the napkin is removed so that the first course can be placed. Without maid service, the first course is often in place when guests are seated; in this case, the napkin is in its usual place at the left of the forks. The long fold is always correct, but many novelty folds are used for fun and flair.

Q. What is the correct routine for using finger bowls?

A. With full maid service, the finger bowl with a doily beneath it, resting on a plate, is placed after the dessert is removed. But it is more usual for the maid to place the dessert plate with a finger bowl on a doily, flanked by dessert spoon and fork. Each person removes the doily and finger bowl and puts them to the left above the fork. The maid passes dessert.

Q. How is after-dinner coffee served?

A. This is a pleasant practice whether you have a small or large dinner party. The group moves to the living room. The hostess has the tray placed on a convenient table top; on it are the coffeepot, the demitasse cups and spoons, sugar, cream and perhaps some thinly sliced lemon or cinnamon sticks, and small napkins. As the hostess pours each cup, the host or someone in the group passes it to a guest.

Q. Why are both a spoon and fork used for dessert?

A. I suppose you might say as a preparation for any emergency. Ordinarily, if the fork will serve, it is used. However, it is correct to use both simultaneously while eating a fruit dessert, a whole pear or peach in wine, for instance. The fruit is kept from sliding by the fork while you serve yourself with the spoon.

Q. How far should a cloth fall over the table edge?

A. This is flexible; fifteen inches makes a pretty line.

Q. Should all creases in a tablecloth be removed?

A. It is correct to have one center fold. For this reason, tablecloths should be rolled, not folded.

Q. What is a service plate?

A. At formal dinners the service plate, also called the place plate, is on the table when the guests are seated; the folded napkin is centered on it. At less formal functions, the smaller plate for the first course may be placed on the service plate; the napkin is then in its usual position on the left. The service plate remains until it is exchanged for the dinner plate. It is often referred to as the "ever-present plate" or the "plate never touched by food." Formerly it was elaborate, gold- or silver-encrusted; now pewter, Mexican tin, wood or even decorative pottery plates are often used.

Dare to be different, try your hand at invention, use what you have and search for exciting tidbits in white elephant sales, auctions and second hand stores. If you like the look of this patchwork quilt, which is used for an occasional Saturday night New England dinner, you will want to experiment with other off-beat ideas.

PERIOD
PORTFOLIO

6

WHAT ABOUT ANTIQUES?

ONCE OF INTEREST only to the few, antiques are increasingly becoming a matter of exciting moment to a vast number of recruits. In fact, more and more people are even beginning to think of them as important investments. *Business Week, The Wall Street Journal,* and staid *Forbes* have carried articles on antiques—which is proof enough that antiques have arrived. Further evidence of broad interest is the growing number of news items in the daily press on the antique market and the twelve thousand or so antique shops in the country at large, not to mention front-yard, shed and barn operations which are indicated only as

"ANTIQUES—100 YARDS AHEAD."

Who finances and supports this thriving industry? First, there are the professional antique collectors. (Type One.) These may be true connoisseurs who buy either for the pure pleasure of ownership or because fine pieces are good investments, or because antiques have status value. This is the group that frequents the important auction galleries and pays fabulous prices for rare pieces. Antique buying in this category is usually done with and through an experienced dealer.

One of the most exclusive groups in this category calls itself the Walpole Society; this is an organization of antique connoisseurs in the million-dollar bracket which is said to be limited to thirty members.

Second, there are the small-time or amateur collectors who have a minimum of money to invest but who love old things and feel in their bones when they see and handle them the lure, the mystery, the stored-up memories of the past.

This group (Type Two) combs the antique shows, the country antique shops and auctions and prowls through second-hand shops for finds and bargains. Its members learn the art of restoration, refinishing, caning and preserving, and seek authenticity in technique and detail.

Third, there are a rapidly increasing number of people (Type Three) who have discovered that a few antiques mixed in with fairly ordinary furniture improve the flavor of a room in the same way that sugar brings out the taste of strawberries. Antiques are increasingly used in interior design as a sweetener of this kind. The original purchase may be instigated by a decorator. After that first sweet taste, sorties into the antique world are almost inevitable.

Dabbling in antiques can be an insidious game, a little like taking dope. It is easy to become an addict. This is a risk one must take. However, if you make wise original purchases you will probably not lose money on buying, trading or selling antiques. They are in a bull market, with resale values on the upgrade.

One Connecticut couple started collecting Early Americana twenty years ago. Because they bought with a thin purse, most of their purchases were crude country carpenter pieces —bargains at that time. Over the years they have traded in or sold not only all of their original pieces but many more—each time for higher prices. Now, with the profits from their trading, they are moving into the fine furniture category. They now own several original Duncan Phyfe chairs as well as other cherry, mahogany, and walnut pieces from the hands of fine early American cabinetmakers—pieces their dealer will take off their hands any time they wish to sell. Such pieces are investments.

Another couple in the Middle West began buying and refinishing antiques as a hobby, a hobby that is now a full-scale business.

What Is an Antique?

ANYTHING THAT WAS made in the nineteenth century or before may be casually called an antique, from a fifteen-dollar child's iron bank, circa 1870, to a $6,700 Louis XVI *petite secretaire*. However, it is not a *true* antique if it is less than a hundred years old. Furthermore, if you are bringing your find through the United States Customs, duty free, or if you are involved in a legal matter, the piece must date before 1830 to qualify as an antique.

It is often thought that 1830 was the date selected because the tariff regulation was made about 1930, a span of a hundred years. But the fact is that 1830 marks the dividing line between the time when almost all home furnishings were hand crafted and when the machine began to take over. In a sense, then, true antiques are handmade and have that peculiar charm that comes from the touch of the hand.

Antiques, like new furniture, can be divided roughly into fine formal furniture and accessories and country or informal things. Fine pieces, whether French, English or American, go together beautifully and are apt to be expensive. Informal or provincial pieces from around the world have a common bond and are less expensive.

There is also a growing interest in the semiold. This is almost the only area where real bargains still exist. A whole roomful of Victorian and Edwardian furniture could be a little overwhelming, but often one or two curlicued pieces —a chest of drawers, a whatnot, or a gone-with-the-wind lamp—can be the making of a room if they are used with imagination and tongue-in-cheek aplomb. The contrast will give the touch of whimsey, "the beauty of affected ugliness." Collectors are taking an interest in everything made up to 1930, when the industrial designer appeared on the scene. Bit by bit these "indispensable" experts are smoothing away all individuality from common household objects, thus making those produced before 1930 seem odd, quaint or interesting.

Five Guides to Authenticity

RECOGNIZING GOOD PIECES is a talent that has to be cultivated. To be a genuine antique, the piece must have been made in the particular period the design represents. It must be well made, original in all aspects (except for a normal amount of restoration), and it must have a fine patina and perhaps even a notable history. The cabinetmaker and first owner may be known. Unfortunately there are a lot of phony antiques on the market, some of which fool even the experts. Others are frankly reproductions; some are made of old wood and still others are almost totally reconstructed. Even china and glass are reproduced, and old pieces can be restored so well that it's hard to see the repair. Furniture can be restored up to 40 per cent and still be classed as "antique," but its value may go down at least 50 per cent.

According to the firm of Israel Sack, handler of fine American antiques, there are five categories into which fake antiques fall:

1. Out-and-out fakes.
2. Basically old pieces which have been deliberately converted to more valuable types.
3. Old pieces with more than 40 per cent of repairs—this downgrades their value.
4. "Married pieces," made up of several pieces of old furniture that did not originally belong together, such as two sections of a chest-on-chest.
5. Copies made at a much later date than the originals; often pieces made 50 or 75 years later are passed off as originals.

The case of the Baltimore ladies' desk which was accepted as a gift by Mrs. Kennedy for the White House is a good example of the need for accurate appraisal. The desk was purported to have been made in Baltimore about 1800. After it was installed in the White House and pictured on page 66 in the publication *The White*

An unusual early nineteenth-century secretary of glowing fruitwood is the dominating piece in this memory-filled sitting room. Wall panels are enlarged photographs of architectural details, posters and photographs.

House (White House Historical Association, Washington, D.C., $1.00) it was found to be a reproduction made in 1880. This completely destroyed its original estimated value of $20,000 and it was removed from its place of honor and returned to the donor.

It may take considerable experience and several questionable purchases before a buyer becomes fully aware of all of the problems involved and realizes why the experienced Type One buyer himself uses an expert to check purchases.

The expert first considers the design to see that it is correct for the period and the region it is supposed to come from. Next he considers the way the piece is put together, drawer construction, the blocks in reinforced areas and the signs of hand tooling of the period. Evidence of shrinking at crucial points and the appearance of all unfinished wood are important areas. The backs of chests and the insides of drawers assume natural coloration of aging which varies according to the degree of exposure to air and ranges from a light to a mellow brown.

There are so many details to check that close study is needed; however, the presence of glue can warn you that a piece is less than a hundred years old. A magnet will distinguish gilded iron from brass. Turnings can be checked with calipers. If they are exactly alike, they are machine made. Experienced fingers and a trained eye will catch the difference between the slight corrugations of hand-dressed lumber and the smooth machine-processed kind. It is surprising how fast you can learn the look, the feel, the language, of old furniture, old china and glass, if you put your mind, eyes and sense of touch to work. Of course, if you like something and the price is reasonable, and if you are not a Type One buyer, what difference does it make if it is only seventy-five years old, or even if it isn't what it is purported to be? If you are a Type Two or Type Three buyer, never buy anything just because it's old—buy only what you like. Use taste, drive a bargain, and after that—go on your emotions.

As you become more interested and involved with antiques, you will want to study books and magazines and actually see as many good pieces as you can. If the garden club in your community has a spring tour of houses and gardens, take advantage of it. Visit auctions whenever you can. You will look at furniture with different eyes once you have seen a single piece of eighteenth-century furniture go for, let's say, twenty-five thousand dollars or a child's tea set made about 1850 go for two dollars. If you hear of a country auction in your locality, go and sit under an old apple tree and have the time of your life, even if you are only an observer. Get acquainted with small dealers within driving range; go to annual antique shows. Should you become a serious collector, it will be helpful to become familiar with several shops and follow their prices.

How to Train Your Eye

ONE OF THE most pleasant ways to become acquainted with the furniture, fabrics, ceramics, glass, metal wares and the thousand and one fascinating household objects that have become our American antiques is to visit museums and restorations of famous homes such as:

THE HENRY FRANCIS DU PONT WINTERTHUR MUSEUM, WINTERTHUR, DELAWARE. This museum houses the largest collection of American furniture and decorative arts in the country, covering two hundred years from 1640 to 1840. For information about tours, write to the museum. It can be visited without making reservations only during five weeks in the spring.

COLONIAL WILLIAMSBURG, WILLIAMSBURG, VIRGINIA. The extensive restoration of the colonial capital of Virginia affords an opportunity to study eighteenth-century English and American furnishings representative of an affluent colonial society.

THE HENRY FORD MUSEUM AND GREENFIELD VILLAGE, DEARBORN, MICHIGAN. All forms of Americana and almost every phase of American history are represented in the collections and buildings in this indoor-outdoor museum.

Rough-hewn, honest and comfortable, honors in this living room are shared by the old carved Canadian cupboard and the amusing farmyard painting over the sofa. The Shaker rocker and the beech-and-elm captain's chairs are old.

This red-walled room has furniture of the same vintage as the one above handled in a more elegant manner. The portrait attributed to Copley, the ample draperies, the tea canister lamp and the plant-filled cradle make the difference.

Other treasuries of the American past are the Shelburne Museum, Shelburne, Vermont; Old Sturbridge Village, Sturbridge, Massachusetts; Old Deerfield Village, Deerfield, Massachusetts; the complex that includes Fenimore House, Farmers' Museum, and the Village Crossroads developed by the New York Historical Association at Cooperstown, New York. This last emphasizes folk life between the end of the Revolution and the Civil War.

Among the great houses and places associated with history and literature are The White House, Washington, D. C.; Monticello, Jefferson's home at Charlottesville, Virginia; the Sleepy Hollow Restoration near Tarrytown, and Boscobel, both in the Hudson River Valley, New York; the fine Adam houses in Charleston, South Carolina; the historic homes at Jamestown, Virginia; the restored colonial homes of Newport, Rhode Island; and the famous houses and gardens of Natchez, Mississippi.

Where to Buy Antiques

NEW YORK IS this country's antique center. Surprisingly, you can often find lower price tags on English and French furniture and silver in New York than you can in the countries of origin. If you are a Type One collector, you will be interested in the Parke-Bernet galleries and the smaller galleries on upper Madison Avenue. Type Two and Three collectors will have a fascinating time browsing through the small shops from the sixties to the eighties on First, Second and Third Avenues, and the auction markets around University Place in the Village. They are all fascinating, whether you are buying or just looking. To see first-rate pieces, the Metropolitan Museum and The Museum of the City of New York have collections that shouldn't be missed, particularly the Early American Wing at the Metropolitan.

Antiquing also adds interest to travel in other countries.

The Care and Repair of Antiques

WHAT YOU DO with antiques after you get them will vary with your point of view. People rarely wantonly destroy the value of their possessions, but they also rarely think in terms of responsibility to future generations. In handling antiques, both points of view are worth considering.

Serious Type One and, for the most part, Type Two buyers will cherish their antiques and use only preservative measures. They will tolerate rickety belongings and, if necessary, spend lavishly on preventing further deterioration until restoration can be made.

The Type Three approach is more imaginative and decorative. For the most part these collectors will avoid things in bad repair because current use is the aim. If a table is too high, the legs are sawed off; if a patchwork quilt is large enough and in good condition, it may be used to upholster a chair; old dessert plates are actually *used* for dessert and are the high point of a meal. Or the solid doors may be removed from a corner cupboard and carefully stored, the better to display a collection of white china.

This crass handling of antiques needn't cause any hysteria if the things tampered with are not great, not of museum quality. The trouble comes only when fine pieces are hacked up. It is said that do-it-yourself restorers are responsible for a serious loss of antiques which should have been preserved indefinitely.

One woman bought a small Louis XV table and had the legs cut off because it was too tall. Another woman had a Louis XVI armchair made into a rocker. A third woman paid several thousand dollars for a fine chest, then had it scraped and stained to match her other furniture.

It is becoming increasingly important for us to guard and protect our heritage. This applies to the preservation of old furniture just as it does to saving some of our fine old buildings. The rules for handling a fine antique are the same as for handling any fine furniture. Coddle it a bit, keep it dusted, cleaned and polished, protect it from cigarette burns, alcohol and water marks, keep it out of drafts and hot, dry rooms. Given such sympathetic care, fine old furniture will survive to serve and inspire many more generations.

Country antiques have a special charm, especially when they are handled in a gay, free way. Here, the old chair frame gains from the hit-or-miss patchwork, the old desk gains personality from the spice chest and accessories strewn around.

ABOUT PERIOD FURNITURE

THROUGHOUT MAN'S LONG EVOLUTION, there has been a need for seating pieces, for surfaces to work on and put things on, for sleeping and for storing things. Solutions changed with the state of the culture and the materials at hand. In different countries shapes took slightly different turns, but in the long term of history, it isn't necessary to go back farther than the sixteenth century to find the antecedents of our furniture today.

All period furniture can be roughly divided into three major classifications. If you are not too good a historian and get mixed up on kings and dates, these three main style movements and the key centuries will help you get through any museum or furniture store: the Renaissance; the Baroque and Rococo; and the Neoclassic. Most large, heavily carved, straight-line furniture goes back to the Renaissance. Gracefully carved and ornate furniture belongs to the baroque and rococo movement. The smaller, slender, straight-legged pieces with flat surfaces are usually of the neoclassic family.

Styles, forms, fashions are logical expressions of the period in which they developed. When kings and queens still had to be reckoned with, furniture and accessories reflected their personality and interests, but economic and social factors also entered the picture, as well as new developments in science and the world outlook. Great styles develop when great movements in all fields are evolving. The twentieth-century invasion of outer space may very well found another great style. Perhaps the early phase of this development can already be seen in so-called "modern" design.

Renaissance means rebirth and describes the development in Europe which started in Italy in the fifteenth century and swept over all Europe and eventually across the sea to young America. After the fall of the Roman Empire the art of living went into an eclipse. Europe slept for several hundred years. Then advancements in astronomy and navigation, the discovery of America and a constantly widening outlook on the world brought a startling change in the economic outlook. Social conditions improved. Life expanded and burst the narrow confines of medieval thought. Artists and writers felt a new freedom; the invention of the printing press helped spread knowledge. A new world was in the making, with more comforts and a hearty, bold outlook. At the same time the classic beauty of the ancient world was being discovered and was influencing design. All this can be seen in furniture influenced by the Renaissance. *Baroque* art and design expresses the full swing of the fashion pendulum away from the heavy straight-line classicism of the high Renaissance. By the middle of the seventeenth century the world had become a fascinating golden plum to plunder. The rich were very rich and the poor had no choice but to serve. Kings and queens were in their heyday. In France, Louis XIV, the Sun King, was at the center of it all. By 1715, when Louis XIV died, the baroque style was waning.

In furniture, lavish ornamentation and the curve rather than the straight line took over, although an architectural feeling persisted. So forceful was the splendor and magnificence of the French court that its influence was felt by designers throughout Europe.

Rococo is the term used to describe extreme baroque forms which are fantastically overdecorated, gaudy and ornate. During the reign of Louis XV (1723-1774) French rococo was at its peak; but to get the real significance of rococo forms, visit Vienna and Germany, where gilt, cupids and ornamentation really got out of hand.

Neoclassicism was a revolt against the soft femininity, endless curves and ornamentation of the baroque and rococo design movements. Simple straight lines swept Europe and America in the late eighteenth and early nineteenth centuries. This style coincided with the French and American surge to democracy.

The straight, trim, military forms expressed the spirit of the period. But the impulse and source of inspiration came through new excavations and discoveries in Pompeii and Herculaneum. Rome, Pompeii and Athens became the mecca of the great French and English designers who were the prime force throughout Europe and America in the development of the classic idea.

All design developments seem to move through a cycle—the steps just outlined. A style begins simply; becomes more ornate, then over-ornate, before it is brushed aside; and straight lines and plain surfaces return. Design movements are a little like the seasons—winter, spring, summer, fall—and may express man's constant need of change or renewal.

For example, nineteenth-century design began with delicate neoclassic lines, moved into heavy straight-line Empire furniture which persisted to the 1830s, when simple, quaint curved-line early Victorian furniture became popular. By the end of the nineteenth century, ornamentation became more extreme. It engulfed furniture, accessories, rooms. The reaction to these excesses came at the beginning of the twentieth century with the straight-lined flat surfaces of mission and early modern furniture. Now, in the mid-twentieth century, ornamentation is becoming increasingly popular. Round molded shapes are being used. Ornamentation will, in turn, be overdone, and simple forms will inevitably return.

In studying furniture learn to look at the over-all form first—its scale and proportions. Then study the shape of the leg from top to bottom, including the foot. Next, look at chair backs and the details of the rails or splat. Consider chests, their ornamentation—inlay, carving, japanning, mountings.

In the design charts that follow, decorative motifs and brasses or medallions are included. These are not only the forms used for carving and pulls on furniture, but are also found in accessories and patterns on wallpaper and fabrics.

Develop quick recognition of period forms, and the whole world of design will develop meaning for you, wherever and whenever you see it.

Cassone

Rope of
Fruit and Flowers

Egg and Dart

Arm Chair

Acanthus Leaf

Dante Chair

ITALIAN RENAISSANCE

Vargueno

Leather
upholstered Chair

Table with
Wrought
-Iron
Supports

Shell

Lantern

Arabesque

SPANISH RENAISSANCE

Melon bulb Legs

Elizabethan Court Cupboard

3.

2.

4.

1. Elizabethan
2.3.4. Jacobean Legs

Yorkshire Chair

Guilloche

Arch

Wainscot Chair

Rose

Gate-leg Table

Strap Work

Mounts

ENGLISH RENAISSANCE

Chest

Wainscot Chair Back

Carver Chair

Bannister Back

Flemish Chair Back

Slat Back

Courting
Mirror

H-Hinge

H-and-L Hinge

Strap Hinge

Candlestand

Trestle Table

Lantern

Andiron

PILGRIM

Settle

FURNITURE OF THE RENAISSANCE FIFTEENTH, SIXTEENTH AND SEVENTEENTH CENTURIES

ITALIAN FIFTEENTH AND SIXTEENTH CENTURIES

The arts had their first great awakening in Italy. Artists and writers, working in a frenzy of creation, influenced all Europe. This was the age of Benvenuto Cellini, Leonardo da Vinci, Michelangelo, Raphael, Palladio and a host of other great men in the art world. The art of living was in its infancy. Spaces were vast, surfaces crude: stone, tile, big timbers, rough plaster were the building materials. Furniture which was architectural in character was big, formal, heavily carved and ornamented, often with polychrome decorations. The principal wood was walnut.

The most important piece of furniture was the chest or **cassone**. A chest with a back was called **cassapanca** and **credenzas** were sideboards with doors below and a drawer above. There were vast damask-curtained fourposter beds, stools, benches and rectangular tables supported with an arcade of columns. There were few chairs; however the Dante and Savonarola chairs are identified with the period, as well as elaborate square-lined, high-backed Medici chairs and simple, straight monk's chairs.

On fabrics and for carvings and painted and gilded decorations, popular designs included acanthus leaves, the guilloche, dolphins, masques, grotesques, amorini, vases, horns of plenty, ropes of fruit and flowers, and classic architectural motifs.

Fabrics were rich velvets, brocades, damasks, tapestries and brocatelles, often interwoven with real gold and silver threads. Fringes, tassels and big upholstery nails were much used.

Accessories included tall gilded wood candleholders, iron candelabra, small, heavily framed mirrors, marble sculpture, and bronze Roman lamps.

SPANISH SIXTEENTH AND SEVENTEENTH CENTURIES

The general character of Spanish furniture was similar to the Italian forms, plus Moorish influences. Walnut and oak were the principal woods. Metal studs and finials, wrought-iron supports on tables, and tooled leather upholstery were used more frequently. Probably the most characteristic piece of Spanish furniture was the **vargueno,** a secretary-chest on legs. The front dropped down to form a desk with elaborate drawers and pockets for paper. Spanish decorative motifs blended classical forms with Moorish arabesques, geometric patterns, animal motifs and the typical Spanish scallop shell and coat of arms. Hand-knotted Alpujarras rugs and bedcovers were brilliant notes in simple white-walled rooms. Red, green and gold were the colors.

ENGLISH SIXTEENTH AND SEVENTEENTH CENTURIES

Tudor, Elizabethan (1500-1600) and Jacobean (1600-1660) influences were the lusty heart of Renaissance England. Living was rough and ready; England was flexing her muscles. This was the age of oak—a sturdy masculine, straight-line period, with honest construction, rough, bold carving, bright colors, strong textures. Forms were inspired by the Italian Renaissance but executed in unmistakably English terms with strong Gothic overtones.

There were few refinements in living in sixteenth-century England. There were long trestle tables and court cupboards with huge bulbous legs that looked as much like squarely built Henry VIII as furniture could look. Heavily carved chests stored the family property, wainscot chairs with carved-wood backs and seats and joint stools with turned legs supplied seating. Beds were heavily draped to keep out the cold damp air. Favorite carved motifs were linenfold panels and the Tudor rose, heart and tulip.

Jacobean furniture (1600-1660) was crude compared with what was to come. By the latter part of this period great lavishness was evident. Walnut was coming into use. Upholstered seats on chairs offered more comfort. Side chairs with open carved crescent-shaped slat backs, called Yorkshire and Derbyshire chairs, had a lighter look. Slant-top desks and small cabinets appeared. Tables were of lighter weight and had twisted rope legs; gateleg tables first came into use in Jacobean days and the average home began to develop more comfort.

Fabrics in the great houses included velvets, brocades, damasks, tapestries, flame-patterned needlework and crewel embroidery. Long fringes, tassels and elaborate galloons-encrusted hangings. The cold stone floors had here and there a bright Turkey or grospoint rug. Linen, linsey-woolsey, cotton and homespun were used by the common people.

Accessories included trophies of the chase, armor, portraits, pewter, brasses, candlesticks and maps.

AMERICAN SEVENTEENTH CENTURY

The Pilgrim period in America (1620-1720) is usually referred to as Early American and corresponds to the arrival of the earliest settlers in this country. Their furniture and the character of the houses they built corresponded to those they had back home.

Oak was the favorite wood, but before long, carpenters began to use pine and maple too, which were easier to work with. The most common article was the chest, a heavy wooden box with a lid which served as a trunk, a place for valuables, a seat, a table or even a bed. It was often the only piece of furniture in the house. Chairs were scarce at first. Stools, settees and benches, which could be easily put together, served. It is said that the first chair in America was brought over on the Mayflower by Governor Carver. Deacon Brewster had a similar one. These chairs had turned spindle backs and were the forerunners of the popular Windsor chair. Toward the end of the period, banister-back, slat or ladder-back and even walnut Flemish chairs were used. Gateleg and trestle tables were typical. Though this early furniture was much cruder than other rich handsome Renaissance furniture, it closely paralleled what ordinary people were using throughout Europe during the seventeenth century.

Houses were built around huge central chimneys, ceilings were low and the huge oak framing beams and rafters were exposed. The fireplace wall was paneled wood, but the other walls were logs filled in with wattle and daub for warmth. Windows were small. Interiors were unpainted. Andirons, hinges and candlesticks were made by the local smithy. The battle for survival was more important than elegance.

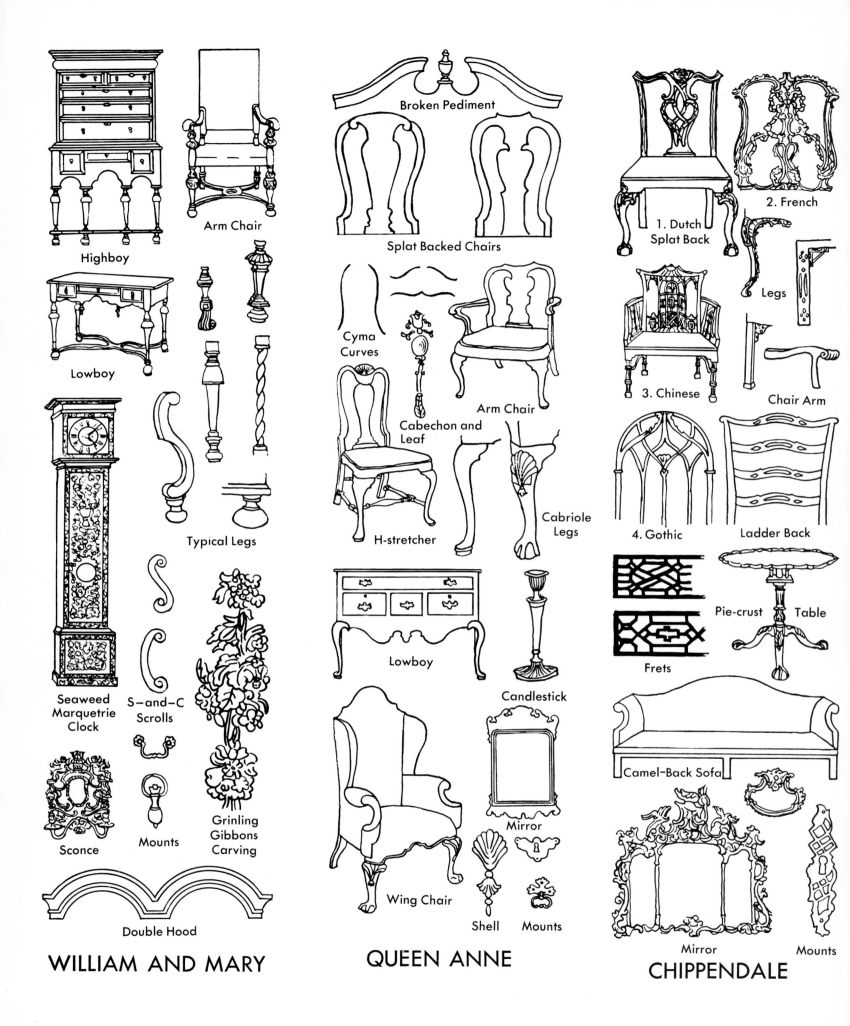

Highboy

Arm Chair

Lowboy

Typical Legs

Seaweed Marquetrie Clock

S—and—C Scrolls

Grinling Gibbons Carving

Sconce

Mounts

Double Hood

WILLIAM AND MARY

Broken Pediment

Splat Backed Chairs

Cyma Curves

Cabechon and Leaf

Arm Chair

H-stretcher

Cabriole Legs

Lowboy

Candlestick

Mirror

Wing Chair

Shell

Mounts

QUEEN ANNE

1. Dutch Splat Back

2. French

Legs

3. Chinese

Chair Arm

4. Gothic

Ladder Back

Pie-crust

Table

Frets

Camel-Back Sofa

Mirror

Mounts

CHIPPENDALE

BAROQUE FURNITURE IN ENGLAND: LATE SEVENTEENTH AND EARLY EIGHTEENTH CENTURIES

RESTORATION (1660-1702)

Charles II came to the English throne in 1660, and with the restoration of the monarchy a gay, new, prosperous life began. It was soon reflected in household furnishings. The new style was baroque and the influence predominantly Dutch, since the king had spent most of his exile in Holland. This period can be recognized by heavy, elaborate design, caning used on seats, and chairs' backs with bold, theatrical carving, and by the use of C and S scrolls, spiral turning, japanning and floral marquetry. The general lines were rectilinear.

The carving of Grinling Gibbons is associated with the last quarter of the seventeenth century. His rich, flowing designs in which birds, small animals, fruits, flowers and leaves were interwoven appeared in palaces, churches and college buildings. Gibbons was employed by Charles II and the architect Sir Christopher Wren.

The William and Mary period (1689-1702) continued the baroque style, but the furniture was lighter and the influence French. Curved lines began to take the place of straight. The highboy, lowboy and desk or writing table were introduced. There was great interest in keeping diaries and writing letters. Characteristic details are flat serpentine stretchers, geometric paneling on drawers, delicate, elaborate carving, scrolled legs and legs with trumpet turning. The bun foot, turnip foot and Spanish foot, which resembles a tassel, were used. Particularly characteristic of the William and Mary period is the fine seaweed or arabesque marquetry on cabinets and such pieces as the tall clock. The double-hooded cabinet is a distinctive piece, and the continued use of caning and the japanned chest on a gilt stand show the Oriental influence, which grew as England increased her trade with the Orient.

QUEEN ANNE (1702-1714)

This period was a continuance of the mood launched in England by William of Orange; now the straight lines melted into simple, feminine curves. The wood was richly finished walnut and the furniture is charming.

The key to the furniture contour is the cyma curve which forms the cabriole leg introduced into England at this time. The knees of the legs were either plain or carved with a shell, a lion's head, satyr masque, or cabochon and leaf. Pad or club feet or claw and ball feet are characteristic. Early in the period chairs had stretchers connecting the legs; later ones did not. The chairs had vase-shaped, unpierced splat backs, often topped with a carved shell. Chairs had broad comfortable seats. Settees were made with two, three and four chair backs.

Upholstered wing chairs with shaped aprons and rolling arms were also introduced at this time, bringing new comfort to the home.

Lowboys and highboys continued as important storage pieces, but the curved broken pediment replaced the straight and double bonnet tops.

Other newly introduced pieces of furniture at this time include tilt-top piecrust teatables, secretaries, bookcases, hanging shelves, writing desks, mirrors and oval dining tables.

Accessories multiplied. China collections became a mania, silver and glass ware were seen more frequently, oil paintings and books were acquired by the best families. Living was developing some refinements and a great deal more comfort.

THOMAS CHIPPENDALE (1718–1779)

Thomas Chippendale was the first of the great furniture designers of eighteenth-century England. His fame dates from his book, published in 1754. It was the first furniture catalogue, and sold for sixteen dollars a copy. This period is often referred to as the Golden Age of furniture design in England. It was Georgian, since it started with the advent of George I to the throne in 1714 and continued through four Georges to 1830. For the first time, furniture carried the name of the designer as well as the king in whose reign it was made.

Early Georgian furniture was a continuation of Queen Anne styling, in mahogany rather than walnut, but designs became progressively more ornate, with a profusion of pierced work and carving. There are four types of Chippendale chairs: (1) Queen Anne chairs with a pierced splat, more carving on the cabriole legs, always mahogany; (2) Louis XV chairs with rococo motifs, delicately turned, highly decorated cabriole legs, scroll feet and ribbon carved, looped and festooned backs; (3) Chinese Chippendale chairs with straight legs often decorated with fretwork, square backs or a top rail with ears or a pagoda-like lift to the ends and fretwork back splats or ladders. The legs often had brackets linking the legs and seat; (4) Gothic Chippendale, also with straight lines, but the back splat featuring Gothic arches and tracery.

Cabinets and commodes were made in the French style with bombé fronts. Side tables and card tables generally had cabriole legs with claw and ball feet. There were piecrust, tilt-top, galleried and tripod-legged tables. Upholstered chairs, wing chairs and scroll-topped sofas and loveseats were popular. Dining-room furniture became more refined and more flexible.

Accessories included exquisite porcelains, silver and lacquer. Portrait painting reached its zenith and is as characteristic of this period as mahogany.

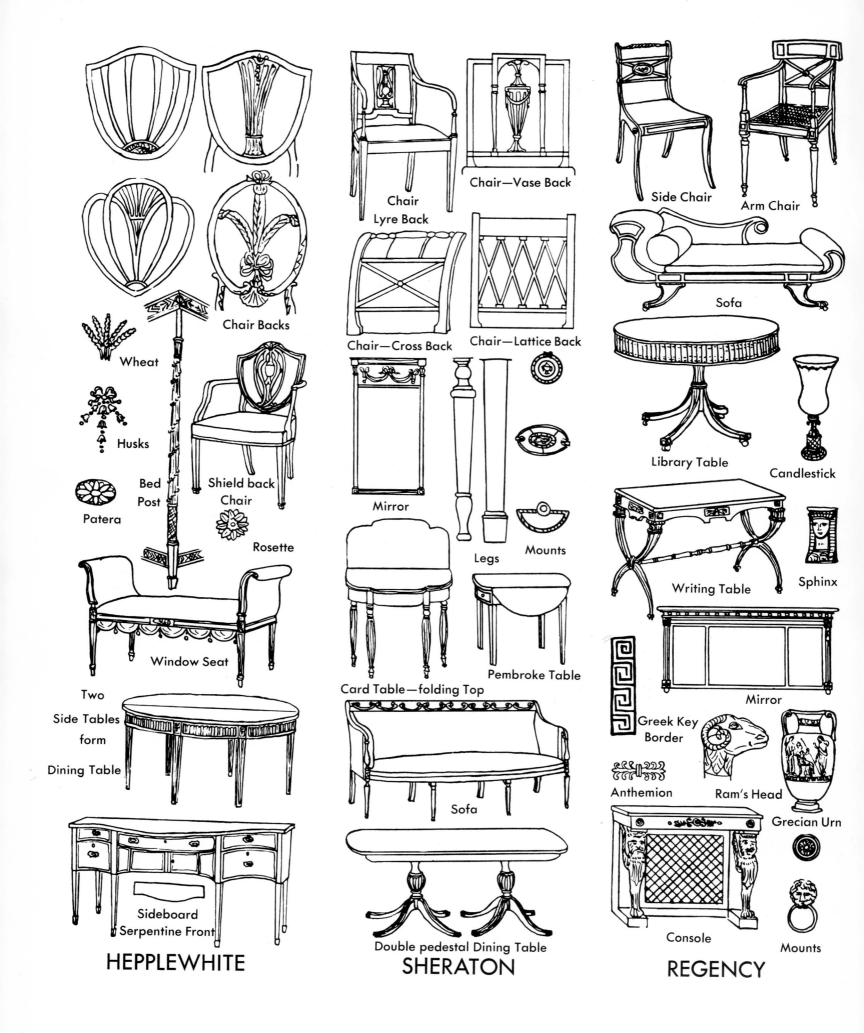

Chair—Vase Back

Chair
Lyre Back

Chair Backs

Wheat

Husks

Bed
Post

Shield back
Chair

Patera

Rosette

Window Seat

Two
Side Tables
form
Dining Table

Sideboard
Serpentine Front

Chair—Cross Back

Chair—Lattice Back

Mirror

Legs

Mounts

Card Table—folding Top

Pembroke Table

Sofa

Double pedestal Dining Table

Side Chair

Arm Chair

Sofa

Library Table

Candlestick

Writing Table

Sphinx

Mirror

Greek Key
Border

Anthemion

Ram's Head

Grecian Urn

Console

Mounts

HEPPLEWHITE

SHERATON

REGENCY

GEORGE HEPPLEWHITE (1715–1786)

The brothers Robert and James Adam were the architects who led the return to classicism. They designed not only great houses but the furnishings as well, and they employed the finest craftsmen, including Chippendale, to carry out their furniture designs. George Hepplewhite was the first furniture designer to popularize their classic style. He used a combination of curved and straight lines, graceful and dignified in manner, which conveyed a more formal feeling than the Chippendale styles. His designs formed a transition between Chippendale and Sheraton, who passionately believed in the straight line. Hepplewhite's wife, Alice, published a book of his designs posthumously in 1788.

The principal furniture wood was still mahogany, but satinwood was introduced for more elaborate pieces and beechwood was painted or gilded.

The typical Hepplewhite chair back had a shield or oval frame with converging bars and a pierced center splat, interlacing hearts or Prince of Wales feathers. Legs were square, tapering toward a spade foot. Seats were generally square and comfortable.

Dining-room furniture was highly developed at this time. There were elaborate buffets, serving tables and china cupboards. Card tables had bowed serpentine fronts. Bedposts were slender, tapering and fluted, and were topped with a carved tester. Chests of drawers had bow or serpentine fronts. There were also secretaries, breakfront desks, and dressing tables.

Motifs used on fabrics, wallpaper and carving were classic. They included patera, rosettes, acanthus leaves and classic architectural details, also pendant husks, floral swags, rosettes and ribbons.

Fabrics were smooth, handsome and elegant satins, moires, velvets and brocades. Unpatterned fabrics, stripes and widely spaced medallions were used for formal rooms, chintz for informal rooms.

SHERATON (1751–1806)

Strong but delicate straight lines characterize Sheraton designs which were strongly influenced by the classic Louis XVI style and the work of the Adam brothers. His furniture lacks the vigor and strength of Chippendale's early work and is more feminine.

Sheraton came to London in 1790 and soon published a book of his furniture designs. He became the rage. He recommended mahogany for dining room, bedroom and library furniture, and rosewood, satinwood and gilded or painted furniture for the drawing room. Inlay was his favorite form of decoration.

His chairs were smaller in scale than Chippendale's, have rectangular backs with a center panel in the form of a vase or a lyre. The backs were sometimes carved, hand painted or inlaid with rare woods or even Wedgwood medallions. Seats were upholstered or caned. Armchairs had down-curving arms and baluster supports. The legs were more often round and reeded or fluted than square. No stretchers were used.

He designed drum tables with leather tops, round dining tables, tier tables and small side tables. For all of these he favored concave tripod pedestals like the dining table shown. In fact, most late English eighteenth-century and early nineteenth-century furniture which is rectangular in form, delicate in construction, uncarved, highly finished and with narrow satinwood inlays is almost certainly of Sheraton derivation.

Motifs included the usual classical symbols: urns, lyres, stars, honeysuckle, laurel wreaths and crossed diagonal banding.

ENGLISH REGENCY (1780–1830)

As a political fact English Regency applies to the late Georgian Period (1810-1820), when George IV ruled as regent in place of ailing George III; but as a style, it began in the late eighteenth century, when George IV was the popular Prince of Wales, and it lasted through his short ten-year reign, ending with his death in 1830. In character and time, American Federal (Duncan Phyfe) and French Empire and Directoire are kin. This was the period when the White House was built and furnished.

Thomas Hope, a Scotsman, was the chief designer in this style. His inspiration came from his early travels and sketches made in Greece and Rome. He adapted designs quite literally from ancient coins, sculpture, vases and cameos to create a strong neoclassic character. Other designers were Holland and Tatham.

English Regency furniture is slender but with flat planes. The finish is glossy with gilding, carving, and metalwork. Other characteristic details include brass galleries on tables, grillwork on cupboard doors, casters on legs, medallion and lion-head mounts and pulls, sphinx bas reliefs, Greek key borders, anthemion or honeysuckle friezes, swans, dolphins and dainty hoofs, also flaring pedestal table bases.

Regency chairs are light and graceful in appearance, with straight or concave backs and carved top rail, and sometimes have cane seats and back panels. Legs are either straight or with a graceful flare, and have no braces or stretchers. The legs are often finished with collar banding, and occasionally have dainty brass animal hoofs. The upholstery is flat, without springs.

Mahogany, satinwood and rosewood are the favored woods. There is some painted furniture. The bamboo motif is particularly popular for chairs and chest frames.

Fabrics: Velvets, silks, and brocades were used with fringe and galloon. Popular colors were dark red, Chinese pink, grass green, white and gold. Walls were painted in dark rich colors.

Accessories: Mirrors were widely used. Tall pier glasses were mounted between windows and gilded —there were also three-part horizontal chimney mirrors. Mirrors called tabernacle glasses, with molded cornice, ball beading and reeded corner columns were also popular. Crystal chandeliers, bronze hanging lamps, glass-shaded candles and mantel clocks may be seen in pictures of the period. Elegance was the outstanding quality.

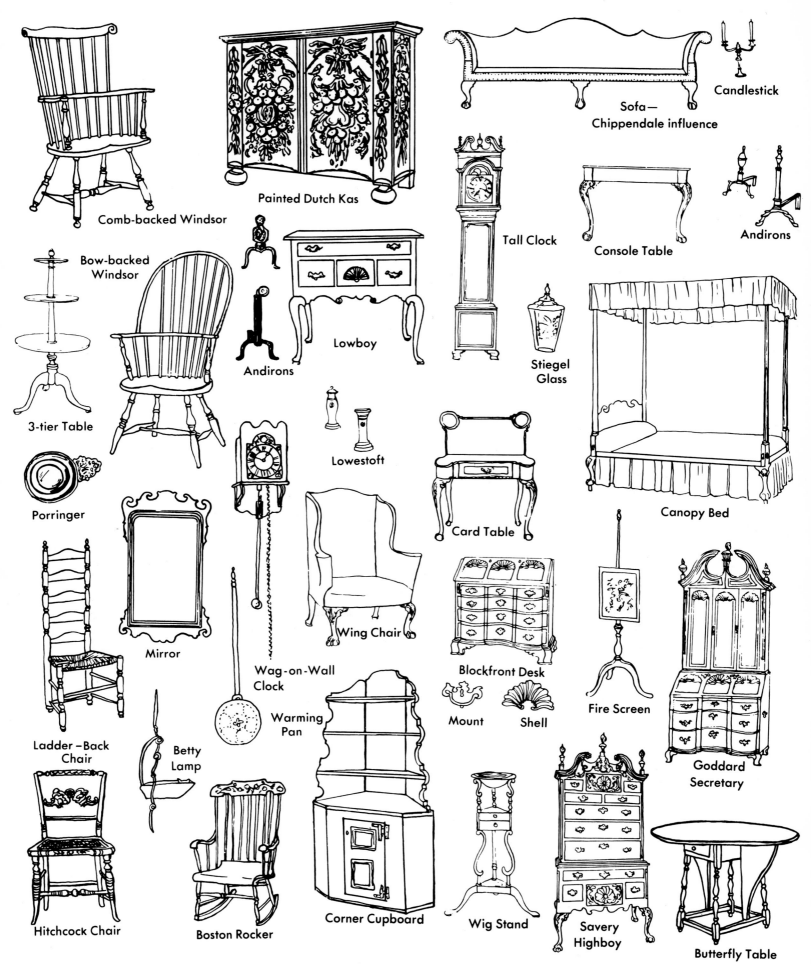

Comb-backed Windsor

Painted Dutch Kas

Sofa—
Chippendale influence

Candlestick

Bow-backed
Windsor

Andirons

Lowboy

Tall Clock

Console Table

Andirons

3-tier Table

Porringer

Lowestoft

Stiegel
Glass

Canopy Bed

Card Table

Mirror

Wag-on-Wall
Clock

Wing Chair

Blockfront Desk

Fire Screen

Goddard
Secretary

Ladder–Back
Chair

Betty
Lamp

Warming
Pan

Mount

Shell

Hitchcock Chair

Boston Rocker

Corner Cupboard

Wig Stand

Savery
Highboy

Butterfly Table

COLONIAL 18th Century English Inspiration

AMERICAN FARMHOUSE (1776–1830)

It took months for a sailing ship to make a round trip from London to Boston and other American ports. Only the wealthy could indulge in extravagant foreign imports. Farmers, villagers and even the majority of the townspeople were on a do-it-yourself basis. They either made the furniture themselves or had a handyman do it. The resulting pieces are casual and gay, and show the influence of the current fashion as well as the national heritage of the maker.

Woods used were those at hand: maple, pine, cherry, ash, hickory, chestnut, elm. Often several woods were used in one piece and there was no such thing as a roomful of furniture all of one wood. Finishes were both natural and painted. Stencil details were popular.

Typical pieces include: Windsor and ladderback chairs, cobbler's benches, washstands, simple corner cupboards, low and high fourposter beds, blanket chests, settles, lowboys and highboys.

From 1826 to 1843 Lambert Hitchcock operated his famous chair factory. He made rush-seated chairs with turned legs and a curving back. The top rail was painted, stenciled or decorated with decalcomanias. These chairs were copied by other New England factories. They are again being made in the same factory today.

The women made fabrics from home-grown cotton and wool. Because cloth was hard won, every scrap was saved. Rags were converted into rugs and patchwork quilts. Girls were taught needlework almost in their cradles. There was a saying at the time that if a girl had not completed her first sampler by the time she was seven or eight she was destined to be an old maid.

There were brass, pewter, and wrought-iron candlesticks, lanterns and fireplace tools. There was enough glass and the Bennington potteries in Vermont were making crude brown bowls and plates. Later the Ohio factories made white salt-glaze dinnerware.

Crude though it is, the touch of the hand and the honesty of the work make furniture and accessories of this time collector's items.

AMERICAN COLONIAL FURNITURE (1720–1776)

In Virginia, Philadelphia, Baltimore, New York, Newport and Boston, furniture styles were inspired by what was being done in London. Communication was slow so that there was a lag of years in actual duplication of fashions, but after each ship's arrival reports on what was going on in England were almost as important to women as the cargo.

Much of the fine mahogany and walnut furniture in fine town houses in the North and the plantation houses of the South was ordered and delivered by sailing vessels from the mother country. However,

there were capable cabinetmakers working in this country. Some of them followed, line for line, an imported Queen Anne chair, Chippendale chair or a design taken from Chippendale's book. Some added their own flourishes and variations and developed such characteristic styles in carving and detail that even without labels and account books the area in which they were made can be identified.

The furniture of colonial America was Georgian and gracious in character. It had simplicity with distinction and formality without coldness. Visit the great houses of this period and it is easy to glimpse the comfortable and pleasant living possible in eighteenth-century colonial America. Mount Vernon, Colonial Williamsburg, and many of the rooms recreated at Winterthur Museum tell the story.

These were truly great houses with gracious entrance halls opening into large drawing rooms and handsome dining rooms. Against cool ivory, pale-blue or green walls, handsome Queen Anne and Chippendale chairs reminded women of home. Portraits and beautiful gilt-framed mirrors hung above the fireplace or buffet. Rich, fringe-trimmed damask festooned the windows and silver candelabra and crystal chandeliers glittered in the candlelight.

Mahogany was the principal wood. It is even possible that it was the first wood used for furniture in this country since it comes from the West Indies. However, other woods easier for the local cabinetmaker to come by give added interest to homemade pieces. These woods include butternut, cherry, beech and black walnut.

Among wanted furniture at this time were lowboys and highboys, corner cupboards, handsome grandfather clocks, desks, chests and secretaries, game tables, upholstered stools, drop-leaf and tip-top tea-tables; high fourposter beds with flat or arched tester tops hung with copper-plate-printed English linen or French resist-dyed linen. There were also many side chairs, knife boxes and mirrors.

Accessories were brought in by captains of sailing vessels. There were all sorts of Oriental novelties in lacquer, porcelain, bronze and brass. There were tea boxes and carved chests of exotic woods, as well as tea and table services from England.

Along with the imported accessories there was a sprinkling of American-made glass. Wisterberg made glass in New Jersey, Baron Stiegel had a glass factory in Manheim, Pennsylvania. This was blown glass of pale blue, deep blue, amber, amethyst and wine. Reproductions are available today.

Motifs or designs used in carving and other ornamentation include flame finials, shells, broken pediments, Chinese fretwork, claw and ball feet, beading, urns, and birds. Elaborate brasses were used for ornamentation.

On fabrics, scenic and damask-type patterns were used, as well as all-over florals. Needlework was popular, including cross stitch, grospoint, petitpoint, crewel work and typical seventeenth-century flame-stitch tapestry.

Pillar and Scroll Clock

Settee—Hepplewhite influence

Secretary

Sheraton Chair (Martha Washington)

Girandole Mirror

Astral Lamp

Swag

Rosette

Lyre Back Chair

Chair Back

Reeding

Card Table

Acanthus

Tabernacle Mirror

Empire Chair

Gilt Mirror

Empire Chair

Sofa—Sheraton influence

Pedestal Table

Sleigh Bed

Lyre Sofa

Banjo Clock

Pineapple Bed Post

Sofa

Lyre Detail

Bed Post

Drop Leaf Table

Laurel

Bench

FEDERAL AND AMERICAN EMPIRE

DUNCAN PHYFE

AMERICAN FEDERAL PERIOD
(1780-1810)

Politically the Federal period developed after the American Revolution. In England it spans the work of Hepplewhite (1790-1810), Sheraton (1800-1810) and the Regency (1800-1820). From France came the classical influence of the Louis XVI style (1760-1790), Directoire (1790-1804), Empire (1804-1815) and Restoration (1820-1840).

The American Revolution halted house construction, which did not get under way again until the beginning of the nineteenth century. Then a group of architects began to develop an "American look." These men were Samuel McIntire, John McComb, Thomas Jefferson, Charles Bulfinch, Benjamin Latrobe, and James Haban.

This group of architects was heavily influenced by classic forms as these filtered through from English and French builders. Proportions were lighter, more delicate and refined. Wood-paneled walls appeared less frequently. Classic details—fluted columns, dental molding, pediments and laurel wreaths—became the fashion. However, the Chinese Chippendale influence persisted here long after it had been dropped in England.

The popular furniture woods were mahogany, satinwood, cherry, rosewood, maple, apple and pear. Fine veneering and inlay work gave furniture a light, elegant appearance. Secretaries, desks, dressing tables and china cabinets had straight lines, and delicate scroll pediments topped bookcases. Cabinets often had an eagle finial on top. There were sewing tables, Pembroke tables with drop leaves, candlestands and pedestal tables with narrow, carved, flaring legs. The tambour desk replaced the secretary. Martha Washington open armchairs, adapted from a Sheraton model, were seen everywhere. So-called "fancy" chairs with stenciled splat and rail backs, no stretchers and cane or rush seats became popular; they are still being made today, with scarcely any change.

The spread eagle, stars and stripes, and color schemes of red, white and blue or gold and white were popular on wallpaper and fabrics. Patterned surfaces were restrained.

Because communications had improved by this time between the bigger cities, variations in style between different sections of the country became less marked.

AMERICAN EMPIRE
(1810–1840)

By 1810 there was a subtle change in furniture. It became more massive, with large undecorated veneered surfaces combined with bold carving. The neat straight-backed Sheraton sofa and Hepplewhite chair-back sofa and settee were replaced with heavily carved pieces with curule legs, scroll arms and exposed wood frame. The sleigh bed replaced the four-poster.

All the neoclassic motifs used by Hepplewhite and Sheraton were duplicated: fluting, reeding, acanthus leaves, honeysuckle, pendants and classic borders. American patriotic emblems were blended with the classic forms on fabrics, china and wallpaper.

Silk fabrics such as damask, velvet and taffetas were imported. Haircloth and leathers were also used, as well as linens, printed cottons and toiles de Jouy. Curtains of fine mull or lawn, embroidered, drawn or hemstitched, were introduced.

Gilt-framed mirrors became increasingly popular. There were rectangular shapes with a painted panel of glass at the top, and large and small convex or bull's-eye mirrors with and without candle brackets. Every fireplace had pierced fenders and a fire screen. There were all types of clocks made by the great New England clockmakers. There were paintings. Portraits were popular as well as miniatures and framed silhouettes, steel engravings and mezzotints. Pottery and china included American-made wares and English, French and Chinese imports. Silver candelabra and good glassware could be seen in all the fine houses.

DUNCAN PHYFE (1768-1854)

The best known of the fine American furniture designers and cabinetmakers was a Scotsman, Duncan Phyfe. He came to this country in 1784, opened his business in New York City in 1792 and did not retire until 1847. His works span the classical styles of Hepplewhite and Sheraton to Empire and early Victorian. He is best known for his classical period, which ended about 1830.

He used mahogany almost exclusively. His work has a delicacy of line with strong Sheraton overtones. His most important pieces were his cloverleaf tables with vase pedestals and brass paw feet, which were made in all sizes from small parlor tables to long banquet sizes. His chairs were much admired. They had in-curving saber legs ending in carved or brass-tipped dog feet. Often the carving was carried up the front legs. The Grecian-curved backs had a crossbar with a rosette or a carved lyre splat.

Armchairs, window benches, sofas and footstools followed the same style. Sofas were of two types: his early models had a straight wood top rail carved with swags or laurel leaves and fluted baluster legs; his later sofas followed an Empire line and had Greek curule or cornucopia legs. The arms were often wood with lyre splats, to match the chair backs. Others had upholstered scroll arms.

Motifs most commonly used by Duncan Phyfe were lyres, acanthus leaves, laurel, drapery swag, rosettes, wheat, dog feet, trumpets, reeding and fluting. The Phyfe style was, and still is, widely copied—so much so that accurate identification of his work is almost impossible. Few of his pieces were labeled. Upholstery fabrics used at the time include silk, damask, velvet, brocade, chintz and horsehair.

LOUIS XIV

Early Chair
Boulle Work
Panel
Transitional Chair
Console Table
Shell
Bench
Double L in Oval
Rayed Sun
Bed

LOUIS XV

Detail
Bergère
Small Table
Shell
Panel
Side Chair
Canapé
Commode with Marble Top
Doe's Foot
Andiron
Foot Stool
Console
Wall Sconce

LOUIS XVI

Symmetrical Mounts
Bergère
Panel
Side Chair
Vase Motif
Armchair
Couch
Fluting
Farm Tool Motif
Gallery-top Table
Rosette
Bed
Chair Leg

LOUIS XIV, BAROQUE (1661-1715)

Through the reign of Louis XIII, French court furniture followed closely the rectilinear outlines of the Italian Renaissance. Flemish, Spanish and German influences were also felt. The advent of Louis XIV saw the development of the first French style.

The Louis XIV period was the most sumptuous and impressive the world has ever seen. The king was the impetus behind its development. He was a small man, who had been firmly restrained as a child by severe tutors. When he finally became king and master, the purse strings were relaxed, and nothing that would reflect glory and magnificence on the king or his household was overlooked. He was variously known as the Sun King (Le Roi Soleil) and Le Grand Monarque.

This style was showy, pompous and masculine, and straight lines dominated the structure. It gave birth to the sculptural baroque feeling but even the deepest carving and most inflated moldings were always symmetrical. Architects were in control, and they designed walls, paneling, chimney pieces, ceilings, doors and furniture. The natural wood paneling common during the reign of Louis XIII gave way to elegant painted paneling picked out with gold.

The reign of Louis XIV covered seventy-two years. Early furniture adhered to straight lines, but gradually smooth curves developed, including the first cabriole legs. Crossed stretchers were used on tables and chairs. There were long and short rectangular tables, consoles, square and octagonal tables—but no dining tables. Tables were gilded and decorated with boulle work (an inlay of tortoise shell and metal), marquetry, marble tops and heavy gilded bronze mounts.

Sofas (canapes) had the same general contour as chairs and had upholstered or cane backs. Beds were upholstered and curtained in silks.

The reign of Louis XIV saw the founding of the Gobelin tapestry works at Beauvais and the Aubusson rug factory. Versailles was expanded and converted from a hunting lodge to a palace during this period.

REGENCE AND LOUIS XV, ROCOCO (1715-1774)

When Louis XIV died, Louis XV, his great-grandson, was only five years old and his uncle, Philippe d'Orléans, headed the regency. There was an immediate relaxation of pomp and by the time Louis XV and his coterie of followers were in control, a gay, extravagant, feminine era was already launched.

The most obvious feminine influences were the smaller proportions, gayer colors and the more intricate detail. Even rooms were reduced in size. There were endless varieties of intimate parlors which called for many specialized pieces of small-scaled furniture.

Furniture was graceful and curving. Legs were elongated S curves with slender scroll feet. There was carving at the center of the back frame, on the rail and at the knees of chair and sofa legs.

There were card tables, consoles, desks, ladies' work tables and dressing tables, cupboards, sideboards, wardrobes, four-poster beds with curtains and alcove beds.

Furniture was painted, gilded, lacquered, veneered and inlaid with wood and metal or covered with marquetry.

The word "rococo" means "rock and shell." These were important motifs used in decoration along with C and S curves, naturalistic flowers and leaves, cartouches and palm leaves. The Chinese influence was rampant. Filtered through the imagination of French draftsmen it became a gay, whimsical form of decoration known as chinoiserie, and was quite different from authentic Chinese designs. It strongly influenced English designers, particularly Chippendale.

Fabrics: Gobelin tapestries were used for upholstery, featuring pastoral scenes, ribbons and flowers. Velvets, damasks and brocades, taffetas, fine stripes and moiré were available in unlimited quantities. For rugs there was a choice of Aubussons, Savonneries and Orientals.

Accessories were unlimited and included gilt and bronze appliqués (candle sconces), cartel clocks (for walls), overmantels (looking glasses with pictures above the mirror glass, the whole set into the paneling above the mantel), Chinese vases and objects of art. There were also bronze and marble busts by Houdon, Sèvres porcelain, paintings by Watteau, Boucher and Fragonard. The names of Madame de Pompadour and Madame Du Barry are frequently linked with design forms of this period.

LOUIS XVI, NEOCLASSIC (1774-1789)

The reign of Louis XVI brought a total change, a reaction against the excesses of Louis XV. The straight line and classic influence were reinstated.

Hunting was the king's hobby; he cared nothing for the pomp and circumstance of court life. All that he turned over to his young Queen, Marie Antoinette. The resulting style is very much more hers than the King's. She carried over from the previous reign the gay colors and informal motifs—the bow knots, shepherd's crooks, garden tools and garlands seen in plasterwork—but banished the cupids, doves and overindulgent curves and asymmetric balance.

Furniture in the reign of Louis XVI was small in scale and backs were straight but softly rounded. Legs were fluted columns topped with a square block ornamented with a rosette. Side chairs sometimes had lyre panel backs. Commodes were rectangular, with small fluted legs and simple marquetry and metal mounts. There were endless occasional pieces, secretaries, poudreuses, screens and footstools. Beds had upholstered panel ends.

Design motifs used on fabrics and in all of the decorative arts included garlands, festoons, swags, wreaths, Pompeian arabesques, Greek frets, vases, honeysuckle, guilloches and scenes of pastoral life. Lacquer, Sèvres porcelain plaques, ormolu mounts, paintings, carving and some marquetry were used.

Fabrics and accessories changed little except to acquire more classic forms. There were Dresden china, Chinese, Indian and Persian objects of art, ancient bronzes and Wedgwood plaques. In addition to Aubusson and Gobelin tapestries, toile de Jouy and silks and tooled leather were used.

Bergère

Chair Back

Day Bed

Swag

Small Table

Lyre-back Arm Chair

Tole Flower Holder

Side Chair

Small Table

Military Motifs

Strawseated Chair

Overdoor Panel

Arm Chair

Fasces

Swan

Side Chair

Bookcase

Couch

Armoire

Rouen Plate

Toile De Jouy

Gilt Mirror

Decorated Door Panel

Circular & Curvle Chair Backs

Empire Details

Plaid

Commode

Greek Border

Console Table

Egyptian   Motif

Escritoire

Bed

Table

Sideboard-Dresser

DIRECTOIRE AND EMPIRE

FRENCH PROVINCIAL

FRENCH DIRECTOIRE (1795-1804)

FRENCH EMPIRE (1805-1815)

In Europe, England and even America, neoclassic influence was a reaction against the excesses which had developed. Directoire furniture is transitional. It has the delicacy of Louis XVI forms, but a greater simplicity. Life in France had suddenly become a deadly business with heads being guillotined day after day. It was no time for playful design, and all suggestions of court life were eliminated.

When Napoleon moved into the picture, he had to have his own style, like the kings before him. The classic artist David and the architects Percier and Fontaine turned the current neoclassic Directoire style into a heavy, masculine and military one. Walls were painted or hung with fabric or wallpaper. Rooms were draped like military tents. Crossed spears were used as decoration. Napoleon's own symbol—a capital N with a laurel wreath or bumblebees for Bonaparte—was used to decorate fabrics, wallpaper and porcelain.

Directoire furniture was mahogany or cherry, often painted a soft gray. Mahogany, ebony and rosewood were the woods of the Empire. Large plain surfaces were given a mirrorlike finish and trimmed with metal mounts, feet and crestings. The forms were large, heavy and rectangular, although some chairs had graceful outward-curved backs and arm supports of swans, lions or sphinx. Animal legs were used with brass claw feet.

Typical sofas had rolled straight backs and arms. Gondola and sleigh beds were used. Tables were round or rectangular and had heavy square legs, often only three, with claw feet. Tall mirrors, sometimes called psyches, were used in bedrooms.

Fabrics of velvet, satin and silk appeared in draperies with lambrequins and upholstery. Muslin curtains were embroidered with stars, medallions, wreaths, bees or Ns. Colors were strong and contrasting—wine red, emerald green, purple, gray, yellow, blue and brown. Marble and porphyry were imitated. Aubusson and Savonnerie rugs were still used.

Accessories included mahogany-framed looking glasses with supporting columns and metal mounts, candelabra, cornucopias, tripod stands, urns, clocks, porcelain, bronze and toiles.

FRENCH PROVINCIAL FURNITURE
SEVENTEENTH AND EIGHTEENTH CENTURIES

French provincial furniture refers to all furniture made in the provinces in any period. Sophisticated Paris styles served as models; but translated by country cabinetmakers country furniture has charm and simplicity of design and material.

There is great variation in the design because provincial furniture, as we know it, spanned a century and a half. There was a vast difference in the capability of the carpenters and the requirements of different regions.

Early provincial furniture, like early American furniture, was Renaissance in character. Later, differences developed. In Lorraine, Gascony and Burgundy heavy Louis XIII styles were popular. In Normany and Limousin the style of Louis XVI was the chief inspiration.

In Provence, Louis XIV and Louis XV styles were adapted and are chiefly responsible for the popularity of provincial furniture today.

Climate, geographic areas and customs also influenced styles. In northern provinces, which were cold and damp, beds were built into kitchen alcoves and open-shelved dressers displayed pewter, brass and pottery; in the dusty south, cupboards had closed wooden doors.

Furniture made in the provinces near the Pyrenees showed a Spanish influence; in the east, Flemish and German forms were borrowed. In Provence along the Riviera there were Italian touches. Brittany and Normandy probably represent the richest and most undiluted French taste.

It is almost impossible to date French provincial furniture because no one knows how long it took for a style to seep into the provinces and how long it was made after the style was dropped in the big cities.

French provincial furniture is sturdy and naïve, with a certain timeless quality. Cabinetmakers used local woods—walnut, oak, chestnut, ash, poplar and fruitwoods. There was no metal appliqué, little carving, veneering, or marquetry, but it is nevertheless largely in the ornamentation that provincial furniture can be placed geographically. No nails or screws were used. All furniture was doweled and joints were dovetailed.

Natural finishes were popular. However, painted finishes were used, too. Small mirrors with a top crest of a vase of flowers or fruit were often gilded. Grandfather clocks were a feature often introduced right in the center of a cupboard.

Characteristic pieces include armoires, tables, chairs, curtained poster beds, buffets, dressers with shelves above, cupboards and straw-seated ladderbacked chairs which are a refined relative of those still made in the mountains of North Carolina. There were open-arm upholstered chairs with padded arm rests.

Fabrics included red and blue checks, toile de Jouy, homespuns, printed cottons and linens, and in wealthier homes, damasks, velvets and brocades. It was easier to buy fabrics by the bolt, so often one fabric was used for upholstery, draperies and even walls. Tapestries decorated the walls of the wealthy, while the less affluent used painted canvas or flock paper.

Accessories were used in abundance. Pewter, copper pots and jugs glinted from tables and cupboards. Colorful pottery from Rouen ornamented shelves and hung on walls. There were hanging shelves, salt and bread boxes, birdcages and every possible kind of container for utilitarian and decorative purposes.

Floors were tiled or of polished oak, with flower-spattered needlework rugs.

EPILOGUE

Now YOU HAVE reviewed the whole—the objects, the materials, the arts, the planning and the historic background that go into designing a room. You have experienced tempting possibilities and extravagances. You have struggled with decisions. Now the room is completed—the dreaming, the planning, the hours of shopping are over, and the installation is finished. You have worried through the painting, the paperhanging, you have watched the curtains, draperies and carpeting being installed. You have waited days, weeks, even months, for the furniture to come. You have at last found the right lamps and have worked out a pleasing arrangement of accessories and pictures. The room is finished, except for one thing. Like the sculptor Pygmalion, who with the help of Venus breathed life into his marble creation, you too must believe in and breathe life into your room, into what you have done.

All the doubts and occasional despair must be swept aside. The only way out of the labyrinth of doubts—the planning, the shopping, the decisions, the might-have-beens and the expense—is to discover your own social self. Like Persephone, you have to re-emerge into the light after four or more months underground and bask in the pleasure of the family and the joy of having friends near.

A room is not something just to be looked at like a model room in a store or a picture in a magazine. To be a success, it has to be used completely, happily, constantly and unstintingly. Its offer of sociability, charm, privacy and comfort must be shared with family and friends if it is to be the room you dreamed of. A room that is only to be looked at is not a success; it is a bitter mistake.

So, have an Open House; have a room-christening; invite the neighbors in; entertain the club; let the children have a party. Don't hold back the family by your fears of this getting hurt or that broken. If you have planned well, the room will hold its own.

Give Loving Care

HOWEVER, THINGS do get soiled, liquids are spilled, and dust does accumulate. A pleasant home is a responsibility. Care is one of the inescapable burdens of civilization. Become slack, and something subtle and important goes out of your life. A sense of quality and standards is worth acquiring and preserving.

There was a time when a woman's dress, her neatness and her carriage were a gauge of her character. Somewhere young people have mislaid their sense of vanity. They slouch around in flats, sweaters and soiled jeans. Women go to the market with hair in curlers, their faces made up with eye shadow and mascara as though they were going to a formal ball. Clothes and make-up, like one's carriage, reveal an attitude of mind. This same sloppiness is beginning to affect housekeeping standards. A newly decorated room can be an inspiration because you are proud of it, because it works. The fam-

298

ily, without being told, will cooperate in keeping it nice, and you will find that a handsome room is easier to keep, easier to clean, than a drab and ugly one.

Be a Critic-at-Large

As an initiate in the realm of home furnishings, you have other responsibilities. You are one of the caretakers of culture in this country. You have a responsibility to the arts which should be considered with every purchase you make—the house you buy, the stores you trade with. If bad taste or carelessness in window displays, in merchandise, in model rooms is condoned, gradually vulgarity pervades an area. If a community's taste is exacting, if badly designed houses are shunned, if women let builders know when the model houses they show and their furnishings are gross and ugly, inevitably a higher level of design will brighten your community.

In the art world it is important to react—to applaud the good, to condemn the bad. In the home-furnishings field we have few critics, and women don't seem to realize the power they have. That power has a cash price tag of billions of dollars annually. If there are applause and acceptance only for good design and fine quality, and boos and stony resistance for badly designed products, then retail merchants and manufacturers will quickly get the message. The blind acceptance, the helpless attitude women appear to have today when they go shopping is neither sound nor healthy, and it is bitterly discouraging to those fighting to raise the design level of the marketplace.

Why, for instance, are the French generally credited with having the world's finest cuisine? The thoughtless answer is, "Because they have the best cooks." But that is only a part of the story. The French cook is willing to take time, to take hours to prepare a meal, and the diner is willing to devote himself completely to its appreciation. The French diner will not put up with sloppy service or accept anything that is put before him. He will not be hurried in ordering, he discusses each dish on the menu with the maitre d' before making his choice. If he is not happy with what is served, he is a most insistent and articulate complainer and will repeatedly send a dish back to the kitchen for correction. A Frenchman is, in short, a cook's most responsive audience and best critic.

Translate this same insistence on quality and design into the architectural and home-furnishings fields, and there would be a renaissance of design in this country. What we need are more hisses, boos and catcalls at merchandise and houses that are beneath our standards. It would delight me to see the women of a town picket some of the ugly development houses which are growing up like toadstools on the fringes of our cities. The design details and plans are so poor that they hurt, and almost no amount of camouflaging inside or out can save them from being scars on the taste of people who live in them.

What we need is more honest criticism, more discrimination, more self-confidence in our taste—self-confidence based on experience, knowledge and enthusiasm for real achievement; in short, a larger aesthetic elite. Only a knowledgeable audience inspires the best.

McCall's is indebted to the following photographers for permission to use the photographs of interiors as listed below:

Haanel Cassidy—Page 57
George de Gennaro—Page 153, page 218 (upper)
Otto Fenn—Pages 115, 156, 255, 258, 280
Richard Fish—Page 218 (lower)
Don Hulin, Alderman Studios, Inc.—Pages 13, 35, 63, 113, 119, 121, 124, 171, 183
Norman Karlson—Pages 222, 227, 228
Vincent Lisanti—Pages 131, 173
Tosh Matsumoto—Page 87
Richard P. Mellmann—Page 215
Pagano—Page 219
Julius Shulman—Page 233 (upper)
Ernest M. Silva—Pages 59, 70, 88, 137 (left), 197

Melvin Sokolsky—Pages 142, 163
John Stanton, Alderman Studios—Page 44
Hans Van Nes—Frontispiece, 3, 9, 10, 15, 21, 24, 27, 28, 32, 39, 41, 47, 48, 50, 55, 57, 64, 67, 71, 73, 75, 78, 83, 84, 91, 93, 95, 99, 101, 103, 106, 116, 123, 126, 128, 137 (right), 139, 141, 145, 158, 161, 165, 167, 175, 177, 178, 181, 184, 189, 191, 196, 200, 203, 208, 210, 211, 213, 231, 236, 238, 239, 240, 243, 244, 247, 251, 253, 261, 263, 267, 269, 270, 273, 278
Nowell Ward—Pages 5, 18, 37, 69, 149, 187, 192, 195, 199, 206

We wish to further acknowledge the fine cooperation of the following stores and manufacturers for keeping us informed about products and for supplying us with merchandise for photography:

Building Materials: American-Standard, Crane, Cyanamid, Eljer, Formica, Marble Institute of America, Morgan Doors and Woodwork, National Oak Flooring Manufacturers' Association, Ponderosa Pine Woodwork, Schlage Hardware.
Dinnerware: Castleton, Franciscan, Ginori, Jackson, Lenox, Melmac, Rosenthal, Spode, Syracuse, Taylor Smith & Taylor.
Entertainment Centers: General Electric, Magnavox, Westinghouse, Zenith.
Fabrics: Avondale, Belgian Linen Association, Bloomcraft, Brunschwig & Fils, Burlington, Cohama, Cone, Conso Products, Continental Felt Company, Dan Cooper, A. L. Diament, Eaglesham Prints, Everfast, Greeff, S. M. Hexter, Irish Linen Guild, Jofa, Kandell, Kravet, Jack Lenor Larsen, Gene McDonald, Herman Miller Textiles, Ottavia, Owens-Corning Fiberglas, Patterson, Riverdale, Ben Rose, Scalamandre, F. Schumacher, Isabel Scott, J. H. Thorp, Waverly, Wellington Sears, Window Shade Manufacturers' Association.
Flooring: Amtico, Armstrong, Bird, Congoleum-Nairn, Flintkote, Kentile, Robbins, Wood Flooring Center.
Furniture: Baker, Bassett, Century, Directional, Drexel, Globe, Henredon, Heritage, Heywood-Wakefield, Hooker, Kittinger, Lane, Morganton, Nichols & Stone, Roundtree, Simmons, Thayer Coggin, Thomasville Chair, Tomlinson, Vanleigh.
Glass: Blenko, Fostoria, Imperial, Libbey.
Lamps and Lighting: Anne Allen, Bradley, Chapman, Georgian Lighting Studios, Paul Hanson, Jim Hurt of Texas, Herman Kashins, Warren Kessler, Nathan Lagin, Lange & Williams, Lightolier, Stiffel Company, Wilmar.
Pillows and Bedspreads: Bates, Clavos, Craig, Fieldcrest, Morgan-Jones, Nettle Creek Industries.
Rugs and Carpets: Barwick, Bigelow, Cabin Crafts, Firth, James Lees and Sons, Loomweve, Magee, Masland, Mohawk, Olson Rug Company, Alexander Smith, Priscilla Turner Rug Guild, Waite.
Silver: Gorham, International, Kirk, Oneida, Reed & Barton, 1847 Rogers Bros., Towle.
Stores: B. Altman & Company, Bloomingdale's, Greenbaum Bros., Lord & Taylor, R. H. Macy, W & J Sloane, Tiffany & Company.
Tablecloths: Ottavia.
Wallcoverings: Louis W. Bowen, Felters Company, Imperial, Jones and Erwin, Katzenbach & Warren, W. H. S. Lloyd, F. Schumacher, C. W. Stockwell, Thomas Strahan, Timbertone.

McCall's is also grateful to the following interior designers for their help and cooperation in making their work and their clients' homes available for photography:

Ethyl G. Alper—Pages 101, 227
James Amster—Page 87
Jane Ashley—Page 126 (lower)

David Barrett—Pages 39, 41, 73, 91, 123, 139, 163, 167, 213, 239
William Beach—Page 158

300

Lee Blake—Page 51 (top left)
Braswell-Cook—Pages 24, 27
Bonnie Cashins—Page 196
William Cecil—Page 280
Robert Chatham of Lord & Taylor—Pages 93, 267
Barbara D'Arcy of Bloomingdale's—Pages 131, 177, 240
Doris Dessauer—Page 142
Jay Dorf—Pages 161, 251
Elaine Kaufman Feiner—Pages 165, 247
Richard Felden—Page 193
John Fitzgibbons of Yale R. Burge—Pages 59, 99, 137 (right), 175 (lower), 189, 231
Robert Flaherty of B. Altman & Co.—Page 116
Richard Frazier—Page 218 (lower)
Jeremiah Goodman—Frontispiece, pages 28, 55, 184, 200, 203
Albert Higgins—Page 149
Randolph Jack—Page 137 (left)
Leona Kahn—Page 57
Henry M. Libhart—Page 51 (upper right)
Robert S. Lindenthal—Page 199

Jerome I. Manashaw—Page 194
Manashaw and Daggett—Pages 103, 238
James Childs Morse—Page 128
Muller-Bachich—Page 95
Mrs. Robert Neely—Page 215
Mary Neveleff—Page 126 (upper)
Joseph B. Platt—Pages 15, 175 (upper)
Deane Pleuss—Page 187
Bette Sanford Roby—Page 228
John D. Root—Page 33
Jacquelin Ross—Page 218 (upper)
Howard Perry Rothberg—Pages 48, 141, 191, 261
Renny B. Saltzman—Page 100
Otho Shaw and Dede Draper—Page 77
Ving Smith—Page 219
Karl Steinhauser—Page 18
Roy Succa—Page 37
H. Rexford Taylor of B. Altman & Co.—Page 88
Mrs. William Van den Heuvel for Tiffany's—Page 244
Kirk White—Page 70
Sally Wynn—Page 69

Line drawings by ANDRE LA PORTE

INDEX